The Most Dangerous German Agent in America

The
Most Dangerous
GERMAN AGENT IN AMERICA

The Many Lives of Louis N. Hammerling

M. B. B. BISKUPSKI

NIU Press / DeKalb, IL

Northern Illinois University Press, DeKalb, Illinois 60115
© 2015 by Northern Illinois University Press

24 23 22 21 20 19 18 17 16 15   1 2 3 4 5
978-0-87580-721-8 (paper)
978-1-60909-176-7 (ebook)

Design by Yuni Dorr

Library of Congress Cataloging-in-Publication Data:
Biskupski, Mieczyslaw B., author.
The most dangerous German agent in America : the many lives of Louis N.
Hammerling / M. B. B. Biskupski. — First edition.
    pages   cm
Includes bibliographical references and index.
ISBN 978-0-87580-721-8 (pbk.: alk. paper) — ISBN 978-1-60909-176-7
(pdf)
1. Hammerling, Louis N., 1870-1935. 2. Jews, Polish—United States—
Biography. I. Title.
DS134.72.H36B57 2015
627.1243073092—dc23
[B]
2015000098

Henrykowi Bieńkowskiemu,
pradziadowi, kawalerzyście, artyście,
skrzypkowi, tę książkę poświęcam.

CONTENTS

PREFACE

MANY YEARS AGO, while pursuing another topic in the archives of
the American State Department, I stumbled upon a character whose
convoluted career at once arrested my attention. I filed this information
away, was diverted by projects for more than two decades, and finally decided that I had accumulated enough material to essay a reconstruction
of the most bizarre life I have ever encountered. It is both fascinating and
frustrating to present the story of Louis N. Hammerling (1870–1935).
Much about him is unknown, probably much of that unknowable. He
usually functioned behind the scenes, and it is a reasonable initial conclusion that he was little more than a petty crook who found himself in
convenient positions. But there was more to this. He was a considerable figure in both the United States and Poland, and he epitomized so
many personae with which we have come to deal: the poor immigrant
boy striking it rich in America, the Polish émigré perhaps always long-
ing to return in wealth to his ancestral Fatherland, the devout converted
Catholic, the successful Jew resented by his Christian fellow immigrants,
the politically adroit greenhorn, union organizer, newspaperman, American power broker and politician, the con man later swimming in a world
of corruption and venality much too common in both America and the
world of interwar Polish politics (1918–1939). He was so many things,
often at the same time: he did so much, so much of it of moment, that he
is impossible to characterize in a single phrase or a few paragraphs. He
deserves a book, and now he has one.

I have been pursuing the elusive and mysterious Hammerling for many
years. In this undertaking, many people have helped; few knew what
in the world I was about. The topic seemed so obscure, his very name
was virtually unknown, the evidence scattered in archives throughout
Europe and America, often only passing references in other stories. Yet,
there were those who sensed that I had discovered an adventure and
were fascinated where it would all end and the many phases through
which it would pass.

I remember driving with a group of friends from Wrocław to Kraków.
The time weighed heavily on us. For some reason, I announced: "Would

you like to hear a good story; it will take a bit of time?" They tiredly assented, and I presented them with an outline of Hammerling. The other passengers, a prominent lawyer, a politician, a government official, all responded that what I had told them was not the making of a book, but the stuff of a film. They urged me to finish it and, a decade later, after consulting seventy-four archival deposits in five countries, and coordinated trial testimony, investigative reports, and blackmail correspondence, I have. Their inspiration encouraged me not to let this story vanish, but to complete it no matter how long it took.

This volume is presented to two quite different audiences. To my colleagues in History, it is designed to be a contribution to immigration studies, particularly the Poles in turn-of-the-century America, particularly Pennsylvania, and to include a large presence hitherto forgotten. Specifically, for my fellow historians of Poland, it is an effort to reconstruct one of that country's most significant émigrés: later a prominent figure in the early years of independent Poland and the target of a national scandal. Apart from the academy, I trust this tale will arrest the attention of the non-scholarly world. This is not a life, it is an adventure, and it has in it all the elements of a fantastic tale but, as the documents demonstrate, it is all true.

My family is very precious to me and—not through my efforts—the three oldest have all grown to have successful careers. There are two very little ones remaining at home, Misia and Staś, who never left my thoughts as I wrote, because they always asked me to tell them one of my stories; and now I do. I wrote this volume, therefore to not one, but all of my dear ones, that they might all enjoy one of Daddy's stories. Their great-great-grandfather, Henryk Bieńkowski, to whom I dedicate this book, should prove inspiration for all of them.

I should like to acknowledge the valuable help given me by a number of people. Roger E. Nixon was my research assistant at the British National Archives; Jeremy Bigwood performed the same tasks at the US National Archives in College Park, Maryland. Edward O. Barnes of the National Archives found some rare papers in the State Department files—where I should never have thought to look. Joseph Hapak provided material on two of Hammerling's key relationships: President Taft and Jan F. Smulski. In the small libraries and historical societies of the anthracite region, I had the assistance of Virginia R. Mitchell, and at the Dutchess County

Court records office, her sister, Joanna L. Mitchell, helped find valuable documents. David K. Frasier of the Lilly Library, Indiana University, was indispensable in locating rare documents in the University archives concerning Hammerling's dealings with the Germans. Renata C. Vickrey, of Central Connecticut State University, deciphered some handwritten letters that were beyond my ken, for which I am very grateful. Ewa Wołyńska, of the same institution, was enormously helpful in retrieving documents. Władysław Bułhak in Warsaw helped track down obscure materials. Finally I should note the CCSU History Department's Katherine Hermes whose advice on discovering legal documents relative to Hammerling was invaluable. Waldemar Kostrzewa and Nick Pettinico were always available for help and good counsel. To all of them I am grateful. I have only myself to blame for errors and infelicities. This work would not have been possible without the generous support of Central Connecticut State University.

I am particularly grateful to the descendants of Hammerling who sent their advice and comments: Jeane O'Donnell, Judith Gold, James Renier Hammerling, Phillip Hammerling, Drs. Solomon and Anne Linder Hammerling, and Victoria Hammerling Rosenberg. They helped by enriching the text and adding valuable nuance. It is a better book thanks to them.

Several people read all or part of the manuscript and offered valuable suggestions. Others provided research possibilities; these include Neal Pease of University of Wisconsin–Milwaukee; James S. Pula of Purdue University Northwest; Anna M. Cienciala of the University of Kansas; Perry Blatz of Duquesne University; Jeanne Petit of Hope College; and the conscientious and painstaking editor Amy Farranto of Northern Illinois University Press.

Colchester, 2015

The Most Dangerous German Agent in America

Prologue

ON APRIL 27, 1935, A MAN OF ABOUT SIXTY-FIVE opened his window on the nineteenth floor of an apartment he owned in New York.[1] His breakfast and newspaper lay on a table by the window. It was about a quarter after seven in the morning. He lived alone, and no one was there when he fell from the window to his death.[2] In Queens, New York, he is buried in a grave with another's name: the name on the stone is that of his beloved son Robert, who did not survive his first year due to the influenza epidemic of 1918–1919. This is the story of that forgotten man.

Ludwik Mikołaj Hammerling, or Louis N. Hammerling as we shall refer to him henceforth, was one of the most influential Polish immigrants in turn-of-the-century America and by far the leading voice and advocate of the eastern Europeans who had come to this country seeking a better life. He was also a pathological liar, crook, swindler, ruthless entrepreneur, and a patriot—of which nation he could never decide. In America, Hammerling rose from the grinding poverty of his youth to the heights of wealth and power. From his arrival in America he was, variously, a timberman and mule driver in the Pennsylvania anthracite coal mines working under brutal conditions and earning pitiful wages, an indentured worker in the Hawaiian sugar fields, one of the major behind-the-scenes powers in the United Mine Workers and a close friend of its leaders, an employee of the Hearst newspaper chain, a powerful figure in the Republican Party, a confidant of the largest and wealthiest brewing and shipping companies in the country, the owner of a major advertising agency whose variegated activities made him a millionaire while still in his youth, a prominent figure dealing with federal authorities in immigration affairs, the most influential immigrant spokesman of the early century, a frequent correspondent of Theodore Roosevelt and William Howard Taft (for whom he supposedly undertook foreign missions), both a German agent, and, by one account, a "Bolshevist agent," and a colorful senator of the Polish Republic who may have brokered the change of government in 1923 Poland.[3] There are many other roles crammed into a relatively short life. He was a devout Roman Catholic, though targeted by anti-Semites as a Jew; he was a probable bigamist married first to an Orthodox Jewish woman and, later, a Polish aristocrat. He told a federal agent in 1918 "I have no children"—at a time when he had several.[4] By his own admission he was a devoted American and, at other times, an intensely patriotic Pole. He described himself as being of several different nationalities. He may well have been the financial source for the success of one of Poland's principal political parties. He was monitored and scrutinized by several state and federal agencies, as well as British Intelligence. He was, in the words of his pursuers, "the most dangerous German agent in America."[5]

CHAPTER 1

Wanderings

From Galicia to Honolulu and Back

LOUIS HAMMERLING WAS BORN IN 1874 — or, this was his assertion for many years, until he changed that to 1870. In a 1918 Senate investigation, of which we shall hear much more, Hammerling gave many details about his life, and yet they were often contradictory. He explained that he really did not know how old he was as a child because he had not gone to school — though he later credited his education to the YMCA.[1] He also said that he came to the United States in 1855 — fifteen or twenty years before his birth.[2] His birthplace was Galicia, the portion of Poland seized by Austria in 1771 — though he later swore he was born in either Germany or Honolulu.[3] His native village, Drohojów, was in an area of mixed population with Poles and Ukrainians and many Jews; the latter would be exterminated by the Germans in the Holocaust. Today, Drohojów, population about 150, lies virtually on the Polish frontier with Ukraine near the large city of Przemyśl. At the time of Hammerling's birth, Drohojów was a tiny hamlet characterized by a colorful history and utter destitution.[4]

We know little about his family in Poland, but there is no question that they were Jewish and abysmally poor. He was the fifth child of his father's third marriage.[5] So impoverished was his family that "I was taken away by a peasant out of a matter of mercy." On at least one occasion he also said that he was "driven out of home" by his "disagreeable family."[6] He put this as occurring in 1879 or 1880. There were apparently many other siblings, though only Samuel, who oddly used the surname "Weiss," seems to have later surfaced in America. Hammerling denied that he was his brother. Louis Hammerling was not above making grandiose claims. He once said that his destitute father was a general in the Austrian Army, and he also claimed to know Emperor Karl of Austria-Hungary, and to have visited him at his hunting lodge.[7]

Though his adoptive father, the "peasant," was obviously very important in the boy's young life, Hammerling later mentioned him only rarely, and never by name.[8] Testifying before the Senate in 1918 regarding his relationship with German agents in the United States, Hammerling gave this bizarre aside: "inasmuch as my people were Jewish by race, I was not, and this peasant took me away to make a Christian out of me, that was his idea." What Hammerling had in mind when he said that his family was Jewish but he was not, is not clear. He told the Senate that he was "brought here" when he was nine by "a man from the village where I came from."[9] Similarly, he never spoke of his actual father, and never mentioned his family in any recorded statement. He would seem to have left his family behind him. However, later in his life, when he was very wealthy, he traveled frequently to Galicia and may well have thus visited his family on a regular basis. At one point an anti-Semitic journal produced an illegible card, purportedly from Hammerling to his father written in Yiddish. This is a mere scrap of what must have been a complicated family background.[10]

Hammerling was always very vague about his ethnic ancestry. At various times he announced with some grandeur that he was an "Austrian" and proud of it.[11] Other times he described himself as "half Bohemian and half Polish." He emotionally proclaimed his American loyalties, and when he later served in the Polish government in the 1920s he was passionately Polish, but the only thing he rarely discussed was that he was Jewish. The reasons for this can only be speculated upon. Hammerling once noted that he never denied being Jewish, he just never mentioned it.[12] It was, he explained, awkward for a Jew to do business with many Christian immigrants to the United States, more than a few with anti-Semitic prejudice. It is interesting to consider what his native language was. In the United States it was noted that his English was heavily accented and occasionally ungrammatical. In Poland, his execrable use of the national tongue drew mocking attention. According to one of his employees, the only language he spoke fluently was Yiddish.[13] His extant letters are rather clumsily written, and apparently when he could afford it, he had stenographers write his letters for him, which he then signed.

Hammerling's movements in the early years of his life are incomprehensibly complex, and filled with inconsistencies. His adoptive father, the unnamed peasant, paid for his passage and went with him to America, leaving via Bremen. This, according to Hammerling, occurred sometime in 1879–1880 when he was very young. The possibility that Hammerling first arrived in the United States as a ten-year-old is accepted by the author of a biographical sketch, Czesław Lechicki. Lechicki has Hammerling spending just a few years in the country, then returning to Galicia in 1884, marrying in a Jewish "ritual" service, and leaving for the United States again in 1891, at the age of about twenty-one.

On his first American visit (ca. 1880), at a very young age, Hammerling stayed briefly in New York, where he arrived and worked in some menial capacity. After what must have been a very short stay he and a friend, in pursuit of more gainful employment, went to Lehigh County in the anthracite region of eastern Pennsylvania, then to Lattimore and other nearby cities. He probably arrived in this area in his early teens and left because "They began killing people there, the Molly Maguires."[14] The Molly Maguires was the controversial and mythologized Irish miners' organization with roots in the homeland. Known for their clandestine and violent behavior, the Mollies gained especial notoriety in the late 1870s, and several were executed after dramatic trials. The violent Mollies added yet another element of danger to the anthracite region in which literally thousands died due to mine owner neglect and abysmal working conditions. Children as young as seven were sent to be so-called "breaker boys" crushing coal into manageable chunks at the pitheads. The Mollies were known to resent the Welsh and English senior miners and reciprocally disdained the more recent immigrants from southern and eastern Europe. Years later, Hammerling would recall his time in the mines with a baleful reference to the Mollies.

According to one report, Hammerling, at the age of only ten, was a mule driver in an anthracite mine. How long that lasted—if it ever happened— is not corroborated.[15] Hammerling was associated with the anthracite region on and off for decades (he claimed to have lived in Wilkes-Barre for twenty-six years). An area once known for its natural beauty, the region by the time of his arrival was filthy, polluted, and crowded by impoverished immigrants.[16] In all of adjacent Luzerne County, and in the city of Wilkes-Barre, the most numerous of these were the Poles, and the Polish anthracite workers were the most isolated and unassimilated of all the immigrants. These were Hammerling's people.[17]

Hammerling probably spent four years in Pennsylvania before returning to Galicia, about 1884. In 1894 he married his first wife, Clara Schächter (Klara Szechter). We know scraps about this episode from a statement by Klara's brother Samuel. Hammerling apparently did not like Samuel, whom he described as "the worst blackmailer that ever lived." This probably means that Szechter was telling the truth.[18] According to him, Hammerling's engagement took place in Mogelnica, Galicia, about 1892. Soon afterwards Hammerling was drafted into the Austrian Army—a fact he vehemently denied in sworn testimony.[19] This denial of his service makes absolutely no sense. He told the Senate that he never served because when he was called to service he had "an abscess" so he was not inducted, "not a day." Seconds later he said he was on "furlough" when he was betrothed, and when the furlough expired he escaped to America.[20] Samuel, however, claims Hammerling served for a year in the Imperial Army, was discharged, and then married his sister. It was almost certainly an arranged marriage. This would have been about 1894. This story comports with Hammerling's apparently accidental reference to the "furlough." In any event, he fled Galicia probably shortly after his marriage and returned to the West—this time to the sugar fields in Hawaii. He recalled writing to Klara in 1897 from Honolulu. If this is correct, it would mean that he was in Hawaii sometime between the ages of about twenty-four and twenty-eight.[21] He left Hawaii for the United States probably in 1898.

Hammerling once suggested that his adoptive father took him to Hawaii because he had relatives there.[22] However, in a statement made only weeks later, he noted that his voyage to Hawaii involved a "German concern" that hired 500 contract laborers, paid them nothing for five years, and then, when their passage was repaid, gave the workers "cloth," "rice," and "different stuff." His sojourn in the Hawaiian Islands was apparently ghastly. He insisted he was at sea an incomprehensible 150 days. He was "sold out by some German crooks" on the Islands and worked under brutal conditions that resulted in 300 of his 500 compatriots dying, and the rest, including our hero, running away. He claimed to bear lifelong scars from beatings. His tale of the Hawaiian experience in his testimony before the Senate is melodramatic, and it is notable that he went out of his way to denigrate Germans in the early part of this testimony. Because at the time he stood accused of being a German spy, reviling them was a handy tactic. However, he had also given an entirely different version of the Hawaiian episode: "the Almighty was there . . . I worked for him [the adoptive father who took him from Galicia] 18 months with the Japs, Chinese, and negroes, in the sugar plantation, and it was good, and I loved it."[23]

While Hammerling was in the Islands, his abandoned wife Klara, then about thirty, left Galicia and sailed with her brother Samuel to Philadelphia. Shortly after their arrival, Hammerling apparently asked them for money to finance his move there from San Francisco, where he had gone upon leaving Honolulu. Census bureau information has Hammerling arriving in Philadelphia in 1894.[24] This date ill purports with the Hawaiian stay and is difficult to explain.

It was sometime in the mid-1890s that Hammerling returned to Pennsylvania to join his wife and brother-in-law in the City of Brotherly Love, where he found work as a labor contractor. After six months he went to Wilkes-Barre to work in the mines as a timberman.[25] He joined the United Mine Workers (UMW) in 1898, or perhaps 1900—he was to claim both dates in public testimony a few years later.[26] Wilkes-Barre was then a burgeoning city with a bright future and a large immigrant population—a perfect place for his boundless energy, unexampled ambition, and utter unscrupulousness.[27]

Hammerling was already involved in Republican political activities in the anthracite region in 1896, but there is no evidence connecting him to the largest incident of the era involving the eastern European miners: the Lattimer Massacre. In September 1897 there was a notorious massacre of striking mine workers by local authorities in Lattimer, near Hazelton, killing at least twenty and injuring scores. Many of the victims were eastern Europeans, in particular, Poles. The incident was a milestone in the history of the nascent UMW and marked the rise to power of the mine workers' leader John Mitchell, who shall figure more in Hammerling's life in the next chapter. One of the several lessons of Lattimer was that the eastern European immigrant miner, previously regarded as docile and beyond the reach of unionization, took an active part in the affair—and represented most of the casualties. Hammerling was moving in the midst of an anthracite world in an era of change and convulsion.[28] The eastern European miners were becoming a significant component of the local mining population.

When Hammerling applied for his naturalization papers in Wilkes-Barre in 1901, he claimed never to have been married and, of course, thus never divorced.[29] He repeated these statements in 1915 when he married for what was really the second time, though he swore it was the first.[30] We know little of the long-suffering Klara save that she was Jewish. Thanks to one of her descendants we know something of her background. She was one of seven children who all emigrated to the United States, with the exception of a brother, who ironically prospered, for a time, by never leaving poor Galicia. He was later killed by the Nazis.[31] Unlike Hammerling, whose Polish was dreadful, the Szechter family spoke Polish as a first language. Though technically Orthodox Jews, the family was not religious.[32] Klara's family life provides us with some insight into the fast-changing world of Austrian Poland at the turn of the century, when the Jewish community was in various states of assimilation to Polonism, and in a kind of linguistic transition.[33]

Because the marriage service was Orthodox, we may conclude that Hammerling had still not converted to Catholicism by his mid-twenties. His attitude toward his marriage and his first wife is most curious. He explained that Jewish weddings were not recognized in Austria, so he was really never married before 1915. He noted that only a few rabbis in Austria were empowered to perform legal weddings. Thus, said his lawyer, the marriage was "void *ab initio*." However, he did later divorce Klara in Austria.[34] Why he would go to the expense and immense trouble to dissolve a marriage that he always maintained had no legal standing in the first place is another curiosity of his unusual history.

According to Hammerling, he was living in the United States, which did not recognize his "Jewish marriage," but by living with Klara he had a "common-law woman" with whom he had three children. She, however, returned to Galicia in 1912, and thereafter they did not live together.[35] He claimed that they had agreed to "some arrangement" whereby Klara released all claim for support, though he was, by then, prosperous. She

would, however, get some sort of "settlement." This, as far as he was concerned, ended the marriage. However, there was a problem. They may
not have been legally married under Austrian law, but in the United
States Klara was his common-law wife. The matter was turned over to
lawyers in 1913.[36]

However, Hammerling went back to Galicia—probably just before the
outbreak of World War I in early 1914, hired an attorney, and obtained
a divorce. According to Hammerling, he had to explain to the Austrian
courts that he needed an Austrian divorce—but before they granted the
divorce they needed to have a marriage to dissolve. Austria, Hammerling explained, recognized a marriage, then granted a divorce.[37] While
involved in these legal proceedings in Galicia, Hammerling met a very
young, very rich, and very beautiful Polish girl. They married in 1915—
as Roman Catholics. Klara, understandably, never understood that she
was divorced. She spent the war years with the three children in Great
Britain and returned to the United States on July 9, 1920, launching legal
action against her estranged husband.[38]

By 1899 the man who was ever reinventing himself had become involved in the newspaper business in Pennsylvania. This was the beginning of the occupation that was to eventually make him rich: he was
now an advertising broker to the immigrant press. How exactly he provided this service is not entirely clear, but apparently he arranged for
businesses to place advertisements in foreign language newspapers, for
which he would receive a commission. Along with the monetary gain
came a newfound authority. Hammerling very quickly became a major
figure in the immigrant community because he had the power of grant-
ing or withholding advertising payments from papers unwilling to do his
bidding. In addition to—or as part of—the immigrant press, he also had
a working relationship with the Hearst newspapers, probably involving
advertisement, but his specific responsibilities are not known.[39] By 1900
he was an agent of the *United Mine Workers Journal*—perhaps already its
advertising manager.

When we consider that Hammerling never attended one day of
school, and may have been largely illiterate, that he spoke a hodgepodge
of different languages, his emergence as a newspaperman is amazing. He

acquired an interest in a local newspaper, probably Scranton's *Górnik*[40] in the anthracite area—quite a linguistic achievement for a Polish Jew who barely spoke English. He may well have gained control of other ethnic papers, but that cannot be corroborated.

Hammerling's involvement in the newspaper business was precocious: it was just beginning to emerge as a significant industry, and the publicity it provided as a major element in business success was of recent vintage.[41] Repeatedly during his career he showed the ability to grasp emergent trends and turn them to personal account. This talent—his entrepreneurial anticipations could not all have been serendipitous coincidences—belies that later characterization of Hammerling as a man of limited intelligence. The reason for this unflattering description could more charitably and accurately be explained by the fact that he was an unschooled, rather than stupid man, one who was always forced to function in languages not natural to him. While overall he seems to have made a poor impression on the intellectual front, there is no doubt that he was a man of considerable native ability.

While Hammerling was living in Wilkes-Barre he met, in nearby Hazelton, an ambitious Irishman named John H. Shea "who was studying [law] at night" and "got interested." Shea was "in love with my eyes, and a good looking fellow."[42] Hammerling described himself as "a child" and Shea "became so affectionate to me as his child that I grew up to be successful." Shea gave Hammerling advice that he later lived by: "Louis . . . the American people have no use . . . for the Polish Jews." Hence, "make your citizenship with any country; if you denounce one, you denounce them all."[43] Hammerling may have been taking this advice when he decided to claim Honolulu as his birthplace and thereby "denounce" Galicia: details did not matter.

In 1901, Hammerling applied for naturalization in Wilkes-Barre and swore to a tissue of lies. When later confronted with these misstatements— Shea was both witness and attorney for Hammerling, and he must have known that the application was a lie[44]—Hammerling claimed that it was the fault of "the parties" and that it was a general practice before elections. Agents for both the Republicans and Democrats would comb the mining districts, find unnaturalized residents, take them to Wilkes-Barre to register, and then a few days later they would take them to vote—presumably for the party that had been responsible for registering them. These agents drove around the area, and thus immigrant votes were cast many times over.[45] Hammerling's reasoning was that "the republicans are making citizens every day, so I thought I would pick a country I live in." "There is nothing I love better than that country [the United States]."[46] Despite this patriotic aside, he chose his American citizenship, it would seem, by happenstance, or cagey advice from Shea. Besides, since he was "disgusted with where I came from," he could "select his own birthplace."[47]

Hammerling's decision to become a Hawaiian probably reflects the regnant prejudice against eastern and southern European immigrants in the coal districts. An 1898 report noting that liquor laws cannot be "enforced" characterizes them as "inassimilable and hard to manage," given to riots, and "turbulent." This description would be repeated many times. They had been "clumped upon our shores by the shipload" and turned the once placid region into "the most mixed population to be found anywhere in the world."[48] Being associated with such a coarse and motley crew was not useful to Americanization and social advancement for the enterprising Hammerling.[49] We may well assume that Hammerling knew exactly what he was doing when he officially severed his Galician Jewish roots and made himself a Hawaiian.

Business, Politics, and Coal

HAMMERLING WAS FRANTICALLY ACTIVE IN POLITICS and business from the time of his return to Pennsylvania in about 1896.[1] Already during the McKinley campaign of 1896 Hammerling held the post of "advertising agent of the Republican National Committee for the foreign language press." His political career appears to date from 1894, which ill comports with other evidence suggesting that he was still in Hawaii then or just returned to Pennsylvania from the Islands. It is a very mysterious chronological problem.[2]

Hammerling began his efforts to act as a conduit between the Republican Party and the immigrant mining population as an organizer of immigrants for political purposes. He was "flooded with letters from Polish people" asking him to gain support for political initiatives.[3] We must remember that the Lattimer Massacre of 1897 had just drawn national attention to miners and the union movement. For the politicians the dramatic events of 1897 also raised the possibility of gaining votes from the eastern European immigrant community—a community previously ignored.

By 1898 Hammerling, in Philadelphia, was "placing Hungarians and other foreigners at work in the mining sections, running an employment agency for this purpose and a steamship ticket office."[4] By 1900 he gave his occupation, oddly, as "clerk."[5] Certainly he was politically involved before then, and by the turn of the century was already what would characterize him for years: a hustler, lighting on one business or another, flitting about but always connected to the immigrant anthracite population. No longer a miner, he was now some sort of multiform businessman.

JOHN MITCHELL AND UNION LEADERSHIP

Apart from the mysterious Shea, the first great influence on Hammerling's life was labor pioneer John Mitchell. This famous organizer of the miners' union became Hammerling's mentor and close associate. Mitchell (1870–1919) was a fascinating character. A poor Irish orphan, he went to work in the mines at the age of six. In 1885 he joined the burgeoning Knights of Labor of Terence V. Powderly. The Knights had a reputation for incompetent leadership and, after a rapid increase, began a striking decline after 1890. They were replaced by the more industry-focused United Mine Workers founded in part by Mitchell in 1890. Mitchell, who worked closely with their legendary Mary "Mother" Jones, was noted for his ability to expand the UMW to include recent immigrants from eastern Europe—his eventual link to Hammerling. Powderly's Knights had not been particularly successful in recruiting eastern European miners.[6] In a relatively short time the UMW increased its membership tenfold to three hundred thousand, and Mitchell became a national figure.

When Mitchell arrived in the anthracite district he quickly saw the need for assistance in recruiting the recent immigrants, and so he began cultivating local "foreigners" including especially "foreign language editors"—editors of the newspapers created to serve the rapidly growing immigrant population.[7] Mitchell entrusted Hammerling with choosing "non-English speaking aspirants" to state positions because Hammerling was "in a better position to select" foreigners.[8] Hammerling had already become a leader of the eastern European immigrant community in the anthracite district by 1900, and he was thus able to arrange for political support from Pennsylvania Republican Senators Matthew Quay and Boies Penrose. He was, quite probably, the most influential immigrant in Pennsylvania, and certainly the most powerful Polish immigrant.

It may be that Hammerling was baptized a Catholic at this time, although he later claimed to have converted to Roman Catholicism because of his second wife.[9] The baptism, if it took place, must have been surreptitious: Hammerling would not have wanted to draw attention to the fact of his Jewish roots. Entering the Catholic Church could only have helped him professionally in his work with the predominantly Catholic eastern European immigrant population.

Hammerling's career as a union leader began with the celebrated anthracite strike of 1902. The nascent United Mine Workers, led by the "talented and modest" Mitchell, had carried out successful strikes in the late 1890s in the Midwest.[10] The infamous Lattimer Massacre of 1897 had increased the popularity and visibility of the UMW as well as demonstrating that Slavs and other recent immigrants—the bulk of those killed and wounded in the episode—were not adverse to strikes and confrontations with mine owners. Another strike in the anthracite regions of Pennsylvania in 1900 succeeded in attracting many workers from the ethnically diverse area, but did not gain recognition for the union.[11] Hammerling played a prominent role among the miners— this even though he was already a petty businessman involved with the newspapers.[12] He had been the moving force behind the effort to build a monument to the victims of the Lattimer Massacre at the beginning of the year, using the Lithuanian-Polish Club, his creation, as its basis.[13] The fact that Poles were prominently featured among the immigrants, forming the backbone of the strike, was a convenience for a Polish immigrant like Hammerling. The press reported that the outbreaks of violence were due to "foreigners," who sang "weird Hungarian and Polish battle hymns," were "eager for fighting," and were generally in an "ugly mood."[14] Election year politics brought the strike to a rapid conclusion as Ohio Senator Mark Hanna intervened vigorously with his fellow Republican mining moguls.

This vision of workers as a Republican constituency was closely associated with Hanna. He viewed workers as a potential cooperative bloc to work with the owners. What Robert Wiebe calls "industrial mutualism" would not only end labor unrest and bring prosperity, but it would Americanize the immigrants and make them Republicans.[15] Mitchell actively cultivated Hanna—who surreptitiously funded him—and established close relations with key members of the Republican Party.[16] In this effort a prominent role seems to have been played by Hammerling. Hanna, in turn, regarded the miners as a key voting bloc for the election of 1900.[17] In this he reflected the notions of President McKinley.[18]

For Republicans like Hanna and later President Theodore Roosevelt, labor grievances were politically dangerous. Mitchell and his protégé Hammerling, Republicans themselves, had a vested interest in working together. The circumstances for Hammerling's advance in influence in Republican circles were created before 1900 by Republican labor policies.[19] In 1896 the Republicans gave Hammerling $196,000 as an advertising budget to use among the foreign born, a very considerable sum.[20] This marked a dramatic start to his career as a political broker.

Becoming the Republicans' liaison to the immigrant community was a major accomplishment. Another achievement was his creation of the Lithuanian-Polish Club. By the late nineteenth century, relations between Poles and Lithuanians in both Europe and America had entered a rapid and bitter decline. The Lithuanians were a minority in the northeastern corner of the once immense Polish Commonwealth. It was this state that rapidly etiolated after 1648 and was erased from the map of Europe by the partitions. The idea that the Lithuanians were a distinctively different nationality with only historic linkages to the Poles, and not part of the Polish-led Commonwealth of prepartition days was horrifying to the Poles, who resented nascent Lithuanian nationalism as an attack on the very historic continuity of the heritage of the great Poland of the past. Soon the two communities were bitterly divided, and their relations had virtually reached violence by the late 1890s: Polish-Lithuanian parishes were dissolved, and the two communities lived in mutual antagonism. Yet in this era of conflict, Hammerling—a Galician Jew—created a joint club of Poles and Lithuanians, which eventually became large and influential. Perhaps if neither side saw him as a true Pole, they would have been willing to accept his leadership. Whatever the reason, Hammerling created a historical anomaly: a cooperating body of Poles and Lithuanians at a time when the two communities had dissolved into mutual acrimony. This was a preamble to his successful efforts to create an umbrella organization for much of the immigrant press. It may also be an early indication of Hammerling's chameleon ethnicity: he was not sufficiently Polish publicly to antagonize the Lithuanians and probably offered himself simply as a Christian.

In 1901 Hammerling's name appeared very frequently in the *United Mine Workers Journal*, making him one of the best-known mine workers' leaders in the anthracite region.[21] He was gaining new subscribers constantly—more than one hundred monthly—and arranged advertising by local businessmen.[22] Hammerling was really not an activist for the miners but rather an organizer and anthracite area businessman who was comingling labor and politics to make himself important and, probably by this point, rich.

THE GREAT STRIKE OF 1902

The "great strike" occurred in May of 1902. It lasted until autumn. The mine owners refused to recognize the UMW, and efforts at arbitration by Mitchell proved bootless. Perhaps 80 percent of the miners walked off their jobs. Relations between strikers and those remaining at work descended into bitter hostility. One woman from the area even claimed that "Polanders" threatened to blow up her home and were shooting at her.[23]

It seems that at the time of the strike Hammerling was no longer working in the mines: his advertising business made unnecessary such brutal work.[24] For reasons he never explained—"That is my personal affair"— Hammerling left the union at the beginning of the strike and was not enrolled during most of it.[25] State and, ultimately, national politics were now his chief occupation. He acted as Mitchell's envoy to Senator Penrose and went to Philadelphia to meet him at Mitchell's request for the first time probably in January 1902.[26] His relationship to Senator Quay was even closer: he was in the man's pay by 1902. Though what he was supposed to accomplish is not known.

As the 1902 strike dragged on, a "coal famine" in the winter was threatened, and large-scale violence seemed imminent. Finally, President Roosevelt intervened. He initially considered using the army to operate the mines, and ultimately attempted to mediate. The strike was suspended on October 24th, and Roosevelt created an investigative body, called the Commission, to take testimony. The details were worked out at a White House meeting that involved both Mitchell and the mine operators early in the month. Hammerling was intimately involved as a facilitator and go-between among the interested parties. The surviving correspondence clearly demonstrates that Hammerling assumed considerable initiative, and sometimes met with the principals without others being present.

This reflects Mitchell's methods, which were not confrontational but sought to gain cooperation among the coal magnates, prominent political figures, and the mine workers through negotiations, frequently highly secretive. This behind-the-scenes action would later characterize Mitchell's protégé Hammerling.[27] Too, we should remember that the strike and its settlement were in many ways negotiations conducted within the upper reaches of the Republican Party: no prominent Democrat was involved.

Hammerling participated in endless secret negotiations involving labor representatives, owners, and prominent politicians, negotiations that led to the suspension of the strike. He had, he admitted, "considerable to do" with the settlement. Hammerling, acting for Mitchell, arranged meetings with Quay and, more often, Penrose throughout the summer of 1902. The meetings moved all about the eastern United States including such places as Quay's hometown in western Pennsylvania, an obscure hamlet by the name of Beaver. There was a major meeting in September in New York with Senators Thomas C. Platt of New York, Quay, and Penrose. Hammerling may not have been at these negotiations; however, Mitchell was also frequently absent. The meetings, arranged via cryptic telegrams—sometimes more than thirty a day—stretched on for months, through the October intervention by Roosevelt.[28] It was then, early in the month, that Hammerling's activities reached their zenith: many telephone calls with New York Governor Benjamin B. Odell were added to the avalanche of telegrams. At various meetings Hammerling represented Mitchell or Quay, sometimes both. He admitted, in 1905 under strenuous questioning, that he was Mitchell's closest confidant at the time.[29]

The so-called Presidential Conference took place at the temporary White House (while Roosevelt had the West Wing constructed) on October 3, 1902. Quay paid Hammerling to be present. Hammerling insisted that he had no recollections of the meeting or events leading up to it.[30] Apparently Hammerling was not in the room with the president, but Mitchell kept him abreast of developments. Triangular negotiations among the operators, the union, and politicians ensued. Hammerling met with mine operators alone with Mitchell in secret conclaves.

The elite of Pennsylvania and New York politics attended a meeting in New York on October 7: Senators Penrose and Quay from the

Commonwealth, and Senator Platt and Governor Benjamin Odell of the Empire State, as well as Edward Lauterbach, chairman of the New York Republican County Committee.[31] Also in attendance were Mitchell and "a man said to be L. N. Hammerling, an independent coal operator from Wilkesbarre, [sic] PA." This statement about Hammerling's occupation may have been simply erroneous, but it is possible that by October 1902 he already had an interest in a small mine. He was also described in the press as "secretary on the Miners' union." Hammerling testified in 1905 that he had no recollection of why he went to the meeting, though he admitted that Quay paid him. He was "sick of the strike" and thus remembered nothing of the negotiations. The impressive gathering was, he noted, not special for him: "I came so often in contact with these people, that it is nothing new to me."[32] Such a statement is remarkable, considering that he had been a menial mine worker just a few years before, and was the only immigrant in the group. The day's meeting had an unusual termination: Hammerling had overlooked registering for a hotel—as had others at the meeting—so he, Penrose, Governor Odell, and Quay's son Dick all slept in the same room.[33] It was a breakthrough in negotiations.[34]

When Mitchell returned from Washington to discuss the planned Commission with the strikers, he met with Hammerling who "acted as a missionary [sic] between Mr. Mitchell and Senators Quay and Penrose in their conference with the coal road presidents." Again, the negotiations were secret.[35] When Mitchell brought the details of the suspension back from Washington to Wilkes-Barre, it was Hammerling who moved their acceptance by the assembled crowd of miners.[36] Obviously, he was in a crucial role in the bargaining. There is even some suggestion that he was in the pay of one of the mine operators.[37] Subsequently, his position in the negotiations became clearer, and he was referred to as "Senator Quay's representative."[38] Since Hammerling was very close to Mitchell, he was the mediator in an effort by Senators Platt and Quay, and also Governor Odell, to encourage Mitchell to attempt to become the president of the American Federation of Labor in November—an arrangement between Republican politicians and labor behind the backs of the owners.[39]

When the end of the strike was announced, Hammerling suddenly emerged from the shadows and spoke quite boldly to the press. He forecast grave consequences if the terms of the agreement were not accepted.

His dire prediction included the UMW becoming a "broken organization," and he declared that "public wants are at stake." As for the president: "he should be trusted, and if he fails to fulfill his promises, the public will mete out its judgment."[40] Quite a pronouncement for the humble mine worker of a few years before. This perhaps reflects the persistent but unverified rumor that the real work of Hammerling during the strike was to serve as the intermediary between the union and Roosevelt. He was the ultimate behind-the-scenes actor.[41] Hammerling, in 1918, told a confidant that Roosevelt wanted to appoint him one of the three mediators to settle the coal strike. This is a claim that cannot be confirmed, and appears in no other source, including the Roosevelt papers.[42]

The Commission hearings lasted from October 1902 until the following March. Over 1,100 witnesses were called, and representing the miners was the celebrated Clarence Darrow, best known for his defense of Leopold and Loeb and, later, John Scopes in the "Monkey Trial." Mitchell was satisfied with the results of the hearings, which gained greater wages and fewer hours for the miners but failed to recognize the union. Hammerling's involvement in these hearings is a notable point of his career. When he was called to testify in an obscure trial in 1904–1905 involving the anthracite settlement, he was able to turn to Mitchell, the governors of Pennsylvania and New York, and even President Roosevelt for information and advice. He was certainly a man with the highest connections.[43]

Hammerling's role in the anthracite strike of 1902 remains an enigma. We know that he was in a unique position among the major actors in settling the strike, but whether he had a decisive role or merely represented other major actors is not clear. The fact that he emerged as someone with friends in very high places suggests that he was not merely a passive go-between. The real role of Hammerling in the strike will doubtless never be known because of the fact that all the negotiations were secret and involved only a handful of people. His later nefarious activities would certainly dissuade other participants from reminiscing about their dealings with him.

THE ENTREPRENEUR

In addition to being a union leader, Hammerling was also a protean businessman. He created his own translating agency (*Translation Bureau for all Foreign Languages*) on the main square in Wilkes-Barre, and was given the contract to translate the "mine laws of the state" into various foreign languages and distribute them to miners. This led to 77,900 publications in the anthracite area alone.[44] He made considerable money in the business and was indefatigable in "networking." For example, he talked Mitchell into giving him a letter of introduction to T. V. Powderly, the pioneer leader of the Knights of Labor and dominating figure in the Bureau of Immigration—a useful contact for an immigrant leader. Powderly had, in addition to his work in labor organization, connections to the Republican elite and was deeply involved with immigration issues. Why there is not greater evidence of the Powderly-Hammerling connection is a curiosity. The only scrap we have is Hammerling's note to Mitchell that Powderly "has so much work in my line."[45] Hammerling was using Mitchell both to further his political career and expand the ambit of his publishing and translating business.

Hammerling himself was soon in a position to dispense favors rather than seek them. In October 1902, as the hearings were going on, he offered to include Mitchell in a business proposition in which he, Hammerling, invested $5,000.[46] By December he wrote to Mitchell asking to purchase 250 days of his time to give an equal number of lectures throughout the country on labor issues "or any other subject." He would pay Mitchell $25,000 and arrange the itinerary, including the British Isles, if Mitchell was interested.[47] This seems to indicate that Hammerling was now some sort of public relations figure, with considerable cash at his disposal. If we remember that Mitchell was a major national figure by 1903, Hammerling's close association with him is an important element to his rapid rise to success. How Hammerling, only a short while in the United States and months after being naturalized, could dispose of such sums is fascinating and inexplicable.

Hammerling also asked Mitchell to write to Quay and Penrose as well as other prominent Pennsylvanians to propose him for superintendent of Public Printing of the State. Characteristically, he did not want Mitchell to admit that he had anything to do with the request: Mitchell should pretend that it was unbidden initiative on his part. Next Hammerling wanted to market a picture of Mitchell—perhaps with Secretary of Labor Wilson—to mine workers. He wanted Mitchell to intervene to get him the contract to print the Immigration Law. He wanted Mitchell to inform him in advance regarding bills proposed to the Pennsylvania legislature so that he could act as go-between with state labor leaders. He also arranged with Mitchell to be part of the delegation welcoming President Roosevelt to the anthracite district.[48] His mentor Mitchell was simultaneously a businessman, unionist, and confidant of the coal barons.[49] The description of Mitchell as "devious, shifty, and unethical," and one who preferred "behind the scenes negotiations" might easily be applied to his protégé.[50] Their cooperation would be lifelong.

Hammerling apparently returned to Wilkes-Barre between 1904 and 1908 but was involved with businesses both there and in Philadelphia. He now gave his occupation as "manufacturer"; no longer clerk.[51] He claimed his advertising and printing income, plus the profits from a small Polish paper he owned in the anthracite district, earned him $200,000 by 1908.[52] He received, he told Congress, "an enormous amount of business."[53] Where his residence was is difficult to determine. He admitted to buying two houses (sequentially or simultaneously is unknown) in Philadelphia, and to opening an office there, but he still made his home in Wilkes-Barre.[54] Since his wife and children lived in Philadelphia, the state of his marriage is obvious. He opened an office on the main square in Wilkes-Barre and lived variously in a rooming house and a hotel. In the city directories he described himself between 1902 and 1908 as "interpreter," general agent, and, later, state representative of the *United Mine Workers Journal* and "agent" of the General Lubrication Company.[55] This all in addition to his booming printing business.[56]

He referred to the General Lubrication Company, in which he was prominently involved, as "the grease business." Mitchell owned one third.[57] Mitchell was supposed to drum up business. Hammerling was a director, owned a major interest in the company, and was angling— ultimately successfully—to have W. S. Leib, Assistant Treasurer of the United States, be the company treasurer. Hammerling would be the president. Mitchell left all the negotiations in this adventure to Hammerling, noting that he would front the money and dump it shortly thereafter and turn a quick profit.[58] However, the company struggled, and Hammerling generously offered to buy Mitchell out, which he did in 1908.[59] The whole affair apparently ended in fiasco with the company folding amidst denunciation and lawsuit.[60] It is with the "grease business" that we first encounter Bertha Leffler, Hammerling's very young female employee in Wilkes-Barre.[61] She will become much more important later.

Hammerling tried to interest Mitchell in starting a correspondence school with him, for which he was prepared at once to invest $5,000 on what he described quite openly as a get-rich-quick scheme.[62] He was still involved with anthracite politics and arranging meetings between Mitchell and representatives of major railroads.[63] He was also intrigued with buying coal lands in Alabama.[64] Indeed, there is some incomplete evidence, as we have noted, that Hammerling may have owned a small mine as early as 1902. He started his own publishing company to issue a history of the Republican Party.[65] He and two others incorporated a business in New Jersey, capitalized at $200,000, to "exhibit coal at the St. Louis Exposition."[66] By 1908 he had a financial interest in at least ten foreign language newspapers.[67] As late as 1910 he was still using Mitchell as a link to powerful business interests: he sent a check for $2,000 to Mitchell and asked, in return, a letter of introduction to the "Virginia Carolina Chemical Co." to solicit business from them for his newspapers. He wanted the company to run editorials about "fertilizer" so that non-native farmers would obtain the best "stuff."[68] He also used Mitchell to gain access for advertising copy to the New York Central Railroad.[69]

The breadth of his activities was astounding, and his constant use of contacts from the anthracite negotiations was striking. He asked Mitchell to get him a job as federal tax collector in Scranton, Pennsylvania, a campaign Mitchell undertook with fanatic zeal, and one that involved a number of senators.[70] Hammerling was involved in seeking the position of "Fourth-Assistant Postmaster Generalship"—or "any other position of the same rank"—an effort in which he mobilized very powerful supporters, principally Mitchell, who was his first go-between.[71] Roosevelt appointed Hammerling to the Panama Labor Commission, but he turned it down for reasons unclear.[72] His enemies later claimed that he was already such a controversial character that one person refused to serve on the Commission as long as he was included. He briefly considered the position of Assistant Secretary of the Treasury but, he lamented, "you have to understand banking," and unfortunately he did not.[73] Perhaps most important, his principal promoter was George B. Cortelyou, Postmaster General, and Chairman of the RNC.[74] Hammerling induced Pennsylvania governor Samuel Pennypacker to turn to Roosevelt asking him to consider him for a federal post.[75] He also worked with Mitchell to select candidates for Congress in Pennsylvania, one of whom was Hammerling's erstwhile friend Shea.[76]

Hammerling was constantly traveling about, staying in the finest hotels in New York, Washington, and Philadelphia. When a threatened strike surfaced in the anthracite region in 1905, Mitchell dispatched Hammerling to Washington to meet with the powerful: operators, Senator Philander Knox of Pennsylvania (Quay had died in 1904), and reportedly President Roosevelt. Hammerling was referred to as "Mitchell's Confidential Man." No details of his activities were ever reported; once again, all negotiations were secret.[77]

Hammerling's town paper described him in 1902 as "a clever young man who is rapidly coming to the front." He was, it continued, "foremost in the ranks of mine workers here."[78] He was general agent of the *United Mine Workers Journal*, which soon featured a large photograph of him on the front page. He appears quite dapper, with center-parted curly hair, a large moustache, and protrusive ears. The *Journal* noted that he had been employed by them since 1900 and had done commendable work. He "spoke several languages fluently" and "has held many offices."[79] He was a rising star in the labor movement.[80] This was reflected in his wardrobe: from about this time and for the rest of his life he dressed very grandly, often with elegant adornments.[81]

Hammerling represented himself to the UMW and the Republican Party as the spokesman of the "foreign people" of the region.[82] A discerning retrospective analysis in 1917 concluded that the Republicans saw him essentially as useful "in suppressing strikes."[83] He admitted to being paid by the Republicans before 1901 for his efforts with immigrant workers. He met with nationally known Republicans as early as 1900, if not before.[84] He was a power broker between the immigrants on the one hand, and both the union and the political activists on the other. He claims that at this time he concluded: "America's great problem was the immigrant."[85] This reflected his translating work as well as his position as founder and president of the large and powerful Lithuanian-Polish Club, which was often involved in labor disputes.[86] Hammerling thus combined his use of immigrants for business and political goals. He was beginning to look upon immigration issues from a national perspective.

Mitchell, too, in his pioneering labor efforts, tried to cross ethnic barriers to create a united class of miners.[87] The immigrants were vital to the strike and by 1902 constituted an enormous percentage of the miners: almost half of the northern district by 1902.[88] Whereas they had been regarded as beyond the reach of unionization, by 1902 "the Great Strike . . . was successful . . . because of the support of the Eastern Europeans."[89] Here Hammerling was a valuable tool for the Scotch-Irish Presbyterian Mitchell. If Harold W. Aurand is correct, after all, it was "immigrant leadership" that created the UMW.[90]

THE POLITICIAN

In mid-August 1903 Hammerling called on President Roosevelt at Oyster Bay and had a substantial conversation without, it seems, anyone else being present. It is tempting to see Quay and Penrose in this event. Hammerling "arranged a meeting" by Roosevelt with Pennsylvania Republican leaders for a few days hence. There was a dinner, and Hammerling ensured Mitchell that he would be invited. Mitchell, in his turn, was to organize a miners' rally to greet Roosevelt. The upcoming event was noted in the local press as the work of Hammerling, "a well-known Republican politician and labor leader."[91] It was now Hammerling who was becoming Mitchell's conduit to the politically powerful.

Hammerling, as a Republican link to immigrant workers, had advantages that Mitchell did not. Mitchell's career, and health, waned swiftly after 1902, and Hammerling, who had gained introduction into powerful political circles thanks to Mitchell, was in a convenient position to replace him. Hammerling was, after all, an immigrant himself, and a respected figure in the Slavic population of eastern Pennsylvania. By contrast, Mitchell was known for his disdain for the common laborer, especially the recent immigrant, and his temperament reflected the owners more than the workers; he considered the immigrants, according to Wiebe, "a drove of cattle."[92] This substantially eastern European community was precisely the element upon which Hammerling's position was built.

In 1901 or the next year, before he was naturalized, Hammerling was a delegate to a Republican state convention, though he later claimed not to remember it.[93] (Memory loss of awkward or potentially incriminating events seems to have plagued poor Hammerling). It was at this time he began receiving money for political "services," though he was evasive in discussing it.[94] The year 1904 was the turning point in his life. He was elected a delegate to the GOP's national convention, and the Republican National Committee, utilizing Senators Penrose and Quay, financed his move to New York where he "handled the campaign for them with the foreign papers—the advertising."[95] He told Roosevelt that he and Mitchell would do "anything" for the GOP.[96] He asked Roosevelt to name a friend as an at-large delegate to the convention and described himself to the president as "manager of the Miner's Paper."[97] He even asked Secretary of War William Howard Taft to buy campaign buttons.[98] Hammerling suborned the ethnic press in the eastern United States and later boasted to Mitchell: "I had every foreign newspaper in the United States supporting the Ticket." After the campaign, he and Mitchell continued to "acquire" the ethnic press, and though the details of this acquisition are not known, it probably involved advertising contracts, or simple bribery.[99]

After Roosevelt's victory, Hammerling was one of approximately one hundred members of the president's "reception committee" at the inaugural ceremonies and, along with others, represented the Republican National Committee (RNC).[100] As early as January Hammerling was invited to the White House in a personal note from Roosevelt.[101] In March he "commanded" a group of anthracite miners who marched in the day's parade.[102] He met with Roosevelt soon after the election and crowed to Mitchell: "the President has assured me to appoint me as Assistant Postmaster-General, or Assistant Secretary of any of the other Departments . . . on March 4th."[103] Why he did not receive a federal appointment is unclear. Hammerling was probably very disappointed.

Journalist, businessman, union star, political organizer, friend of the mighty, Hammerling would soon leave the narrow confines of Wilkes-Barre for the national stage. He was also about to become very rich. He would establish himself in the Galicia of his origins as well as the United States.

Hammerling left his business and traveled to Europe in 1909. He claimed that he waited for the "amnesty" so he would not be taken back into the army. Of course, he had testified that he had never served in the army. Traveling in Europe, Hammerling later claimed he did not know where he went. When he was asked whether he planned to return to Austria in 1909, he responded: "I do not remember."[104] Hammerling again traveled to Austria in 1911 and purchased a large estate worth, by various estimates, from $200,000 to $500,000. He insisted that he bought it for his wife—a generous gift.[105] This estate, however, seems to have been in Hammerling's possession until at least 1923, and what kind of "gift" it was to Klara is unclear. He told an American businessman that he inherited it from a rich uncle, a high-ranking Austrian soldier. Since Hammerling's family was poor, there seems to be no question that he bought the estate.[106]

CHAPTER 3

Business Tycoon and Republican Leader

IN 1908 "AT THE INSTANCE OF THE REPUBLICAN cam-
paign," Hammerling left Pennsylvania for New York. There he met a
certain "Grilla" (or perhaps "Grella") who ran an advertising agency for
the Italian language press in the United States.[1] Hammerling apparently
bought out Grilla and transformed the small concern into the American
Association of Foreign Language Newspapers (AAFLN). As Robert E.
Park has noted: it was the first time "that the majority of foreign-language
papers received any consideration from the national advertisers."[2]

THE ASSOCIATION OF FOREIGN LANGUAGE NEWSPAPERS

The AAFLN was incorporated in New York and issued stock.[3] Hammerling apparently moved to Brooklyn. The negotiations with Grilla
began in May and the AAFLN appeared in November; the events of
the interim have never been uncovered. Whether this acquisition was
of his own motion and at his own expense was never determined by
the various investigative bodies that later questioned him. Hammerling claimed he bought Grilla out for $20,000 from his own pocket.[4]
He said that, at the time, his assets were $200,000.[5] He was now a "me-
dia mogul."[6]

We have one piece of evidence that sheds some light on Hammerling's acquisition of the company from Grilla. In 1908 during the negotiations Hammerling approached Herman Ridder, the most powerful German publisher in the country, and sought his cooperation in the enterprise. According to Hammerling—recounting this story years later when it was politically profitable to have anti-German credentials because America was at war—Ridder told him: "Do you think I want to tie up with dirty Dago rags? I am the head not only of the German press, but I make the English [language] papers come to me." Later the number of German language papers fell by over 90 percent. Hammerling was gloating that his AAFLN now represented more papers than the number of German organs being published.

What do we make of this? Despite Hammerling's obvious intention of disparaging Ridder—and with it the American Germans—the story had the unintended consequence of demonstrating that in 1908 Hammerling turned to the powerful German press to be his allies in a newspaper network. Through the company he was deeply connected with the German community long before World War I made this fact very awkward for him.[7] Under federal investigation in 1918 Hammerling claimed that he founded the AAFLN because he had come to realize that "the immigrant" was an enormous problem for America.[8] An enemy, however, said that the whole purpose behind the AAFLN was to make Hammerling a "dictator to the foreign language press"—an obviously political goal.[9] It is also clear that by now Hammerling was moving beyond the Polish-Lithuanian core of his press network by acquiring Italian—and, unsuccessfully—German language papers. His press empire eventually included publications in a great many languages, representing numerous ethnic communities, including those long resident in the United States.

John Higham summarized Hammerling's ascent to a crucial position in GOP election politics: by an arrangement with Senators Mark Hanna and Boies Penrose, Hammerling received "a subsidy which he used to influence foreign language newspapers in favor of Republican candidates ... He served so well in the campaigns of 1904 and 1908 that some of his wealthy Republican friends then helped him set up an advertising-agency, the American Association for Foreign Language Newspapers, which placed national advertising in the pages of the immigrant press. ... Through lucrative contracts which were his to give or withhold, Hammerling acquired a power of life and death over struggling foreign language newspapers."[10]

As we have seen, Hammerling had boasted that he virtually controlled the foreign language press in the country as early as the 1904 election. The AAFLN was an official version of an existing reality. Judging by his 1908 activities and long-established close relations with the leadership of the Republican Party, it is almost certain that the AAFLN's creation was sponsored if not arranged and financed by the GOP.[11] The first meeting of the AAFLN was, incidentally, at the Republican Club.[12] The Republicans were actively buying immigrant votes, and Hammerling was their agent.

The AAFLN was aggressive in securing advertising for its clients. In turn Hammerling demanded that the foreign language press he represented print "practically anything they were requested to do."[13] In addition to commercial advertisements, Hammerling inserted pieces on political matters during election years—always pro-Republican. He boasted to potential advertisers that he had the ear of literally millions of immigrants, and his similar message to the GOP leadership was not unheeded as powerful Republicans paid court to him. The AAFLN was a business and a political tool, and Hammerling stood at the nexus.[14]

The extent and specifics of Hammerling's election activities in 1908 are very difficult to reconstruct. As in 1904, Hammerling was a delegate to the national convention representing Wilkes-Barre (the 11th congressional district). We know that the Republican State Committee of Pennsylvania published figures indicating it paid him only $250 for his work in the state. Given his innumerable connections there, this is absurd.[15] Doubtless there were "unofficial" payments.

In a letter obviously intended for public distribution, Hammerling explained the AAFLN as having four goals: to guide recent immigrants to suitable areas for settlement away from "congested" areas ("rural settlement" was endorsed, which reflected the views of proponents of immigration restriction, then very popular); to fight against "anarchy" and "socialism" to make the immigrant become a "desirable citizen"; to launch a "systematic campaign" to encourage the immigrant to deal with "established American business firms"; and to provide "free daily bulletins" on "important events." These goals clearly reflected the business interests behind the AAFLN and can easily be seen as an attempt to break down the self-sufficient economic settlement characteristic of urban ethnic neighborhoods. The AAFLN also aimed to make the immigrant less "foreign" by integrating him more fully into American society, thereby combating the image of the recent arrivals as dangerous and incomprehensible—themes that were repeatedly raised in the 1902 investigation of the anthracite strike and elsewhere. Hammerling called on Mitchell for a letter of endorsement of the AAFLN to be published in the ethnic press and noted his support from Governor Edwin Stuart of Pennsylvania and from Senators Penrose and Knox of Pennsylvania—all staunch Republicans.[16]

In addition to its advertising business, or perhaps as an extension of it, was the publication of a slick bimonthly entitled the *American Leader*. The journal carried articles by major business and political figures—including Charles Nagel, the former Secretary of Commerce and Labor; Ira Bennett, editor of the *Washington Post*; and the prominent journalist, George Creel—and adopted an editorial position that was very clear. The *American Leader* was opposed to the growing prohibition movement, and to immigration restriction. In its own words the journal "extolled the virtues and hardships of immigrants, detailed political controversies of immigration and strongly offered editorial suggestions for legislative changes. In addition, the periodical drew from newspapers affiliated with the AAFLN to translate and publish selected stories in English."[17] Prominent advertising agencies published letters in the *Leader* as well as many public officials including President Taft and Attorney General George Wickersham.[18] The staff included prominent journalists. Nonetheless, the foreign language press in America, and hence its master, Hammerling, have been largely ignored.[19]

The advocacy of the "wet," or anti-prohibition, cause (what advocates called with refinement "personal liberty") put Hammerling in association with the brewing interests, particularly that of Busch Beer, which advertised liberally in the *Leader*. It was probably Adolphus Busch who—at Nagel's suggestion—launched his anti-prohibition campaign. Hammerling told Busch: "I am your boy."[20] The *Leader* also carried regular advertising from German-owned steamship companies like North German Lloyd and the Hamburg-American Line (of which Hammerling may have been a director).[21] For the rest of his career in the United States, these myriad connections with German business—and later

German government—representatives were to characterize him. The brewers had a close working relationship with the German-American Alliance and contributed generously to a special Alliance fund. This, in turn, brought the brewers and the Alliance into touch with Hammerling and the AAFLN.[22] Hammerling rather crudely told the brewers that they should give the AAFLN their advertising business because it was the heavy-drinking immigrants who "built up this great industry."[23] He bombarded Congress with telegrams from his papers opposing prohibition.[24] The brewers were also interested in politics. British Intelligence later discovered that their money went to Hammerling during the 1912 presidential campaign; unfortunately, details are lacking.[25]

But it was not only German-related concerns that advertised in the *Leader*. Standard Oil, the American Tobacco Company, Liggett & Myers, and others appeared regularly. Hammerling had some of the wealthiest manufacturers in America sponsoring his journal. He also carried political advertising for the GOP. In 1911–1912 he received $128,000 worth of business from Tobacco and Standard Oil alone.[26] By 1912 he was being referred to as an "agent" of Standard Oil. Evidence suggests he helped Standard Oil head off strikes among immigrant workers. He may have done this for other advertisers, drawing on his anthracite years.[27]

Within a year the nascent AAFLN was holding banquets with many publishers present—"every one of them from New York and Philadelphia and all of the neighboring places," Hammerling crowed.[28] There were also "many prominent business men." The organization grew to represent almost 800 papers, in 33 languages, with a claimed 20 million readers. Hammerling was on his way to becoming a millionaire. Cabinet members and officials of the Republican National Committee were frequent guests at these banquets. Even an enemy noted that Penrose "eulogized" Hammerling at the 1910 banquet, as did the politically powerful George Cortelyou (then president of Consolidated Gas) and Melville E. Stone, general manager of the Associated Press, among others.[29] At the same banquet letters of regret from President Taft, Vice President James Sherman, Secretary of State Knox, and Postmaster Frank Hitchcock were read.[30] But, Hammerling noted, the banquets avoided all the "crooks."[31]

The *Leader* functioned in an unusual manner.[32] Authors were paid, rather modestly, for their contributions. The articles were then translated into more than two dozen languages and republished in the ethnic press associated with the AAFLN. Hammerling neither paid for their republication nor was he compensated. They were merely part of a web holding the AAFLN together and allowing Hammerling to influence the political direction of the ethnic press. It was the advertisement he placed in the press that was a major source of their revenue and made the papers virtually dependent upon his favor. Hammerling explained his ability to run a business with so many Roman Catholics, despite the fact that he was Jewish, in a most matter-of-fact manner: "Among my 500 editors there are more than 200 Roman Catholic priests. They may all know that I am a Jew, but that's nothing. So long as I don't go on record with it, they can vote for me as President of the Association. . . . But, if only once I admit to being a Jew, they could no longer vote for me."[33]

The business structure of the AAFLN was bizarre. Hammerling was the president. Bertha Leffler, his teenage secretary from Wilkes-Barre, was treasurer.[34] The AAFLN issued $50,000 of preferred stock, and a like amount of common. The foreign language publishers were asked to subscribe to the preferred stock, but not pay for it. The cost for the 1–4 shares, at $100 a share, was to be compensated out of 50 percent advertising revenue placed in the papers. Hammerling thus ensnared the publishers in his corporate web. Of the 500 common shares outstanding, Hammerling held 290. Mitchell also owned shares, the publishers none. The common was not purchased but given away by Hammerling to friends. Hammerling owned all the preferred stock. "Stock was held by his employees in escrow and endorsed in blank. Whenever he felt like calling the stock in, he just called it in."[35] He declared whatever dividend he wanted, acting at random.[36]

The company had no directors, only "honorary directors" appointed by Hammerling. They had no meetings, nor did the stockholders. There were no minutes, though someone was designated to prepare them. Meetings were announced in English in the foreign language newspapers—thus no one came. Hammerling paid stock dividends to those who "expected" them, but ignored the others. He also regularly distorted the books, giving himself a cut of the expenses recorded. The business records, insofar as they existed, were essentially fraudulent. Every year Hammerling took what records he had to the boiler room of the Mansfield Building in New York and had two employees, Arthur Gabryel (Artur Gabrylewicz) and Sigismund (Zygmunt) Dattner, burn them.[37] The supposed "secretary" of the corporation, Albert Jaudon, quit his job with Hammerling because his boss was essentially a crook.[38] The company had many "vice presidents"— they changed constantly—but they were really just "by name." In reality all officers were clerks.[39] Hammerling thought that by giving his clerks the title of vice president, it would give them greater weight in business dealings. Their titles were thus fleeting, and bogus.

His involvement with the brewing industry was extraordinarily confusing and revolves around Percy Andreae, who represented the brewers. Andreae would write articles opposing prohibition, but not sign them. Hammerling would put his name on the articles, publish them in the *Leader*, and then have them translated for the foreign language press. The articles were billed to the brewers as advertising though they purported to be nothing of the kind.[40] He charged Andreae a regular fee for his service and also had him pay rent on one his offices. He also required him to provide generous Christmas bonuses to his employees.[41] Incidentally, Hammerling would charge Andreae for the translation fees, but pay the translator considerably—sometimes astoundingly—less and keep the overage.[42] He also charged his advertisers huge sums and paid the foreign language press a pittance for carrying the advertisement and kept the difference. His profits were gigantic.[43] The brewers via Andreae were indirectly paying a portion of Hammerling's business costs.

Thus Hammerling was able to carry liquor advertising without registering it as such—a violation of an act of Congress. In addition he charged the brewers a fee for organizing a bombardment of Congress by the foreign language papers regarding prohibition. At Andreae's expense, Hammerling also traveled to different parts of the country to make speeches opposing prohibition. One of the senators, examining the myriad of evidence in 1918, accused him of "graft," though he was never prosecuted.[44] On the other hand, Andreae would make appearances as a vice president of the AAFLN to disguise his employment with the brewers.[45] In fact, Andreae eventually became vice president of the AAFLN; however, it is unknown what that title actually meant. Hammerling made $83,000 from the brewers from 1913 to 1915.[46] It was a mutually profitable arrangement.

Typical of Hammerling's complex multipart schemes is his proposal to the Brewers' Association of November 29, 1913. Charles Nagel wrote a series of articles on "personal liberty" for the *American Leader*—always over Hammerling's signature. The AAFLN would "inaugurate a campaign" to have these articles appear in the foreign language press. The 1,500 breweries in the Association would, in response, subscribe to "four copies each issue" of the *Leader*: $12,000 per year.[47]

In a fascinating episode, Ludwik Bernstein, a boy from Hammerling's home village of Drohojów in Galicia, was sent to the United States to work for Hammerling. Bernstein's father had become indebted to Hammerling's family. To repay the money, and without the son's knowledge or consent, Bernstein Senior virtually sold the boy to Hammerling. Hammerling employed him in a new mail-order business he had created in New York to serve the immigrant community. Young Bernstein was in awe of Hammerling's blasé corruption, particularly his adulteration of the firm's books. What makes this story the more fascinating is that Bernstein later changed his name to Namier, was knighted in Great Britain, and as Sir Lewis became one of the most prominent and respected historians of modern England.[48] He is our principal unbiased witness to Hammerling as crook; curiously, Bernstein-Namier tended to downplay Hammerling's associations with the Central Powers when the former served as an advisor to British Intelligence during World War I.

IMMIGRANT CHAMPION

Hammerling worked to ingratiate himself with both the immigrant community and important figures in the government who dealt with immigration. In 1909, representing the AAFLN, Hammerling joined a group of prominent immigrants to meet with the Acting Secretary of the Department of Labor and Commerce, which oversaw immigration issues through the Immigration and Naturalization Service (INS). The meeting was to protest "unjust exclusion" of immigrants.[49] In subsequent meetings Hammerling acted as spokesman for the group. He was in touch with influential senator William P. Dillingham, who wrote to him over the issue. In an aside that demonstrated the conflicted relationship Hammerling had with his Jewish origins, he explained to the INS that "Christian people" were not gouging immigrants coming to the United States. The clear implication was that Jews were.[50] Hammerling nonetheless played a leading role in legal issues involving Jewish immigrants.

In 1913 he spoke at the Hebrew Sheltering and Immigration Aid Society, which condemned the "educational test" administered to arrived immigrants at Ellis Island. In 1910 Hammerling, leading a group of twenty-five editors of the ethnic press, met with Nagel and Taft in Washington to protest immigration restriction (the Hayes bill).[51] After the 1911 Dillingham Commission report urging immigration restriction via a literacy test, Hammerling's *Leader* became a champion of the notion that "overeducated, neurasthenic Anglo-Saxon men" lacked the virility to confront exertion that immigrants exhibited: the immigrant as a stimulating racial transfusion.[52] He founded something called the Liberty Immigration Society, which met with Secretary Nagel.[53] Early the next year, Hammerling brought his AAFLN editors to Congress to protest against restriction.[54] He was doubtless the most public immigrant in the fight against restriction.[55]

When, in 1913, the Jones-Dillingham quota bill was introduced, discriminating against immigrants from southern and eastern Europe, Hammerling was one of three delegates to journey to Washington to address President Taft. The delegation included Scandinavians and Poles, and Hammerling, representing the AAFLN, spoke for all immigrants.[56] When a large group of immigrant leaders met with Taft the next day, Hammerling "filed a brief," asking that a lack of education not be a factor in refusing immigrants.[57] His was, according to the *Washington Post*, "the principal brief against the bill."[58] The same delegation met with the new president, Woodrow Wilson, a few weeks later.[59] Hammerling's priceless linkages to prominent Republicans including President Taft were broken by the election of Democrat Wilson. The new president came to know a good deal about Hammerling and neither liked nor trusted him.

Two years later, with Wilson president, Hammerling was again at the White House arguing against restrictionist legislation.[60] He made efforts to see Wilson in 1916 over the issue, and in January of that year, provided a fascinating testimony before the House.[61]

Hammerling cultivated both Jews and Christians. In 1913 he successfully intervened to reopen the St. Joseph Home for Polish Immigrants in Brooklyn after federal authorities had closed it and barred its representatives from Ellis Island. All other efforts to reopen the organization, including those by the highest Polish clergy in the country, had been in vain. Hammerling had the matter reviewed by Congress, and the Office of the Commissioner of Immigration allowed the Home to reopen in 1915. Hammerling was clearly a very powerful ally with the immigration authorities.[62] This service to the Polish community reinforced his particular linkages to the Poles, and when a Polish cleric in New York was elevated to Monsignor, Hammerling was prominent at the ceremonies.[63]

He worked with other groups as well, such as the Russian consulate, to find the families of Russian immigrants in the United States.[64] It was immigration restriction that linked Hammerling to powerful Jewish leaders like the Zionist champion Louis Marshall.[65] He also published an article in support of the innocence of Menahem Mendel Beiliss, thus associating the AAFLN with pro-Jewish causes.[66] Beiliss, a Ukrainian Jew, was accused of the ritual murder of a Christian child, and the infamous trial led to the widespread condemnation of Russian anti-Semitism. Hammerling also led a committee negotiating with the immigration authorities regarding the treatment of immigrants at Ellis Island.[67]

In September 1909 there was a hearing regarding "the method of executing the Immigration Laws." Three officials of the Immigration Commission were present, and eight immigrant leaders, including Hammerling.[68] He always spoke in the name of "the newspapers that I represent."[69] He was perhaps the most frequent and lengthy speaker. His central argument was to have representatives of various eastern European groups serve on the commission at Ellis Island, the so-called Board of Special Inquiry.[70] He offered himself as the voice of eastern European immigrants, representing them through the AAFLN. He was a member of the "advisory committee," and the AAFLN was its link to the readership of foreign language newspapers."[71] That organization was represented on the powerful National Liberal Immigration League (established in 1906) with Hammerling as its delegate.[72] Woodrow Wilson was also a member along with a number of members of Congress. Hammerling had become one of the key immigrant leaders in the country, a representative of this variegated community to federal authorities.[73]

He had testified before Congress five times by 1916. The January 1916 session of the House gave him the opportunity to lead an eighteen-person committee to Washington.[74] He had "D. S. Mormon"[75] read a statement that claimed the AAFLN represented newspapers with a circulation of over 8 million, almost half of the 18 million immigrants in the United States. The statement contained a protest against barring "desirable and worthy immigrants" from entry because it would "prove detrimental to American interests"; these "sturdy and virile" immigrants had been an economic boon to the country. He enumerated various industries where immigrant workers were common—vital because of the "scarcity of labor" in the country. The 1916 bill was virtually the same as the one Wilson had vetoed in 1915.[76] The statement was signed by a long list of Hammerling's editors.

Hammerling insisted that his committee was "more against the admission of any undesirables" than Congress "will ever be." This because any wrongdoing by an immigrant would reflect badly on the whole foreign community. His minions were teaching language, loyalty, and patriotism, and their opposition was a reflection of their "Americanism." He made an aside criticizing the American Federation of Labor's Samuel Gompers for his support of the bill, and insisted the labor organization would be ten times larger if not for his stand against immigration. The immigrants were afraid to join the Federation, which had long opposed immigrationand regarded newcomers as "inassimable and therefore a threat to American institutions."[77] Hammerling had made an intelligent, though much exaggerated and optimistic case for opposing the new version of the immigration bill, which had already been vetoed by three presidents.

He also issued a fascinating statement about his support of Wilson that deserves quotation. "Unfortunately" he did not vote for Wilson since he was a delegate for Taft, and Hammerling did not want to "betray his party." "But I will now." He assessed that "50,000 people" had sent small amounts of money to Wilson for vetoing the bill as it made them feel safer and hopeful that the rest of their families could eventually join them in America.[78]

The *American Leader*, the AAFLN's journal, carried constant articles on the benefits of immigration, the evils of restriction, and literacy requirements. In fact, that was the essence of the *American Leader*: a celebration of immigration and a damnation of efforts at its restriction. When he was not writing about "personal liberty," Hammerling was publishing editorials condemning the likes of the "obnoxious" and "pernicious" Burnett Immigration Bill.[79] Despite these efforts, the bill passed in 1913; Taft vetoed it, but Congress overrode the president's action. And despite two vetoes by Wilson, the literacy test was passed by Congress, motivated by wartime jingoism in 1917.[80]

BANKER: THE CARNEGIE-SAVOY SCANDAL

By 1910 Hammerling was a prominent businessman in New York. His advertising business involved him deeply in the Carnegie-Savoy banking scandal of 1911. On March 28, 1911, Joseph B. Reichmann of the Carnegie Trust Company was indicted for "official misconduct."[81] Reichmann had sworn that the Carnegie Trust had no outstanding debt in a September 1910 report. As a matter of fact it was liable for over $100,000 to another bank, which it disguised. Carnegie subsequently failed. The scandal soon implicated the Savoy Trust Company, of which Hammerling was a director. The City of New York had made deposits to Savoy at the express solicitation of Hammerling, including one for $50,000 in September 1910, though there had been earlier deposits of $75,000.[82] Savoy paid 2 percent on the $50,000, which it immediately loaned at 6 percent to William Cummins of Carnegie. Reichmann was involved in the loan.

The night before the deposit, Cummins met with Hammerling and assured him that he could arrange a City deposit at Savoy, which accomplishment Hammerling had tried long and vainly to gain.[83] Hammerling's previous efforts to gain deposits were facilitated by his friendship with Charles H. Hyde, the city's chamberlain, who was responsible for handling municipal assets.[84] However, he needed Cummins to get the additional $50,000. As soon as Savoy got the money it would lend it to Cummins. Hammerling, in return for what appears to have been a "deal," bought 100 shares of Carnegie with which Cummins was associated. Reichmann's Carnegie was one of the recipients of such deposits and was thus implicated. The circle was closed.

The deal soon became public knowledge. Savoy's books were seized by the district attorney, and Hammerling and another Savoy director were required to testify behind closed doors. Savoy's success in getting the City's deposit of $50,000 set off a series of investigations of how City money was being invested. Hyde managed to extricate himself, but Hammerling's association with gaining City deposits to turn a quick profit became public knowledge. Cummins went to Sing Sing for seven years; Reichmann followed him into prison.[85]

But the episode showed Hammerling to be more than a smooth operator with powerful connections in the financial world. An anonymous analysis reports that the loan was originally refused by Savoy and only made when Hammerling threatened to resign and promised to guarantee the loan himself. Carnegie soon thereafter went into bankruptcy, and Savoy quickly followed. Savoy asked Hammerling to pay his guarantee; he refused and was sued. He was able to settle for a mere $5,000.[86] The story has a final twist, and fortunately we have a (biased) eyewitness testimony for the events.

Liston L. Lewis was Hammerling's attorney and close friend. He was also counselor for the fast-failing Carnegie Trust. Two days before Carnegie went under, Liston came to see Hammerling. The AAFLN had $50,000 deposited at Carnegie. When Liston left, Hammerling hurriedly called occasional vice president Arthur Gabryel into his office and handed him a check for $50,000 drawn on Carnegie. Hammerling told Gabryel to go at once to Carnegie and cash the check. The culmination has comic overtones: "Mr. Gabryel went down to the Carnegie Trust Co., withdrew the money, and handed the amount in cash to Mr. Hammerling who was waiting at the corner of Wall St. and Broadway, whereupon Mr. Hammerling went with Mr. Gabryel to the Bankers Trust Co., which then was at 7 Wall St., and opened an account there with the said money, and Mr. Gabryel was told by Mr. Hammerling not to say a word about this transaction to anyone." This left the AAFLN with $26 at Carnegie. Hammerling's exposure was limited.[87]

THE AAFLN MENAGERIE

The AAFLN—situated in Manhattan in the World Building and, after 1914, in the Woolworth building—must have been a scene of utter chaos: mysterious figures came and went, company officers changed titles constantly, large monetary gifts were doled out for unclear reasons, employees were dispatched on confidential missions, Hammerling held secret meetings, and he was constantly manipulating the company's records. Odd people of every conceivable nationality speaking innumerable tongues crowded the office. Even Mitchell's two sons were milling about. According to one detractor "the whole office is nothing but a whorehouse."[88] (We assume he is speaking metaphorically, because no other source confirms Hammerling's service of this sort to the ethnic community.) After the war started German officials, and perhaps Austrian ones as well, called on Hammerling in his offices. A famous Russian revolutionary also came calling. Hammerling's own words capture the scene eloquently: "He [Leon Trotsky] ran about wearing a blue serge suit that looked like a mirror. . . . He wore a red ready-made tie that kept dropping out of its place in his celluloid collar because of the gyrations of his arms as he wind milled socialism from soap boxes. He came to my office with a proposition so shady that I chased him out."[89] Given Hammerling's own dubious business practices, one can only wonder what Trotsky had in mind.

A year later Hammerling enlarged the story. Trotsky now came by twice and threatened to "organize unions to destroy manufactures." He also threatened to kill him. Hammerling seized Trotsky by the neck to eject him, but the clever revolutionary was wearing a "rubber collar," which somehow resulted in Hammerling cutting his hand. Hammerling related this story to the Senate with much emotion. By now Trotsky was a well-known figure, and tossing him about would make Hammerling more heroic in American eyes.[90]

The story of wrestling with Trotsky is just one of the uncountable Hammerling legends that the man himself put into circulation. Among his other reputed activities was diamond smuggling. In 1907 he allegedly returned from one of his yearly trips to Austria with "an enormous number of diamonds including brooches, rings, pendants, five caret stones, etc." Where and how Hammerling obtained this trove has never been verified or explained. It appears preposterous on its face. But, then again, Hammerling apparently smuggled money into Poland in 1919.[91] What makes the jewelry smuggling more than the tittle-tattle it appears to be is that in 1918 Hammerling admitted that he had been charged with diamond smuggling but he "did not know" the outcome of the case.[92]

The Trotsky affair lasted a short time. Accusations of diamond smuggling were a mere annoyance. Hammerling's AAFLN was also the site of two far longer-running escapades involving his employees. One involved a mystery that was never solved. On March 9, 1918, Hammerling was interrogated by Norman H. White of the Military Intelligence Division of the United States Army over alleged involvement with the Central Powers.[93] He was asked to identify another man seated in the room. "Samuel Weiss," he answered, and noted that he had known the man for "eight or nine years." That would make their meeting in about 1910. Under further questioning he said that Weiss was from Austrian Poland—as was Hammerling. When asked whether Weiss was related to him, Hammerling answered "no."[94] Now the situation began to become difficult. Weiss entered the United States under the name of "Hammerling," and as our hero admitted, "people claim that he is a brother or some other relative." On his citizenship papers Samuel again gave his name as Hammerling. When pressed, our Hammerling noted rather cavalierly that he did not trouble himself with the details about clerks, "especially him." A strange aside.[95]

The same day Weiss was interrogated by White.[96] He did not know whether or not he was Hammerling's brother. He also did not know when he arrived in the United States or on what ship. He also was unsure of his age. He had a brother but knew nothing about him. He lived in Philadelphia from 1904–1906—the years Hammerling was either living there or commuting from Wilkes-Barre. Hammerling's first wife and brother-in-law were then in Philadelphia as well. Weiss, who seemed to know nothing of his own biography—confusion characteristic of Hammerling—said he was from "Darachow" in Austrian Poland, almost certainly a corruption of Drohojów, the tiny, largely Jewish, village that Hammerling came from. The likelihood that a village of a few score would produce two men named Hammerling who were not related strains credulity.

When asked about his employer, Weiss knew nothing. He thought Louis Hammerling was a "Bohemian" and knew absolutely nothing about him except that Hammerling once brought a mysterious boy named Adolph with him from Austria—another relative, also shrouded in mystery. When asked about his real name, Weiss said that he had been working in the "ladies waist" business, but it failed and he had to return to his original employer: Hammerling. He thenceforth used the name Weiss (his wife's maiden name) rather than Hammerling because "he did not want people to know that he was working as a clerk." He also said that he used the name Weiss because "he thought if Louis N. Hammerling knew his name was Sam Hammerling, he would not be employed by Louis N. Hammerling." At this point the investigators became nonplussed and began to consider the queer possibility that "we did not believe Louis Hammerling's name is Louis Hammerling." The investigators began to show signs of total disorientation. Suddenly, no one knew who anybody was. Weiss had simply introduced evidence that overwhelmed the analytical capacities of the federal authorities.[97]

Hammerling's other employees knew that Weiss was Hammerling's brother—or at least a close relative—despite his denials.[98] The reason for these denials and the ignorance of Weiss regarding basic facts are very hard to understand. They left Hammerling open to yet another charge of perjury for giving knowingly false statements. He obviously did not want others to know about this man, and probably coached him to answer in an obfuscatory manner. What conclusion may we draw from this strange episode in which Hammerling probably left himself open for subsequent charges? One possibility is that Weiss knew too much and had to be distanced from Hammerling lest he be examined too closely. In 2006 the Hammerling family stated that Samuel "Weiss" was Hammerling's brother.[99]

The other human resources escapade at AAFLN involved Bertha Leffler. Bertha went to work for Hammerling in Wilkes-Barre when she was in her early teens. He either brought her to New York in 1908 or she came of her own motion. Like her sister, Margaret, she had a number of impressive posts at AAFLN, but in reality these were empty titles. In fact, both Bertha and Margaret were at various points treasurer: "every year it was someone else."[100] Under questioning by White, Bertha corroborated the report from other Hammerling employees that he disposed of his account books every year "because they had no room for them." Hammerling visited Bertha at home, and her mother was "aware of all her connections with him." These seem to have included romance, though Hammerling dated both sisters at the same time. He presented Bertha with a four-hundred-dollar diamond ring—quite a prize a century ago.[101] One can only speculate whether this gift was acquired in the alleged diamond smuggling of 1907. Bertha averred that she knew "nothing" about Hammerling's "personal affairs."[102]

This statement was contradicted by the testimony of the AAFLN's vice president, Gabryel. According to him, Bertha Leffler was intimately aware of all of Hammerling's personal life. Other sources confirm that she was present at most if not all of Hammerling's private business dealings, which would make her perhaps the only person who knew what Hammerling was doing.[103] It would also make her a perjurer. The Justice Department learned that she was "absolutely conversant . . . with

Hammerling's most private affairs." The employees of the AAFLN regarded her as his mistress.[104] Hammerling gave her "large sums of money" and jewels. She also took vacations lasting months. Bertha was, in the words of one of Hammerling's key employees, "everything to him."[105] She had had "dishonorable connections" with him and was "sent away" to a "private hospital" as a result of their "improper relations."[106]

Hammerling was obviously concerned about Bertha speaking too openly. She telephoned him about her interrogation. She was distraught; Hammerling indignant. Motivated either by gallantry or by fear for himself, the next day he reported to the examiners that the allegations regarding sexual relations with him had driven her to a "serious condition." "The poor girl has just absolutely gone to pieces," Hammerling emotionally stated.[107] Hammerling later "jilted" her, and the hopes of federal investigators that she would provide exhaustive evidence never happened. Love runs deep.[108]

The Leffler affair provides an eloquent testimony to Hammerling's secretive and disorderly business dealings. His secretary knew everything but did not produce evidence damning to him, despite their personal adventures. The AAFLN saw people come and go; Leffler never left. Her loyalty to Hammerling suggests that, for all of his mischief and corruption, he had the ability to inspire love and loyalty. He would soon need both.

CHAPTER 4

National Politics

HAMMERLING CANNOT BE UNDERSTOOD other than as an agent of the Republican Party who connected his own financial interests with the electoral success of the GOP and the consequential cultivation of the politically powerful. In 1912 Hammerling was deeply involved with the reelection efforts of William Howard Taft.[1] This placed him in an awkward position as he had earlier worked for Roosevelt—though this was a dilemma shared by many Americans who were asked to choose between the romantic Rough Rider and the stolid behemoth. Hammerling told Congress in 1918 that Teddy "wanted us foreigners to get down on our knees and bow to him, and I wouldn't do that."[2] Taft was thus Hammerling's clear choice by 1912, or at least so he claimed in 1918. Hammerling worked for the party candidate, Taft, and, in the primaries, the target of Hammerling's activities on behalf of the GOP was New Jersey's governor Woodrow Wilson.

It is difficult to establish what Hammerling's official position with the Republican campaign was. In 1918 when he testified before the Senate, nothing potentially embarrassing to the GOP was discussed. In fact his bizarre political role was conspicuously ignored. The only other time Hammerling testified under oath was in 1905, years before the election. Thus we are left with bits and snatches.[3] Republican efforts in 1912 to garner the votes of Poles and other recent immigrants were unprecedented. Wilson had written despairingly of these immigrants in his *History of the American People*, singling out Poles, Hungarians, and Italians for special opprobrium.[4] The issue came to haunt him in early 1912 when he ran in the Democratic primary, and reappeared with a vengeance in the general elections. The Republicans were convinced that Senator Hanna's prediction would come true: the immigrant becoming a Republican, labor and capital in unison, the corporate state.

A special "adjunct organization" was created for work among the "foreign born"; and to counter the traditional charge that the Republicans favored immigration restriction, the chairman of the Republican National Committee, Charles D. Hilles, promised that if reelected, Taft would veto restrictionist legislation.[5] A well-financed campaign to influence the ethnic press to support the Republican Party was also pursued. Hammerling worked directly under Hilles, who was also Taft's private secretary and campaign manager, to win—or perhaps more accurately, force—the foreign language press to support the Republican ticket. Ostensibly, Hammerling did nothing more than place advertising in the various newspapers, but his methods were essentially bribery.[6] In addition, Hilles relied on Hammerling for advice concerning the immigrant community.[7] Hammerling later claimed that the RNC's Frank Hitchcock "depended on him in several campaigns for the foreign vote."[8] In addition to Hammerling's special assignment to the immigrants, he was a member of the campaign's "publicity bureau."[9] By 1912 Republicans in Pennsylvania were reminding Hilles fervently of the vital role Hammerling had played in the 1904 and 1908 elections.[10]

Hammerling raised money, arranged advertising, planted articles, published pamphlets, and suborned the ethnic press. The *American Leader* became virtually a Taft campaign journal.[11] He claimed, probably with more accuracy than he realized, that no one "would do what I am doing for the President."[12] It was Hammerling who issued a blistering attack on Wilson entitled "Woodrow Wilson Has Insulted You! Will You Vote for Your Slanderer?" that called Wilson "our greatest enemy." He tried to convince Poles that Roosevelt could not win, and hence a vote for Taft was the only means to punish their detractor, Wilson.[13] Hammerling was, after all, a Polish Jew, and while his business activities were not complicated by scruples, his national sensibilities may well have been aroused by Wilson's insulting references to recent immigrants.

In 1912 Hammerling placed a considerable amount of Republican advertising. The National Committee paid for it, and Hammerling collected and withheld a 10 to 15 percent commission for himself. In 1912 that amounted to $105,000.[14] Despite this, Hammerling claimed he had absolutely no influence on the foreign language press, though, as we have seen, he claimed exactly the opposite when earlier corresponding with John Mitchell.[15] One report indicated that Hammerling had placed $360,000 of Republican advertisements in the foreign language press since 1896. Much of this was his profit.[16]

Hammerling and Hilles maintained a vigorous correspondence in July-September 1912, which illustrates clearly what Hammerling—and the GOP—were doing in the election. In July Hammerling offered Michał Kruszka, one of the most important Polish publishers in America with papers in both Milwaukee and Chicago, $3,000 "worth of exclusive advertising space in behalf of the president." Hammerling was pressed for more money, but had expended the funds the Party had given him.[17] As a matter of fact, by September he had placed $106,750 in the foreign language press, and the Party and he had to hector the national campaign committee to repay him his costs.[18] In September, chairman Hilles appointed Hammerling "solicitor," and Hammerling sent letters to "a few hundred of my friends" and would thence turn the contributions over to Hilles. The original contributors—we do not have the full list—were "Jewish businessmen."[19]

The Polish paper in Syracuse, New York, promised Hammerling it could "get all the Polish voters in the county to favor Mr. Taft and the Republican ticket and will publish anything we send them." The paper's editor, W. Kozłowski, however, wanted "$400.00 worth of advertising space," and Hammerling advised Hilles that he thought they could get it for $100 less.[20] Hammerling also bribed the Polish press in Buffalo (Polak w Ameryce), an effort that put him in negotiations with W. S. Rylski, one of the leading members of the Polish Falcons, a major fraternal organization. Rylski was a popular figure with a considerable following. He promised to carry only pro-Taft material and support the Republican Party editorially if Hammerling gave them $1,000 worth of advertising. The deal was cut.[21] In addition to the Polish language press, Hammerling was active in bribing Ukrainian, Hungarian, Italian, and Jewish newspapers, and probably others. Hammerling reported to Hilles that by August he had "contracted" with 131 papers. He also gave Hilles a list of those papers that refused, appending a note of "what they want." He had run out of funds and even spent $500 of his own money.[22] The AAFLN was a very convenient network for his campaign activities.[23]

The Falcons—indirectly through Rylski—were not the only Polish group Hammerling tried to influence. It was even later bruited that the Republican Party had paid $5,000 to certain officers of the most influential organization of American Poles, the Polish National Alliance in Chicago, in exchange for active support of Taft's candidacy in 1912.[24] If true, this would have been a major coup: the National Alliance was the largest and fastest-growing Polish fraternal organization in the United States. It also had its own newspaper, the *Dziennik Związkowy*, nationally circulated. Taft made a campaign stop in Cambridge Springs, Pennsylvania, home of the Alliance's newly opened college and spoke to a large gathering of Poles with praise and respect—a far cry from Wilson's disparaging remarks in his *History*.

Hammerling's adventures with the foreign press were not a secret to his political enemies. In the fall of 1911 the Senate created a subcommittee to investigate campaign contributions.[25] Joseph Dixon, chairman of Roosevelt's campaign committee, damned both Democrats and Republicans for suspicious contributions and announced a list of those he wanted to testify. Among them was Hammerling, who "might be called to tell why 242 newspapers published in foreign languages in this country have been purchased." Since Dixon also wanted Hilles to testify, the hearings may well have proven very awkward for Hammerling. With the election soon over, the investigation faded away as did the public exposure of Hammerling as tsar of the immigrant press.[26] Nonetheless, Dixon later damned Hammerling because he "delivered the foreign press to the Taft managers exclusively." Hammerling claimed to have acted impartially.[27]

Hammerling's relations with Taft were more intimate and frequent than might be assumed. During 1912 the two exchanged forty-three letters, sometimes writing daily. These letters included discussions of issues related to the campaign, criticism of appointments already made, requests for Taft's support of a job seeker, requests that Taft send congratulatory letters to (mostly Polish) ethnic organizations, requests for random advice, requests for meetings—which were usually answered very promptly and affirmatively—and other matters.[28]

THE ELECTION RESULTS

Hammerling's efforts among the Poles must be placed in context. Nationwide the Poles in the United States had been a very strong Democratic voting bloc. Democratic candidates received up to 90 percent of the Polish vote. Roosevelt had been the exception, and the Poles supported him enthusiastically. But in 1912, the Poles in large part abandoned the Democratic Party. The results of the 1912 election thus showed a drastic decline in Polish support for the Democrats.[29] Edward Kantowicz's careful calculations for Chicago indicate Wilson received 33.08 percent; Taft, 33.13 percent; Roosevelt, 20.09 percent; and Eugene Debs, running on the Socialist Party ticket, 12.53 percent. It was the worst showing ever for a Democratic presidential candidate among Chicago's Polish voters.[30] In Milwaukee, Wilson received only 34 percent of the Polish vote to Taft's 21 percent, but this was only two-thirds of the Democratic votes, and fewer than Debs, who carried Milwaukee's Polish wards.[31] In heavily Polish Erie County, New York, Wilson ran six thousand votes behind the state Democratic ticket.[32] Debs won 40 percent of the vote in immigrant districts of western Pennsylvania, which included many Poles.[33] A national Democratic Party poll of Catholic priests shortly before the election indicates Roosevelt was a better than two to one favorite over Wilson, with Taft a distant third. Despite the extremely small sampling, this indicates a surprisingly weak showing for Wilson among a usually strong Democratic group.[34] There are also more general indications of the low level of his support among Polish voters.[35]

Nationwide studies of voting patterns indicate that in 1912 "Italian and other newer immigrant votes appear to have gone to the Bull Moose ticket."[36] Roosevelt support also appears to have been heavy among the Poles and other recent immigrant voters in New York City.[37] Dr. Wojciech Morawski-Nałęcz, who directed the Democratic effort among the Poles in both 1912 and 1916, estimated that Wilson received 30 percent of the Polish vote nationwide. This would compare closely with the calculations for Chicago and Milwaukee.[38]

Though Taft lost—and it was not by much—Hammerling was probably instrumental in decreasing Wilson's vote among Polish voters and winning them for Taft. Had Taft won, Hammerling may well have been a very significant figure within the administration. Instead, he went to his estate in Galicia.[39] It would be the last national campaign in which Hammerling would play a significant role.

THE ROLE OF CHARLES NAGEL

We know that by 1910 Hammerling was in direct contact with Taft, or the president's Secretary of Commerce and Labor, Charles Nagel. Nagel was a key member of the Republican National Committee and a major figure in Taft's reelection efforts. As Secretary of Commerce and Labor, Nagel oversaw immigration issues and therefore was very important to Hammerling, who was prominently involved in the matter. Nagel, like so many of the people with whom Hammerling dealt, was of German ancestry.

More, Nagel was also counsel to the Busch Brewing Company, and Hammerling, Busch, and Nagel worked together closely regarding political and other issues. Hammerling used Nagel to negotiate with Busch over advertising issues, though the extent of their talks is unknown. Percy Andreae's name surfaces now and again, suggesting the discussions probably concerned the "wet" issue and Hammerling's convoluted editorial endorsement.[40]

It was, it seems, not always Nagel aiding Hammerling: the latter intervened on Nagels's behalf with the brewers.[41] During 1911 Nagel and Hammerling were in regular correspondence, and Nagel often pressed Hammerling to meet with him. Nagel wrote him letters seeking his views on immigration issues and soliciting his political advice.[42] At one point Hammerling apparently tried to get Nagel to involve three members of the cabinet in some undertaking; Nagel thought it bootless.[43] Unfortunately, we have no corroboration of what appears to have been a major notion by our hero. It was probably with Nagel that Hammerling reached the apogee of his influence in the political sphere: he was advising a member of the cabinet, dispensing wisdom to a presidential campaign director, and, during a presidential campaign, he had close contact with a major RNC member. Nagel was Hammerling's conduit to the White House and passed his letters to the president.[44] It was probably at this time that Hammerling considered running for Congress, though he spoke of this only once.[45] Indeed, there is evidence from as early as 1910 that he had direct access to the White House without going through Nagel. In at least one instance, Nagel asked to accompany him to a meeting with Taft that Hammerling had already organized. More, Hammerling would write to the president and ask for a meeting at the White House with only a few days' notice, sometimes requesting a meeting the next day. As noted above, he seems usually to have gotten his request.[46] Nagel was a veritable agent for Hammerling at Taft's side. However, Hammerling himself was not far away.

THE HUGHES CAMPAIGN

We know very little about Hammerling's involvement with the 1916 presidential election. He made money from the same kind of advertising he had done previously. This time, however, he contributed a very generous $8,000 to the RNC.[47] Hammerling, we know, paid the Czech press to support Hughes, and therefore likely did the same to other ethnic journals.[48] However, unlike 1912 when the *Leader* carried pro-Taft material constantly, 1916 did not see the same lavish coverage of Hughes. He may have handled Hughes advertising beyond the confines of the immigrant press.[49]

By the time of the campaign, the Military Intelligence Division of the Army General Staff (hereafter MID) was monitoring Hammerling and discovered that he used $90,000 of RNC money for Hughes advertising in foreign language newspapers. However, reports indicated that the real amount to pass through Hammerling for these purposes was $250,000. The claims cannot be confirmed.[50] One of these not particularly reliable reports indicates that after the scandal over his "appeal" publicity on behalf of the Germans in 1915, Hammerling had difficulty in convincing some foreign language papers to take the Hughes advertising. This, in turn, raised the issue of what Hammerling did with the checks he sent out to the various editors, checks that were returned to him.[51]

CHAPTER 5

One of the Most Dangerous German Agents in America

DR. E. A. RUMELY WAS A FASCINATING MAN. Born in Indiana of German ancestry, he was heir to the family agricultural business and invented something called the Rumely Oil Pull Farm Tractor. Despite the fact that he was superbly educated (Notre Dame, Oxford, Heidelberg, and Freiburg), he was an incompetent businessman and lost the family firm while still a young man. Undeterred, Rumely concentrated on an unusual institution, the Interlaken School, which combined education with physical exertion. He also had strange notions about diet, medicine, and economic matters.

Rumely had passionately pro-German views regarding the war and was especially interested in having the German position placed before the American public, which, in his opinion, was being presented with pro-British propaganda. In 1912, while he was a delegate to the Republican national convention in Chicago, Hammerling was approached by an employee of the Rumely Company about advertising in the foreign language press. Soon Hammerling met Rumely, who invited him to his factory at Interlaken and arranged for Hammerling to make a speech to the boys. Rumely's business disaster, Hammerling later implied, temporarily severed contacts between the two. In reality they maintained regular correspondence and social intercourse.[1] Hammerling was transfixed by Rumely: "He was going to be the biggest man on earth in America.[2]

Hammerling did not want to admit, in 1918, with the United States at war with Germany, that he was on intimate terms with a prominent pro-German who was even involved in German propaganda activities during the war. Hammerling and Rumely were closely involved as early as 1915, but not about Oil Pull Farm Tractors.

As early as 1909, Rumely had been working with German representatives in the United States, as well as the government in Berlin, to improve the German image in the American press.[3] Soon after the war broke out, Rumely joined with a number of German representatives and businessmen in America to buy the *New York Evening Mail*.[4] Efforts were also made to obtain the *Washington Post* and the *New York Sun*.[5] The German Foreign Office agreed to devote considerable funds, and it was determined that the purchase negotiations would be through a third party—Rumely. In these negotiations Rumely worked closely with German ambassador Johann Heinrich von Bernstorff.[6] Rumely, in turn, engaged Hammerling to act as his agent. What exactly Hammerling did is unknown.[7] Rumely was ostensibly the owner of the paper; he was after all an American citizen and a seemingly successful businessman. In reality, the purchase was financed by Berlin, with Rumely acting as front man.[8] The MID learned that Hammerling had actually negotiated the sale.[9] The paper, according to the report, subsequently became pro-German—hardly a surprising turn.[10] It also went into steep financial decline. The only source we have regarding Hammerling's involvement is a few scant references in the MID files.[11] The whole issue of Rumely and the paper is very difficult to reconstruct.[12] The important fact we may derive is that it was one of the activities launched by Hammerling in the first months of 1915, activities that were financed by German funds surreptitiously expended.

THE APPEAL

In early 1915 Hammerling by happenstance met with Rumely in New York. They spoke of the war, which they agreed was ghastly. The manufacture and shipment of munitions in the United States was particularly regrettable. American munitions were sent exclusively to the Allies, which made the United States an undeclared supporter of England, France, and Russia. This led to a discussion of how to affect this deplorable situation. Hammerling advised Rumely that articles in newspapers would be the best way to stop munitions manufacture, and he did not have in mind just arms intended for the Allies, but for Germany, too. When Hammerling was later told "everybody in the United States that was endowed with a moderate amount of intelligence knows that the complaint was that these munitions were being shipped to France and England, to the allies," he responded that he had had no idea that was true.[13] In all his testimonies Hammerling claimed to be unaware of what was in effect common knowledge: American munitions were being shipped exclusively to the Allies. And Hammerling knew it. A campaign against munitions shipments was, *pari passu*, one in support of Germany. Hammerling's claimed ignorance may have allowed him to avoid awkward admissions, but it made him appear disingenuous and evasive, which, of course, he was.

Rumely approached Hammerling about a major advertisement in March of 1915. He had come to Hammerling's office to discuss the war. He told Hammerling that it was tragic that, in the United States, companies were producing munitions that were responsible for inflicting casualties in Europe. Hammerling agreed. Rumely then suggested that an appeal be sent to the president and Congress of the United States to urge the manufacturers to stop munitions production. In Hammerling's later words, the purpose of the appeal was that the American people "should not manufacture munitions or powder, or anything, and sell it to the warring nations, for the destruction of humanity. That is about it."[14]

However, Hammerling told Rumely that such an article could not appear as a news item but only as an advertisement.[15] According to Hammerling, Rumely said he would speak to "friends who are Americans" about the proposition. On another occasion he said that Rumely mentioned that Paul Craveth (an attorney) and "[the prominent banker Paul] Warburg" were involved.[16] Warburg was an intimate of German ambassador Johann Heinrich von Bernstorff.[17] Hammerling now explained that to publish it in both foreign language and English papers would cost over $200,000. Hammerling claimed that when he discussed the idea with various publishers associated with the AAFLN, they told him that before issuing the appeal he should "find out where the factories making munitions were located and to ascertain, more or less, if they employed foreign born people who read these different American foreign language newspapers." Hammerling said he did not know where munitions factories with a foreign work force were, so Rumely provided him a list. Hammerling, at his own expense—or perhaps with financing from Germany and Austria—organized the brief mission of his agents, but the results were meager.[18] This action of Hammerling's made him indirectly, via Rumely, a German agent, and one associated with the German efforts to carry on industrial sabotage in the United States.

Rumely returned to his mysterious friends and procured the money. Hammerling swore he would "give his life" in support of the statement that he had no idea that Germans were involved.[19] He was, however, "suspicious."[20] He admitted that he had financial dealings with Dr. Heinrich Albert (the paymaster for secret German activities in the United States), though claimed he did not know who he was. Hammerling's story had become preposterous. By 1918 he lamented that Rumely had made a "sucker" out of him.[21] Only later did he bewail: "I was pulled into it."[22]

Although Hammerling denied ever meeting German ambassador Johann Heinrich von Bernstorff, later testifying: "If you can prove it, I will be dead right here," the two met in February 1915 at Hammerling's office. Rumely was also there but whether simultaneously or not is uncertain.[23] Other visitors who were there at approximately the same time included officers of the Hamburg-American and North German Lloyd Lines and the German naval attaché, the notorious spy Captain Karl Boy-Ed. There was at least one call from Hammerling to German Military Attaché Franz von Papen.[24] (There is a scattering of reports that Hammerling was also in regular communication with Austrian representatives, but these have proven impossible to track down, and the Austrian archives are no help.)[25] Though the details of Hammerling's involvement have never been clearly discerned, we have enough circumstantial evidence to reconstruct at least the outlines of the undertakings. Both Boy-Ed and von Papen were very active in building German spy networks in the United States and Canada and recruited various ethnic groups, particularly the Irish, to join the endeavor. Hammerling's immigrant connections would thus make him possibly attractive to the German agents. By the end of 1915 Boy-Ed and von Papen had been expelled from the country.

On April 4, 1915, with the signature of 431 members of the AAFLN—about half of the organization, all Hammerling's clients—there was issued an "Appeal to the American People."[26] Their ranks were joined by a number of English-language newspapers, many of them large.[27] The costs of the Appeal, it was claimed in the text, were "voluntarily given in the shape of small contributions by our people who are actuated by a sense of humanity and justice and a patriotic desire not to have this peace loving nation directly or indirectly the cause of further loss of life or destruction of property." The MID later quoted this passage, an outright lie, as a particularly damning example of Hammerling's service to the German cause in the United States.[28] Rumely agreed to pay Hammerling $205,000 for publishing the Appeal. Through Rumely, Hammerling met Albert, the German Commercial Counselor. Hammerling claimed he did not learn that the money for the Appeal had come from Albert and was baffled when Rumely asked him to give receipts to Albert and not Rumely himself.[29] Hammerling, after expenses, reportedly pocketed an enormous $150,000 from the deal.[30]

The Appeal deserves to be quoted *in extenso* as it is the zenith of German propaganda in the United States and the reason Hammerling has long been considered a German agent. In the name of hundreds of editors and publishers of foreign language papers it implored that: "The pleas of the millions of widowed mothers, the appeals of the fatherless children and orphans and the prayers of the starving thousands of Europe directed to us, we believe, in making this appeal in the name of humanity and justice." Further, "We appeal particularly to the American manufacturers and their workmen engaged in manufacture of any of these articles, to suspend at once the manufacture of powder and bullets which are being made for the cruel and inhuman purpose of mutilating and destroying humanity. Therefore, we appeal individually to the workmen of such factories, even at the sacrifice of their positions, to go on record as being unalterably opposed to being employed for the purpose of manufacturing ammunition to shatter the bodies and blot out the lives of their own blood relatives." The American people were further asked to "do everything in their power . . . to influence the manufacturers and workmen in the United States engaged in the manufacture of powder and bullets for use by any of the warring countries, to end this manufacture, the selling and shipping of such materials." Finally, the country was called upon to "stop producing armaments for profit, and thus end our own participation in the war." In closing it was noted that the Appeal was financed by "voluntarily given . . . small contributions by our people."

There followed an enormous list of foreign language newspapers.[31]

Forty-eight editors, more than 10 percent of the signatories of the Appeal, represented Polish newspapers. A review of these is instructive: ten were from Pennsylvania, where Hammerling's influence was strongest; none of the large Polonia publications appeared. An analysis of the Appeal was provided for the British government by, of all people, Lewis Namier, Hammerling's former employee. Nobody knew better than Namier how Hammerling operated. Namier had become a minor advisor to the British government by 1915 regarding minorities—especially Poles—in the United States. Hammerling was "notorious," and the Appeal was paid for by the Germans.[32] Hammerling's close association with German-owned businesses with the *American Leader* also damned him in British eyes: they "represent and act for the German government."[33]

Many papers refused, some stating explicitly that it was German propaganda. This Hammerling repeatedly denied both to the editors and then to the general public. Hammerling's explanation of the Appeal went through a considerable change. According to him, it was funded by a collection from churches and other organizations including the AAFLN itself. He insisted that the effort began in 1914 and absolutely no German money was involved. Of course, this was a skein of lies.[34] Sometimes he said—as we have seen—that it was small contributions that financed the Appeal; other times, it was rich Americans. It was also, alternatively, Rumely's friends, and German agents, specifically Albert. However, Hammerling told Congress in December 1918 that he should like to be "hanged" if it could be proven that he knew Germany was behind the effort.[35] The source kept changing.[36] Later Hammerling preferred to be "shot" rather than hanged over a different acquisition.[37] Albert wrote Hammerling thanking him for the "work undertaken in America in behalf of the cause of Germany and Austria."[38] Hammerling would, on the basis of this letter, have to be both shot and hanged.

A paper in Omaha, owned by Senator Hitchcock, carried the advertisement for free "as a service to humanity."[39] Hitchcock was one of Hammerling's closest friends. The senator, Hammerling once observed, had depended on Hammerling to produce the foreign vote for the Republicans in a number of elections. However, he also had offered a different explanation to the *New York World* in April.[40] When that paper denounced the Appeal as the work of German propagandists, Hammerling vehemently denied the charges, claiming that "he personally paid the more than the $100,000" it cost to publish the advertisement. Indignantly he denied that the press had any right to investigate the matter further. Then, with a certain grandeur, he added that "he has two or three million dollars and can afford such expenditure."[41] Perhaps the most stupefying lie he provided in 1918 was his claim that he thought the munitions were intended for Germany![42] Thus, preventing their shipment would aid the Allies.

BRITISH INTELLIGENCE

Early in the war the British government had become interested in the value of the ethnic minorities in the United States in gaining American popular support, and thereby access to the American government. An even greater motivation for British interest in these minorities was the fear of German and Austrian influence among the powerful German- and Irish-American communities in the United States. Among the groups regarded as at least potentially anti-German, the Poles were the largest, and hence, as Eustace Percy of the War Office wrote in March of 1915, "The Allies want Polish opinion in America as a makeweight to the German vote."[43] Sir Arthur Cecil Spring Rice, the volcanic British ambassador, was especially concerned about the disaffection of ethnic minorities in the United States, and constantly bewailed the lack of active British policy to counter their increasing hostility.[44] Hammerling had been an object of British investigation for some months before the Appeal. He was assumed to be in the pay of the Central Powers, but no direct connection was established.[45] Some reports suggested a conundrum: Hammerling was known to be a "paid German agent" and also subvented by Standard Oil and North German Lloyd, but publicizing this was dangerous "in view of their connection with American internal politics."[46]

British work among the anti-German minorities in the United States was directed initially by Captain Guy Gaunt, the Naval Attaché in Washington and Director of Intelligence in the United States. During the first months of the war, Gaunt gained the active cooperation of certain Czech and Serbian leaders, especially Emmanuel Voska of the Bohemian National Alliance.[47] The British succeeded in closely monitoring

German activities aimed at the minorities, aided by their many agents drawn from the immigrant population.[48]

In March the British retained a certain Martin Egan, an American, to investigate Hammerling and tell London exactly what they were dealing with. Egan's report, meandering and full of errors, nonetheless gives us an idea of what image the British government was forming about our hero. According to Egan, Hammerling invested $2 million in his Galician estate (i.e., he was very rich); he traveled recently to Berlin and Vienna (i.e., he may have been an assigned agent of the Central Powers); his AAFLN was difficult to follow because they were in "weird languages"; and he was definitely not a German agent. Not a very useful report.[49] Shortly thereafter, the unreliable Spring Rice added a few lurid touches but did not disclose his source. Hammerling was "a Galician with probably a slight Jew strain"; his English was so bad, that others wrote his letters; he was a "servant" of the German steamship companies; after he returned from Europe at the start of the war, he was suspiciously quiet for some time. And, just to complicate matters, Spring Rice added that the German press had accused Hammerling of being a British spy. The only useful reference is the insistence that Hammerling was close to "Herr Ballin."[50] Ballin, a German shipping tycoon with the Hamburg-American Line, had been involved in the Rumely purchase of the *Evening Mail* in which Hammerling was alleged to have played a central role.[51]

The British had a dossier on Hammerling weeks before the Appeal: he was possibly a German agent; he exaggerated his family's position; he "controlled" large numbers of immigrants; he made a great deal of money from political campaigns; he was "clever, powerful, and unscrupulous." London had already made up its mind before the Appeal that he "controlled the foreign press."[52] Thus, when it appeared, claiming the support of several hundred foreign language papers, the British wished to know who was behind Hammerling's action, and what effect it would have on the immigrant population. The answer to the first question at least seemed quite clear. In early April, almost immediately after its appearance, Spring Rice cabled Foreign Secretary Sir Edward Grey that German and Austrian agents had arranged the Appeal. As to its importance, Spring Rice was unconcerned: "It seems to have had no effect whatever."[53] Though dismissed as insignificant, virtually a waste of German money, the Appeal suggested subversive activities by enemy agents.[54] Hammerling's influence was thus pernicious: "The first change necessary," wrote Spring Rice, "is to emancipate the Slav Press from the control of the Austrian Jew Hammerling."[55] The British government shared his view and resolved to destroy Hammerling's influence in the immigrant community.[56] However, the Foreign Office knew of Hammerling's powerful political connections and decided to work cautiously.[57] By May, London was more worried about Hammerling, suspecting he might have influence among immigrants in Canada. Ottawa was to be warned. More, the Foreign Office worried over "more activities" by Hammerling, which, though unspecified, it nevertheless had collected information on. These additional efforts have never surfaced, and the Foreign Office's concerns seem very vague.[58]

Spring Rice even had larger horrors in his vision. The logic went something like this: Hammerling was from a laboring background; socialists in the United States among the immigrants have been enlisted by Hammerling and his German financiers to work to suppress the manufacture and export of arms. Hammerling—a Taft man, let us not forget—was part of a socialist conspiracy directed by Imperial Germany.[59] The socialists, Spring Rice explained to Grey, were really creatures of the Jews, but the foul influence of the Roman Church was visible as well.[60]

The British campaign to discredit Hammerling assumed two forms. Successful pressure was brought to bear on various immigrant groups, primarily the Czechs and Yugoslavs, to repudiate publicly the Appeal earlier published with their endorsement.[61] A far more important method, however, was a sensational press campaign aimed at alarming the American public over the actions of German spies and saboteurs in their midst. Hammerling's Appeal was an early target in this campaign.

The chief element in this undertaking was an arrangement between Gaunt and John R. Rathom, editor of Rhode Island's the *Providence Journal*. Rathom, an Australian by birth and a fanatical partisan of the Allied war effort, agreed to publish disclosures about German intelligence activity in the United States in the *Journal*, without mentioning the source. The information was ultimately obtained from Voska's Czech counterintelligence network working in cooperation with the British.[62] These stories were given increased attention by their previewing in the *New York Times* under the heading "The Providence *Journal* Will Say Today."[63] Rathom also passed his reports on directly to both President Wilson and the State Department.[64] Doubtless Wilson's later disdain for Hammerling dates from this era.

On April 12 the *New York Times* published a front-page article in anticipation of the *Journal*. Beginning with a denial of Hammerling's assertion that no German money was behind the "Appeal," the article made specific charges: the notorious Boy-Ed had approved the draft of the Appeal and personally selected the papers that were to carry it; German money financed the whole operation; and finally, the foreign language papers only carried the story lest they lose their advertising subvention from Hammerling.[65] Although Hammerling immediately denied any knowledge of Boy-Ed, the *Journal* and the *Times* soon returned to the attack, claiming that von Bernstorff wrote the Appeal personally.[66] If the British had evidence of a Hammerling–Boy-Ed connection, it would be a decisive element in the German plan to subvert minorities. Unfortunately, the British documents offer no further information in this regard. The Secret Service discovered—or at least reported—that $3 million had been spent by German agents on the foreign press and associated matters,[67] including "over $200,000" to Hammerling.[68]

Just a few weeks earlier, the American Secret Service had acquired the briefcase of Albert, which contained revelations about attempts to disrupt munitions manufacture by utilizing German and Austrian immigrant workers, and influence public opinion through the surreptitious subvention of newspapers and journals, and other violations of American neutrality. In this effort Hammerling was a major actor.[69] The notion of interfering with munitions work was more frightening than issuing hortatory appeals largely in the immigrant press.

As a result of these disclosures, there was a massive public reaction that Charles Seymour has described as the public's feeling that: "Germany and Austria were . . . through their agents virtually carrying on warfare in the United States."[70] The specter of well-organized German activity in America even affected the administration, which reacted with "genuine alarm," exemplified by Wilson's ridiculous comment that the country was "honeycombed with German intrigue and infested with German spies."[71] The public's arousal at the activities of the Central Powers in America was considerably exacerbated by the furor over the sinking of the *Lusitania* in May of 1915, the *Arabic* in August, and the *Hesperian* in September.[72]

By early 1918, however, with the United States already a belligerent, Hammerling convolutedly explained the Appeal as part of his patriotic attachments. A secret agent of the MID visited Hammerling, and he began underscoring the services of the AAFLN. It had no German language papers among its number, but instead was uniformly pro-Allied: "Think what this means in making this country safe for Democracy," Hammerling announced with more enthusiasm than coherence. But, asked the investigator, who had introduced himself as a journalist from the *Evening World*, "had you not fathered a campaign in the newspapers . . . to reach to the American people with paid advertisements urging neutrality for this country?"

Hammerling's answer was devious and dismissive but, in retrospect, probably true: "I placed such advertisements it is true. But let us be fair. This was early in the war, at a time that the President and many other prominent Americans were advocating neutrality. I was a business man, asked to place advertisements for which an appropriation had been made. These advertisements did not express my sentiments, any more than they expressed the sentiments of the World which accused me at the time, but which accepted the advertisements. It was business with me and it was business with the English printed papers which were only too anxious to obtain part of the appropriation." Of course, this only discloses a portion of the February-April 1915 activities. Why did Hammerling purposely misrepresent the source of his "appropriation"; why did he wish its German origins not to be known? Why was he engaged in secret negotiations with Germans and German-Americans before the Appeal? None of these was explained by Hammerling's statement.

Who wrote the Appeal? One source says he saw it on Hammerling's desk shortly after a visit from von Bernstorff.[73] Gabryel, Hammerling's disgruntled former employee who later associated with his enemies, testified that it was written by a certain Donald Momand (one of Hammerling's rotating officers) together with Hammerling.[74] Hammerling testified that Momand, the advertising executive William H. Rankin, Rumely, and he were the authors.[75] Its language is far more eloquent and grammatical than anything Hammerling was capable of, which Gabryel noted. Rankin, who apparently was Hammerling's link to the English language press, was frequently in Hammerling's office at that time. Gabryel mentions no Germans or Austrians.

Hammerling was very concerned. He randomly doled out "bonuses" to buy silence, sometimes with checks of $500 to $1,000; even the office boy got money at the time. This was four to eight times the monthly salary of many of his employees. When Gabryel reported that the Poles in New York all knew Hammerling was in German pay, he told him to "keep your mouth shut."[76]

When the Appeal was being readied, Hammerling sent one of his employees, Momand, to canvass the foreign language press to see which papers would carry it. Those papers that had already been receiving a subsidy from the Austrian or German governments—and there were several—signed at once. Those that demurred were bribed, usually $100 to $200. Grella's Italian paper was expensive: $5,000, or half of the entire bribery fund.[77] Others were threatened with loss of advertising revenue or other reprisals.[78] Only when enough signed on was the Appeal published.

The conclusions reached by the Foreign Office regarding Hammerling are worth examining because they indicate clearly that they regarded him as dangerous and powerful. In a May 12, 1915, memorandum we read:

> All shipping companies in the United States advertise in the foreign language press of the US through the AAFLN, the president of which is Mr. Louis Hammerling, a German agent. The association is practically owned and directed by the German shipping lines and the German interests in such large corporations as the Standard Oil Company, and the St. Louis breweries. It is a corrupt organization of the worst reputation, but it is politically powerful and exersizes [sic] great influence especially in immigration centers and hence its use of by the shipping companies.

As for Hammerling, he was "actively working in German interests both by propaganda and by spying. He was responsible for the recent manifesto of the foreign language press against the export of arms. His influence over the Polish and other Slav as well as the Jewish and Italian elements in the US has recently led the FO to consider how his activities might be counteracted."

In a strange reference, the memorandum concluded that London had told the Cunard Line to "sever relations with him," but Cunard "did not trust their own New York City Office" because "that office was almost certainly staffed in part by German clerks in Hammerling's pay."[79]

THE ZOTTI AFFAIR

The request for publication made by Hammerling's agent was really a threat. According to an enemy of his, Franjo Zotti, publisher of a Croatian paper *Národni List* (National Letters), claims he accused Hammerling of working for German money and bodily ejected Hammerling's representative from the office.[80] This was the beginning of a war between Hammerling and Zotti. Zotti invited two of Hammerling's clerks, Gabryel and Dattner, to meet with other editors to expose Hammerling. Zotti threatened them if they were to report the meeting to Hammerling.[81] Zotti soon published a letter denouncing Hammerling in the *New York World*. It was the first of many. He wrote to the president.[82] The situation was getting out of hand. Zotti was, it seems, blackmailing Hammerling for $10,000, and he, in turn, was being threatened by Hammerling's political friends to desist.[83] According to Zotti, one of Hammerling's powerful friends, Carl Byoir of the Committee on Public Information, induced the Department of Justice to raid Zotti's office: they took his phone book. Zotti continued undeterred.[84] In one, perhaps indiscreet letter, Zotti called Hammerling "coward," "perjurer," "fraud," "imposter," and an "eel."[85] Zotti was an extremely unpleasant man, and in this case one cannot help rooting for Hammerling. The MID's notes on Zotti were eloquent: subsidized by Austria and Germany, "dangerous," a "swindler and paid German agent." He was, however, anti-Hammerling. The conclusion was "The whole outfit appears to be thoroughly rotten."[86]

The Appeal led to an uprising of criticism from his virtual dependents in the press. Zotti was not alone. The source of the criticism may well have been sincere, but outrage at receiving no or paltry subvention seems to have been an equal if not superior motivation. Italian, Greek, Serb, and other papers representing minorities on the Allied side also were outraged. Milwaukee's *Kuryer Polski*, owned by the influential and erratic Michał Kruszka, labeled the Appeal as German work and denounced Hammerling in its pages.[87] Agostino De Biasi waited until September to renounce Hammerling in the *New York Times* in the name of the Italian papers in the country. Italy was now at war with the Central Powers, and De Biasi's readership would have no sympathies with Austria. Hammerling's AAFLN was an "association in name only." It did not speak for the Italian press; indeed, the members of the AAFLN were never consulted about anything. Hammerling was the leader of nothing, and the association was really "fantastic." He made the foreign press appear "disgraceful."[88] A Serb, Dushan Popovich, claimed Hammerling tried to blackmail him to carry the Appeal, but he refused as a "loyal Serb." Hammerling virtually ended Popovich's advertising subsidy.[89] These charges shook Hammerling's previously obedient coalition of the immigrant press.

MYSTERIOUS SECRET AGENTS

A few weeks before the Appeal appeared, Hammerling organized a series of strange missions. He sent Gabryel to Bethlehem, Pennsylvania, whence he was to take his wife and "spare no expense." In fact he *wanted* his agents to spend money.[90] Gabryel's job was to "Find out the percentage of foreigners working in the munitions plants up there. Go to saloons, go to headquarters, and go to the priests and rabbis if necessary, and bring me back the data there whether they are satisfied with the working conditions, the average earning, what they are earning per week, and bring that data back."[91]

At the same time that Gabryel was sent to Pennsylvania, Dattner was dispatched to Bridgeport, New Haven, and Hartford in Connecticut; G. H. Berg was sent "through the New England states," Momand to Brooklyn, Leon Wazeter to the Philadelphia area, and Henry Gabriel (Arthur's brother) to Utica, New York. There may have been others.[92] When they returned, Hammerling was away, so they met without him. They prepared written reports of their missions.[93] Hammerling claimed he received only oral reports (no written documents have ever been unearthed), which he somehow communicated to Rumely.[94]

Hammerling's explanations of his agents were self-incriminatory. He said these missions were not "investigations" but rather "inspections." They were carried out to anticipate what the reaction to the Appeal would be. Rumely supposedly worried that it would not reach "these foreigners." Rumely purportedly furnished Hammerling with a list of where he wanted "inspections." Thereupon he dispatched his agents. One press report contends that Rumely was apprehensive lest the Appeal not reach the right elements, and Hammerling's survey was his answer to calm Rumely's concerns.[95] The results of the investigation were rather disappointing. Most of the workers were not "foreigners" and "did not give a damn what they were doing as long as they made good money."[96] When asked what the agents did, Hammerling rambled on: "These men were to find out where these places are, and what there was there, and the priests, or the newspapers, or whatever there was there—what these fellows have in this work and to inquire of the priests or the papers or the saloons." The reports were quickly gathered, and insignificant. This amateur sociological investigation was rather perfunctory: the man assigned to Brooklyn spent two hours in research; the others two days.[97]

Hammerling denied that the investigations had any real purpose at all, certainly not to survey the efficacy of propaganda among foreign workers. If this effort was undertaken to convince Rumely of the possible value of the Appeal, he must have been badly disappointed. However, it is obvious that Hammerling undertook the survey—as ridiculous as it was—at Rumely's behest to ascertain the possibility of successful propaganda among munitions workers. Hammerling's claim that he was oblivious to this is preposterous. He made a disastrous slip when replying to Senator Josiah O. Wolcott. The senator noted: "You wanted to stop the [munitions] shipments." Hammerling responded: "Not me: the advertiser wanted to stop the shipment." "Yes, the advertiser," Wolcott said. To which Hammerling lamely answered: "Yes."[98] Then, in another flourish, Hammerling admitted that, had the Appeal worked, it would have caused "industrial trouble." "I'm not responsible for that," he noted.

If this were not enough—Hammerling was his own worst enemy—he admitted that the investigation by his employees was "absolutely foolish and irrelevant." He agreed, imprudently, that had the Appeal been successful, it would have meant that "workers in munitions factories would have quit working on munitions." But then he denied wishing to stop munitions manufacture.[99] This was obviously in obedience to a German order.[100] The federal authorities attached considerable significance to these "inspections" concluding, by late 1918, that: "this so-called 'Appeal' was merely a cover up for payments made to Hammerling to arouse the labor element in the munitions factories to strike."[101]

By this exchange Hammerling admitted he knew that the purpose of the Appeal was to hamper munitions shipments; he knew that he was being paid for this work; he knew that his investigations were designed to canvass foreign workers as regards their sentiments concerning arms manufacture. The issue of arms manufacture was particularly damning because on September 1, 1915, at Falmouth, England, the British seized papers being carried by an American journalist, James J. Archibald, who had been acting for some time as a courier for the Central Powers between America and Europe. Among these were letters from Constantin Dumba, Austrian ambassador in Washington, and from several German representatives, including von Papen. They contained plans to foment strikes among the immigrant population working in American munitions factories.[102] It was not until early October 1915 that Berlin decided to stop efforts to cripple American arms manufacture. The Austrians were duly informed. Hammerling's agents were therefore one of the last steps in a German effort.[103] Coupled with his earlier confession about knowing Albert, Hammerling had just admitted that he was a German agent.

A GERMAN AGENT

In 1918 the Senate concluded that the "main objectives" of German efforts in the wartime United States fell into three categories; viz., "to prevent the sending of munitions of war and supplies of various kinds to the allied Governments," to "keep the United States on a peace footing and at all hazards prevent the United States from entering into the European war as an ally of France and England," and to "maintain its solidarity of the German and Austrian elements of our population and to retard their assimilation."[104] This constituted a damning indictment for Hammerling. The Appeal epitomized the first two attributions, and the very existence of the AAFLN seemed to represent the third: an association to cater to the peculiar needs of insular ethnic communities despite its ostensible goal of assimilation.

In all of these actions Hammerling is linked to German propaganda and—as in the case of his agents reporting on munitions manufacturing centers—with possible German espionage and sabotage. The Senate concluded post factum in 1918 that, in 1915, the German and Austrian representatives in the United States conspired "to prevent the production and shipment of munitions." They created a "Labor Relief Bureau" to take "Austro-Hungarians and Germans out of munition and other factories." The bureau had several branches. This led to the serious charge that "The German Government, no doubt, counted largely upon the fact that in the various munition and other manufacturing plants in the United States there were employed a large number of Germans and Austrian subjects, whose sympathies would be for Germany, and who would act in accordance with the wishes of the German Government, even to the point of destructive methods."[105]

Of course, the basis of this argument is problematical, if not fatuous. To cite merely the most obvious point, the immigrants from Austria-Hungary had, with virtually no exception, no loyalty to Vienna. The American investigative authorities never seemed to understand this during the war, nor apparently after. For a Pole from Galicia living, for example, in the industrial city of Bethlehem, the idea of a Central Powers victory in the war was anathema. However, Hammerling was violently opposed to continued Russian rule over Poland and thus would be willing to work with the Austrians to combat the Russians. His motives were Polish patriotism—and profit—not Austrian loyalty. The American investigative authorities were completely ignorant of the complicated intricacies of eastern European politics when the war broke out in 1914, and had no way of learning them under the pressure of events. Therefore they saw simple conspiracies where, in fact, there were complex political manueverings. Moreover, the notion that the Germans had the ability to entice the entire work force from munitions plants is absurd. Despite its efforts, and some notable successes, like creating the Liebau Labor Relief Bureau to provide jobs to German and Austro-Hungarian immigrants, thereby luring them away from work in munitions plants—an action that attracted several thousand workers—the Germans had neither the funds nor abilities to work a reconstruction of the American labor market.[106] Such charges are not only fanciful; they border on paranoia.

However, Hammerling's actions fit the paradigm of what German propaganda, espionage, and sabotage were seemingly about at the time. The fact that "spy scares" were convulsing the country in 1915—the year that saw the sinking of the *Lusitania*—made his activities of that spring all the more damnable. Jules Witcover has compiled a succinct list of Central Powers acts of sabotage directed at American arms manufacture and transport. Between "April and July of 1915," eight ships caught fire at sea, and "bombs were found on at least five others. In addition, explosions ripped munitions and powder plants in Wallington, Carney's

Point (three times), and Pompton Lakes, New Jersey; Wilmington, Delaware (twice); Philadelphia, Pittsburgh and Sinnemahoning, Pennsylvania; and Acton, Massachusetts. Also, a munitions train was wrecked at Metuchen, New Jersey, and an incendiary fire destroyed a railroad grain elevator at Weehawken, New Jersey."[107] In 1916 the pattern continued: German attempts at sabotage of American munitions ships; the spectacular explosion at Black Tom, the huge ammunition dump; the Kingsland fire a few months later. All of these exposed the large German sabotage network alive in North America.[108]

The American intelligence community had made up its mind about Hammerling by the end of the war: "has charge of all German propaganda in the United States in the Press and elsewhere," "very insidious and dangerous," "prosecute if possible," "a very dangerous agent of the Germans."[109] Besides the public propaganda there was a German sabotage movement in the United States. Hammerling's Appeal, and his sending of agents to major manufacturing centers, suggested that he was involved in both. Besides, his name was German.

THE AUSTRIAN CONNECTION?

The question remains whether Hammerling had any links to Austrian activities during the war. Was he an Austrian agent or did he serve only Berlin? All of our evidence is inconclusive, but taken together it provides cause for speculation. In one document he is referred to as a "friend of Dumba," but this is not developed.[110] We know that in August 1915 he attended a birthday celebration for Franz Ferdinand, which was presided over by Dumba, but this is a very slender thread indeed.[111]

We begin with the fact that Hammerling was in Austria when the war erupted and returned promptly, arriving on August 26.[112] Apparently he was rather sensitive about this issue and told people he had been in China. Did he confer with the Austrian authorities in Vienna? We have no evidence, but we know that the Austrians met with other Poles bound for the United States at approximately the same time, though these negotiations have not been recorded in Austrian records.[113] Did Hammerling return after having met representatives of the Austrian intelligence system?

First, we know that Austria carried on a wide variety of surreptitious propaganda activities during the war. It had, for example, subsidized a number of foreign language newspapers.[114] Subornation of the press was one of Hammerling's specialties. In addition, the Consul General in New York (Alexander von Nuber whom Hammerling knew for years[115]) was instrumental in smuggling Poles from the United States back to Austria to serve in the Polish Legions, which were a contingent of the Austrian Army. However, we must note that the chief actor here was the New York consul, Eugeniusz Rozwadowski, who was a patriotic Pole as well as being an Austrian diplomat. Helping Poles get back to Galicia thus served both of Hammerling's loyalties. He always claimed he never met Dumba; perhaps it was the truth.[116] No evidence has ever surfaced that Hammerling was involved in smuggling patriotic Poles to Europe to fight. Indeed, he was that rarest of Poles: one who did not actively involve himself in the turbulent politics of the Polish emigration in America.

Hammerling's 1915 activity with the agents sent to East Coast factories also links him to the Austrians. The immigrant population of these cities was not overwhelmingly German, but many were from the Austro-Hungarian Empire: Poles, Ukrainians, Hungarians, Croatians, and others. It would be their sensitivity to propaganda from the Central Powers that would be at issue. The Department of Justice accused Dumba and von Nuber of "agitation among foreign residents" to cause disturbances in munitions plants.[117]

There are a number of personal links. Hammerling was close to John Nemeth in his anthracite days. Nemeth, a Hungarian whom Hammerling later dealt with in New York, had been the Austrian consul in western Pennsylvania. Then there is the strange character of Gmernicki, regarded by the MID as an "Austrian Enemy Alien" by 1917 if not earlier. According to MID reports, Gmernicki, a Pole, worked in Wilkes-Barre before coming to New York, though his anthracite years probably followed Hammerling's residence there. Gmernicki next came to New York where he worked for a number of papers (*Robotnik* and *Telegram Codzienny* among others) all associated with the AAFLN. During the war, he was sent to Austria, purportedly on a mission from Hammerling.[118] He was regarded largely as a mercenary for hire, rather than a devoted Austrian loyalist, though his motives may well have been Polish patriotism, using the Austrians to advance the Polish cause. The Justice Department, however, designated him "a spy. Class 1."[119] Hammerling had a large number of contacts in the suspicious world of Austrian-Polish collaboration in North America.

These Polish connections with the Austrian Embassy and consular network were not the paranoid invention of the American investigative services. In 1912 American Polonia had created a national organization (the National Defense Committee, or KON from its Polish initials), which openly supported the Austrian war effort. In 1915 a similar organization in Galicia sent agents Feliks Młynarski and Artur Hausner to America to establish linkages to the KON. These agents worked assiduously to win American Poles to support the Austrian war effort, contribute funds for Polish units fighting in conjunction with the Austrians, and smuggle young Poles to Galicia to join the Polish Legions, military units formed by the later very famous Polish leader Józef Piłsudski. The KON worked with the Austrian official network in the United States, and Hausner and Młynarski cooperated with both, closing the circle. Hammerling, an Austrian Pole, would seem to be a plausible member of the Austro-Polish machinations in America. It is not surprising that federal authorities were convinced that he was an Austrian agent: he should have been.

And finally, there is Dumba, the Austrian ambassador, who was notoriously involved in un-neutral activities and who eventually returned to Vienna at Washington's insistence. Several people claim to have seen Hammerling with Dumba, although he always denied any association.[120] But, then, he denied many things. A source that is not particularly reliable insisted that there were Austrian spies in the United States who worked from the Imperial consulate in New York and were also Hammerling's agents. The chief of these was a certain Gregr. Gregr used Hammerling's money, possibly of ultimate Austrian origin, to buy smaller immigrant newspapers to assure that they would support the Austrians.[121] Although the evidence is fragmentary, it suggests that Hammerling was deeply involved in acquiring or controlling newspapers for Austria.

THE LAST VIENNESE WALTZ

There is, perhaps a postscript on Hammerling and Austrian activities in the United States. After the United States declared war on Germany in

April 1917, Adam Count Tarnowski, an Austrian diplomat of Polish origin, was sent by Vienna to replace the discredited Dumba who had been sent packing in 1915. Tarnowski's arrival coincided with the fatal worsening of American relations with Germany, and his status as ambassador-designate of Berlin's ally was most awkward.[122] He tried repeatedly to gain official recognition by the administration, but was repeatedly rebuffed.[123] Meanwhile, he met with a Pole named Jerzy Jan Sosnowski—a very peculiar fellow, and not without useful connections to the Wilson administration—who counseled him that, should the United States declare war, he should try to remain in America, albeit unofficially, as a link between Vienna and Washington.[124] In this capacity he might work for some version of a separate peace for Austria, and promote Polish interests as well.[125] Tarnowski made such an offer to Secretary of State Robert Lansing, who, after some consideration, rejected it, and he left in 1917 having accomplished nothing.[126]

This is a minor episode, but a document unknown to scholars studying the Tarnowski affair allows us to see a new aspect: the role of Hammerling. Before Tarnowski left he sent for Hammerling. Tarnowski told Hammerling that a substantial faction in Austria regarded the prospect of a German victory as a "calamity." Then Tarnowski told him to expect a "message" in the future "that would enable him to render a great service to the country of his nativity and to the country of his adoption." This conversation was in the spring of 1917. It is useful to recall that Wilson made his famous Peace without Victory speech in January 1917. In this speech Wilson endorsed the cause of Polish independence, which instantly made Wilson a hero to Poles of virtually every political faction. It is not surprising, then, that Tarnowski wanted to build a relationship with an administration led by Wilson.

In early 1918 Hammerling received a call from a Swiss who said he came from Tarnowski and repeated segments of the spring conversation to establish his verisimilitude. He then passed a message to Hammerling from Tarnowski that Austria wanted peace with the United States on any terms devised by Wilson. A German victory was Vienna's greatest fear. Wilson was to send a representative, "preferably an American Catholic Cardinal," to the pope—officially or unofficially. Austria was prepared to "meet" such an offer. The undertaking must be secret for fear of Germany. A few particulars were noted, including "a free Poland." Hammerling explained that he would willingly be "held as hostage [and was] ... willing to be shot if his information was not accurate." It is unclear who Hammerling thought should perform the execution. His interlocutor noted that he appeared under great strain and was very emotional. A new message from Tarnowski was anticipated very soon.[127]

A few months later Hammerling again addressed the Austrian issue. Whether it was on his own initiative or under the influence of Tarnowski is unclear. This time Hammerling had yet more elaborate designs. He sent the White House, on June 17, 1918, a plan for "fomenting a revolt in Austria-Hungary."[128] Hammerling argued that the "break-up" of the Habsburg monarchy was the key to the war, and Austria was the "weak spot" of the Central Powers. This could be done by rallying the nationalities of the empire, which would rise up if they knew the "true significance of America's entrance into the war." This, in turn, could be brought about by a campaign among the nationalities in the United States who would then inform their co-nationals on the Danube. The American foreign language newspapers would be the central actor in this completely preposterous plan, but others would be involved.[129] One can only hope that Tarnowski, an intelligent and sophisticated man, had nothing to do with this. Hammerling's means may have been without merit, but the goal—concluding peace with Austria through American initiative—had been Tarnowski's precise plan. Hammerling may have been attempting to find a means for an end not devised by him. He may have been Tarnowski's inept tool. This is perhaps not so ridiculous if we remember that Tarnowski then described Polish foreign policy as "tragikomiczna."[130]

Wilson passed the memorandum to Creel of the Committee on Public Information, the federal propaganda ministry, and asked what he knew about Hammerling, the president noting that he already knew "a good deal."[131] Creel had been originally a defender of Hammerling against the criticism from federal authorities, but by this time he had come around. Hammerling was a former "agent of the German Imperial Government," and close to Dumba. He would do "anything for money." He had "reversed" his position because of the American war declaration, and now was actively involved in patriotic work.

The frightened Hammerling, Creel reported, would divulge all he knew about German agents—and more—in the United States in a private meeting with the president, which Creel urged.[132] He believed that Hammerling was in touch with the Austrian government—the possible Tarnowski link—and Vienna wanted a separate peace.[133]

Wilson's reaction was curious. He did not wish to meet with Hammerling in person because he was "slippery" and he could use the fact of the meeting for all "sorts of uses." However, Hammerling was not to be rebuffed: "it is very important that the Government should hear Mr. Hammerling's story."[134] He decided to ask for a detailed memorandum and assure Hammerling that it would be given the president's "personal consideration."[135] Hammerling responded with a lengthy memorandum reiterating his harebrained scheme of having representatives of the various Habsburg nationalities in the United States try to influence minorities in Austria. He said nothing about high-level contacts.[136] Wilson curtly rejected the whole ridiculous plan with some choler.[137]

It is tempting to regard this all as another of Hammerling's concoctions, but certain aspects of it are fascinating. We know that Tarnowski was in close touch with Poles in the United States in 1917 and wanted to serve as some sort of liaison between Vienna and the White House.[138] The idea of a Vatican intermediary, a Swiss envoy, a collapsing Austria fearing German victory, highlighting the freedom of Poland as a goal, all reflect what we know of Austrian peace overtures in the last year of the war. It also suggests that Hammerling, as was often suggested, did indeed have close contacts with the Austrians in the United States and Tarnowski was aware of it. There were a number of peace feelers during the war, and Austrian Poles figured prominently among them. Hammerling was an American who was also an Austro-Polish Jew, convert to Catholicism, and by all reports rather devoted to his faith. He would be a plausible vehicle—especially if his services had formerly been utilized. Finally, why would he make up such a preposterous, and detailed, story? To make himself appear more important at a time when he needed to prove his loyalties to the United States? Perhaps, but it might all have been true. Tarnowski's private papers are silent.

DUET WITH PADEREWSKI

In March 1915, in the midst of all Hammerling's machinations with the Germans, Ignacy Jan Paderewski arrived in New York from London. Paderewski was not just a great musical celebrity, he was the most famous and respected Pole in the world. Since 1910 Paderewski had been drifting away from the piano and taking up a new passion: political service to

Poland. When the war broke out in 1914, Paderewski joined his almost equally famous countryman, the novelist Henryk Sienkiewicz, to create a relief agency for Polish victims of the war.

Poland was, in 1914, under the occupation of the three partitioning powers of Russia, Austria, and Germany, and their imperial territories met in the midst of historic Poland. Thus the war, in a real sense, began in Poland. The movement of troops, massive relocations of the civilian population, casualties, and the breakdown of the normal structures of peacetime life left the population bereft. Destitution became general, and death frequent. Poles in western Europe, like Paderewski and Sienkiewicz, felt compelled to create agencies to channel relief to war-ravaged Poland. Hence in January 1915 they created the *Comité général des victimes de la Guerre en Pologne* (better known as the Vevey Committee from its Swiss headquarters) to collect monies worldwide to succor their countrymen. The effort did not begin auspiciously. Efforts to expand the committee to France and Great Britain were complicated by Russian efforts to control everything pertaining to Poland; the British blockade prevented relief shipments from reaching Poland, and the world's attention was focused on Belgium, to such an extent that the far more egregious suffering in Poland—or Serbia for that matter—went virtually unnoticed, including in the neutral United States.[139]

Paderewski came to the United States in 1915 to raise money for Poland, to replace the several worthy but isolated and small relief committees with one large body, the Polish Victims Relief Fund (connected with Vevey), and to be the spokesman for Polish necessity. However, Paderewski's motives were not only eleemosynary. Paderewski, vain, ambitious, and frequently ruthless, wanted to use a relief organization to create a basis to market the idea of the restoration of Polish independence: If Polish suffering made it a good cause, perhaps its eventual independence was a reward for its long travail?

Based on this, but with yet further reach, was Paderewski's plan for himself. He wanted to take control of the large Polish population in the United States, gain access to powerful political circles—including the Wilson administration—and create for himself the foundation for his emergence as leader of a postwar free Poland supported by the statesmanship of Washington, and the sympathy of the American people. The Poles in America would be his army to begin this quest.

Paderewski had been to the United States a number of times before 1915 and had a reasonably close relationship with President Roosevelt. But given the fact that his trips corresponded to the years of Republican ascendancy, Paderewski's influential contacts, in both commerce and politics, were all Republicans. This brings us to Hammerling.

In 1915 Hammerling was not yet derided as a German agent, but admired as a successful Polish immigrant controlling a large and influential network of public relations. Paderewski saw in him a means to reach a wide audience, in which there were many Poles. In addition to the hoi polloi, Paderewski realized that Hammerling had a network of contacts among the mighty in the United States. Hence, soon after arriving in the country, Hammerling and Paderewski began cooperating. Hammerling, who had already become known as someone willing to help the Polish relief cause,[140] provided the maestro with lists of prominent Americans who might be useful.[141] He even offered to accompany Paderewski on visits to solicit money.[142]

This was the beginning of a long relationship between Hammerling and Paderewski. At first the violently anti-German Paderewski seems an odd companion to a reputedly paid German agent like Hammerling. The relationship allows us an insight into Hammerling's motivations for serving the Germans when there is nothing in his background to dispose him favorably toward them.[143] After 1908 he was close to shipping and brewing interests dominated by Germans and established a lucrative business relationship with them. This eventually led to contacts with German political agents: Rumely, and through him Albert, and probably von Bernstorff. But this did not mean that Hammerling was pro-German regarding the war. An analysis of the *American Leader* during the war found it neutral. A similar investigation of the editorial policies of the scores of papers in the AAFLN found them to be, in large part, anti-German. Hammerling's young second wife—he remarried in 1915—was a passionate supporter of the Western Powers and outspokenly pro-Allied. No, Hammerling was not really pro-German—he did their bidding to make money, not to further their cause. He was unscrupulous, and if he had any views regarding the war, he kept them to himself. In fact, when he did speak of the war—conveniently after the United States had become a belligerent—he was condemnatory of the Germans. Hammerling and Paderewski had no impediment blocking their cooperation; both were Poles who were after larger goals: for

Hammerling money, for Paderewski power.[144] Perhaps Hammerling was a Polish spy as well.

As for Paderewski, his tendency was to surround himself with questionable advisors including, most strikingly, the elephantine Jan Maria Horodyski or the unscrupulous "Count Stanisław Józef von Wasilewski." But he was just one of many. Hammerling would not have been a striking exception.[145]

CHAPTER 6

Dreams and Ruin

OF ALL HAMMERLING'S EFFORTS the largest and most ambitious is the one that died aborning: the postwar advertising campaign to market Germany to a war-weary world. Hammerling, as usual, claimed he had no knowledge as to the source of the idea, nor its funding. He said in March 1918 that after the appearance of the Appeal three years earlier, "I had nothing else to do with anybody in this matter and I dropped it altogether."[1] This was another fabrication.

About February 1, 1917, Hammerling called on the Van Patten Advertising Agency in midtown Manhattan to see Harry J. Pruden who handled "space purchasing."[2] Hammerling had known Pruden for more than a decade, and they had worked closely together. Hammerling proffered a "very large and profitable account," but he could say nothing about it save that it would amount to $1.5 million annually for five years with 15 percent commission. The advertising would cover the entire Western Hemisphere. A few days later, Hammerling told Pruden that the parameters had expanded to a "much larger sum" than the $1.5 million, but for mysterious reasons, Van Patten could not handle the additional amounts. The remainder would go to two other firms.[3] When asked the rather obvious question, what was this all about, Hammerling said he was unable to say. Van Patten later mused that whereas Pruden enjoyed a fine reputation with the press, Hammerling knew *he* did not and therefore he needed Pruden to front the campaign. The situation was bizarre, but soon things became clearer.[4]

In late February Hammerling again visited the Van Patten office but now to discuss politics. The war, he explained, would be over in June—that was a certainty—due to the German submarine campaign. In Hammerling's succinct analysis: "the submarines will put the quietus on England and then good-bye France."[5] One week after peace was established, Hammerling wanted the advertising effort to begin; at the latest, July 1.[6] Soon thereafter Hammerling explained that no copy and artist work would be necessary, because the campaign "was already prepared and in plate form" and that *he* would send the advertising to the publishers directly, but that they would bill Van Patten—a curious arrangement. For someone who vehemently denounced "kaiserism," Hammerling was prepared to make a profit from its success. Incidentally, Hammerling boasted to Pruden that he knew von Bernstorff.[7]

Now Hammerling was prepared to furnish more details. The advertising would carry the signature "Hamburg-American Steamship Company." The account of the other two companies would be signed North German Lloyd and another sponsor that Van Patten could not recall during his later testimony. Hammerling was reluctant to provide this information and did so only under pressure. Van Patten was worried about credit risk, and in response Hammerling, astonishingly, told them he would pay cash, in advance, out of his own pocket to cover any risk![8]

The advertising campaign was to have some curious features. It was to avoid large cities and newspapers and be carried in places with a population of 100,000 or less. Hammerling provided a list of 25 to 30 cities where he did *not* want advertising, but he wanted all others to be targeted. The advertisements would be placed in perhaps 250 journals.[9] The campaign would also be in a great many foreign language papers.

Van Patten was becoming very suspicious by this point, and told Pruden that he could not understand why his company would make so large a profit: "I did not like the looks of this thing."[10] Van Patten wanted to see any copy before sending it out. "It looked to me like German propaganda."[11] Van Patten reserved the right to reject anything he did not like. He calculated that he would gross $750,000, but "the whole thing looked queer."[12] Van Patten began to indulge in paranoiac fantasies about Hammerling, noting, with agitation: "Hammerling's offices in the Woolworth building are a good observation point on activities going on in the New York Harbor."[13] But, unfortunately for Hammerling, in the midst of these fantastic negotiations, the United States declared war on Germany. Hammerling denied every aspect of this episode.[14] Of course, why the two advertising men would make up such a detailed story is inexplicable.

PATRIOT

Hammerling disappeared briefly, but almost immediately turned his advertising efforts from promoting Germany to peddling of the American patriotic cause. He was particularly zealous that the foreign language press demonstrate its patriotism by giving advertising space to the government. He was appointed to the Associated Advertising Clubs of the World—to which he donated $5,000 to help coordinate publicity, and wrote to publishers exhorting them to cooperate. His tone was perfervid.[15]

In 1917–1918, Hammerling's world of mystery and intrigue collapsed. Once the United States joined the war, he was frantic to prove his Americanism. Days before he was to be questioned by the Department of Justice, he wrote a pitiful letter to Wilson pleading that his 1915 "Appeal" was at a time when the United States was neutral: "Great harm can be done me by raising issues of two and one half years ago in present atmosphere. I believe that in view of my loyal support of all war policies my attitude in the situation two and one half years ago when our country was neutral should not now be questioned. Will you not accept my pledge of unlimited cooperation in the spirit of assurances of loyalty transmitted to you . . . and speak a word for me in present situation."[16]

Wilson told Tumulty he had "no confidence in this man" and would pay no attention to him.[17] Hammerling tried a direct appeal to the Department of Justice, which also aggravated Wilson because Hammerling was using the prominent Chicago industrialist Cyrus H. McCormick as his supporter.[18] There is a fascinating series of connections here. McCormick was a friend of Jan F. Smulski, probably the most important Pole in the United States and a fellow Chicago banker. McCormick was asked, in late 1917, to involve himself in an investigation of Polish politics in the United States. Smulski was the man he turned to. Smulski was close to Paderewski—indeed his lieutenant. He was also an associate and friend of Hammerling. This gives us a tenuous link between Hammerling and Paderewski that will resurface at the end of the war.

In late 1917 Hammerling gave the press an emotional interview in which he denounced the ethnic press for not being sufficiently patriotic and demanded they all make public declarations of their loyalty. The man who had issued an appeal to aid the Central Powers war aims declared that German papers should have, in 1914, issued a declaration of loyalty to the United States.[19]

By the spring of 1918, Hammerling composed a gigantic list of his service to the war cause, which he marketed about. It goes on for pages and contains thirty major points. Its very extremity proves that Hammerling knew he was under close scrutiny and probably in danger of prosecution and at least public obloquy; he was a desperate man. He recited his services and sacrifices: he gave up his house and car and moved into a two-room flat; he bought a farm to raise produce for the war effort; he purchased Liberty Bonds and War Savings Stamps, and in fact he spent 35 percent of all of his money on these purchases; he snitched on disloyal ethnic papers; he contributed to the relief funds of Poles, Jews, Italians, Canadians, French, and even the Knights of Columbus; he gave "ten million four hundred thousand cigarettes for the Italian army"; he organized the "American-Syrian Loyalty League"; he published hundreds of advertisements for Liberty Loans.[20] There was more. All his employees volunteered for the military; he promised all he would hold their jobs, and some he even continued to pay. He went on a nationwide speaking tour. He clamored for volunteers among immigrants. This was, he concluded, "my bit."[21] In another letter to the Committee on Public Information's Carl Byoir, he boasted that he had arranged free advertising for the government in 443 foreign language newspapers and assured Byoir he could convince the rest to cooperate if "I have authority in my hands to speak to these papers more frankly," which sounds unpleasantly like an offer to threaten.[22] He, or his associates, arranged a letter of tribute to him from 400 editors of foreign language newspapers extolling his virtue in the *Official Bulletin* of the CPI.[23] He also, grandiloquently, asked Byoir if he wanted him to organize "a great meeting in New York," which by careful preparation would be nothing less than the "greatest day in history."[24] He was clearly losing control of his reasoning.

Hammerling was trying to get a government job—and he was willing to accept no salary—to prove his zeal. However, he was repeatedly refused when the MID quietly exposed him to other governmental agencies. Thus he lost positions at the Food Administration and the Liberty Loan Committee, but he did get an appointment at Creel's Committee on Public Information, as Assistant Director, to the MID's utter consternation.[25] As early as January, however, the Justice Department publicly mused over revoking his naturalization. Hammerling was increasingly in jeopardy.[26]

DID ZOTTI PROVOKE THE INVESTIGATIONS?

Evidence suggests that it was Zotti's denunciations that first prompted the intelligence community to renew their interest in Hammerling.[27] The original conflict of 1915 erupted again in 1918, but now accusations of aiding Germany were much more dangerous than they had been before American belligerency.

By the spring of 1918 Hammerling was a sick man. Constant campaigning by Zotti and Michał Kruszka of Milwaukee,[28] and latterly the editorials of the Italian paper *Il Cittadino*, had driven him to a virtual breakdown.[29] As noted above, Zotti was almost certainly blackmailing Hammerling for $10,000. More, the *New York World* seemed to publish anything Zotti wrote, thus expanding the audience for his accusations.[30] Cleverly, when Zotti included a denunciation of Hammerling, he printed in English on the first page of an otherwise Croatian language journal. The *World* ran front-page headlines such as "Hammerling Exposed!" and "Another of Hammerling's Schemes Exposed," and "Some More of Hammerling's Dirty Work."[31]

Hammerling was being accused of a stupendous series of crimes and transgressions, some serious, many simply embarrassing.[32] According to these sources Hammerling was a German agent, an Austrian agent, a manifold liar, "brazen, arrogant and deceitful," given to "hysteric patriotic utterances," a "fakir," a suspicious convert, and a man "every American [should be] afraid to have anything to do with." His lies were uncountable: naturalization, exaggerations of his ancestry, relationship to the Austrian poet Robert Hammerling. He is guilty of graft, malversation, bribery, blackmail, theft, and corrupt business practices with "hundreds" of clients. He falsely claimed to represent the foreign language press in the United States and, by inference, the immigrant community as a whole.

In May 1918 Hammerling sued Zotti for libel. He also contemplated suits against an Italian editor, and Kruszka, the Polish journalist. Significantly, he announced his suit by claiming that he hesitated because he did not think Zotti would be taken seriously, and went on to stress his recent patriotic activities. He did not discuss the issues of the earlier era that Zotti had emphasized.[33]

A few of the editors came to Hammerling's defense, motivated, it seems, by their revulsion for Zotti.[34] More significantly, Hammerling became close to Creel, and the Committee's Byoir became a key defender, dismissing all the charges launched against him as emanating from Zotti. That resulted in another of the endless controversies that characterize Hammerling's life. Creel and Byoir tried to defend Hammerling to MID, but failed completely.[35] Their efforts to exonerate him and praise his (current) patriotism resulted in a damning indictment by the MID that dismissed Zotti as a source and recited only Hammerling's admissions or other "matters of record." These included the Rumely affair with the Evening Mail, the Appeal, running German and Austrian propaganda, encouraging munitions workers "not to work," threatening editors in order to dominate the ethnic press, being in German pay, being on the British "Black List" because they considered him "one of the most dangerous German agents in the United States," obtaining his naturalization through perjury, attempting to create a huge German press campaign in 1917, and several other ornaments.[36] For London, Hammerling was in "charge of all propaganda in US."[37]

Byoir finally could bear the defense of Hammerling no longer. He prepared a memorandum for Creel in which he tried to separate the Hammerling of an earlier day from the ardent patriot he had come to work with. He also tried to eliminate charges emanating from Zotti. Hammerling, Byoir wrote, was "an agent of the Imperial German Government and . . . was in close personal contact with Ambassador Dumba." Subsequently, he has "reversed his position." Byoir raised the possibility that Hammerling was involved with the efforts by Austria to gain a separate peace, an issue in 1917 to which we have already referred.

Hammerling, Byoir argued in a striking paragraph, knew a great deal of information about German actions and agents in the United States and was willing to divulge it—but only to the president in person. While awaiting Wilson, Hammerling mentioned that banker Paul Warburg was currently "the financial head of all the German intrigue" in the United States. Hammerling even cast suspicion on Adolph Ochs of the *New York Times*. The former is certainly plausible.

Zotti, Byoir claimed, was a swine and, more, was in Austrian pay. By contrast Hammerling still enjoyed trust among his editors and their readers: "he has tremendous influence, probably more than any twenty other men, among millions of the foreign born."[38]

But now Hammerling was bereft and betrayed. The Republican Party, to which he was devoted, had not come to his aid in the various investigations. He would "talk to no one but the President." He was "badly frightened."[39]

Hammerling's frantic efforts to prove his patriotism reflected the sudden exposure of his wartime activities during a number of public interrogations, including, in early March 1918, that of the MID in New York. A number of his associates were also questioned: Gabryel, whose testimony was damning; Dattner; Bertha Leffler; the mysterious Sam Weiss; and a few others. Gabryel's affidavit was a concise inculpation of Hammerling: he met with von Bernstorff, the mission to munitions plants were supposed to discover discontent, he gave bribes, he was in the pay of the Austrian government, he was not born in Hawaii, Boy-Ed visited him, his employees burned his books, he had an affair with poor Bertha, and his common-law wife lived in England. Hammerling had a lot of explaining to do.[40] No investigators testified. Zotti's excoriation of Hammerling reached its apogee at the same time and, despite public denials, probably encouraged the MID to hold the hearings.[41]

Hammerling adopted a fascinating style of dealing with questions: sometimes evasive, other times bluntly honest, but most frequently simply confusing. Certain facts, like his supposed birth in Honolulu and false naturalization, he admitted. Other matters, like receiving money from Albert for the Appeal, he claimed he did not know at the time but had just learned.[42] He denied any Austrian connections, which was wise because Austrian spies had been a national hysteria as early as 1915. He said nothing about the Van Patten–Pruden issue and was able to avoid a few other pitfalls. Smaller issues, like being Sam Weiss's brother, he either dodged or obfuscated. He also never admitted that his agents prepared written reports of their missions to munitions centers.[43] He was really, he indicated, a victim of Rumely's perfidy, Albert's treachery, and

Weiss's name problems. He only lied once, and that was because he liked Hawaii. In sum, however, the rumors of 1915 became facts in 1918. He continued to explain his earlier activities as misunderstood, irrelevant, or taken out of context, some of which is probably true.

We must bear in mind that the British were still very suspicious of Hammerling and warned the Americans that his control of the foreign language press still left open the possibility of "sedition being preached." It was probably now that the British suggested that Voska their little Bohemian spy-chaser be turned on Hammerling. The former mayor, John P. Mitchel, had placed him on a reception committee to welcome distinguished foreign guests to New York City. At Hammerling's recommendation two others, both of them Hungarians, were added. Both had been in German pay.[44] After intervention by the secretary of state, all three were removed.[45] It was a stunning failure of judgment on Hammerling's part. His world was collapsing. The MID was finally destroying him.

Reeling from the MID investigations, Hammerling was tortured by another public inquisition launched by the New York State's Attorney General's Office, an undertaking that was bemired in Byzantine squabbling in New York politics. Deputy State Attorney General Alfred L. Becker was a Republican political fanatic and caused the investigation to assume large proportions. Hammerling came to loathe Becker, which does not appear to have been difficult. During the examination, Hammerling continued to claim that he did not know that Rumely represented the Germans when he readied the Appeal. He also denied any knowledge of the Van Patten advertising campaign. The latter, when called to the stand, contradicted Hammerling's testimony.

However, a diversion soon entered the hearings. Becker wanted to implicate William Randolph Hearst, a Democrat, in German propaganda. Hammerling had worked for Hearst in his Wilkes-Barre days. Becker indicated that the money Hearst paid to Hammerling was from an account in the name of von Bernstorff deposited at the G. Amsinck & Company bank. The bank's representative was one Adolph Pavenstedt. This bank, in turn, especially Pavenstedt, also handled the funds of the extraordinary Bolo Pasha, formerly in the employ of the khedive of Egypt, and after 1914 enmeshed in German propaganda. The French ultimately tried and executed Bolo for treason.[46] Thus through Hammerling, Becker tried to link Bolo Pasha with Hearst.[47] This association of Hammerling with Bolo could have further damaged the former's reputation.

The investigative agencies were undecided as to what to do about Hammerling. The MID wanted him prosecuted for a variety of reasons. They shared the British view that he was "one of the most dangerous German agents in the United States."[48] The MID considered arranging to have his citizenship revoked. Joseph Tumulty, President Wilson's secretary, had foul memories of Hammerling from the 1912 and 1916 political campaigns and wanted to be involved in the anti-Hammerling machinations.[49] The Justice Department, however, wanted the issue dropped. The MID was appalled.[50]

Hammerling attempted a final counterattack. He denied most of the minor charges against him, though not the Appeal, and concluded that "the attacks that have lately been appearing in the public press against me and others is a part of propaganda work inspired by pro-German conspirators whose aim at the present moment is to discredit the Czech-Slovak, Polish and Slavonic leaders who are working for the success of America and its Allies."[51] Here Hammerling has perhaps overreached himself in his efforts at exoneration: he is a poor Polish boy being attacked by pro-Germans because of his American patriotism.

However, the Justice Department wanted the case closed.[52] MID was stupefied by Justice's conclusion and fought on. They had thought that Hammerling should be interned. Shortly thereafter, the State Department asked Justice to revoke his naturalization, but they emphasized his recent patriotic work to deny the suggestion.[53] Byoir, reluctantly, accepted his resignation from the CPI.[54] Privately, rumors abounded that it was only Hammerling's immense network of friends and associates, especially the powerful members of the Republican Party, that saved him.[55]

Finally, at the end of 1918 Hammerling was examined before the Senate subcommittee on the Judiciary examining *Brewing and Liquor Interests and German and Bolshevik Propaganda*. The results of Becker's inquiry were a starting point, one filled with contradictions.[56] Hammerling testified for hours and admitted a great deal, although he was variously apologetic, confused, remorseful, offended, contradictory, and incomprehensible. As is typical of all such hearings there was endless repetition, but three things dominated: his 1901 citizenship gambit, the Appeal, and the involvement with Van Patten and Pruden. The latter two are really examples of the same theme: his being in German pay. Curiously, his campaign work from 1896–1916 was not discussed. The Senate committee was created to uncover spies not scold political racketeers.

Perhaps indicative of Hammerling's desperate attempts to make himself appear the eternal foe of the Teutonic enemy is the fact that he claimed he had written an editorial early in the war denouncing Austria. The only problems were that he did not write the piece, and when he discovered that it had been published, he had it retracted and issued an apology to Austria. The article, "Austria's Crime," was reprinted on August 13, 1917, to demonstrate Hammerling's prescience and anti-Austrian sentiments.[57] It was perhaps not a good example for Hammerling to boast of this to the Senate.[58] In conclusion the Senate decided that Hammerling knew he was in German pay, and knew the purposes of that employment. His efforts to deny or ameliorate that connection were mendacious. He was guilty.[59]

Hammerling resigned from the AAFLN in March 1919 in the midst of the investigation. What to do now?[60] It was strangely appropriate that he gave an incomprehensible explanation for his resignation. Many foreign language newspapers, he noted, were going to campaign to have their co-nationals return to their fatherlands now that the war was over. Hammerling, the die-hard American, was going to fight this danger to the United States, and only outside the AAFLN could he do so effectively.[61] It was absurd. Of course, Hammerling's first action after the war was to return to his fatherland, doing what he promised he would urge others not to do.

A FOND FAREWELL FROM A SINKING SHIP

Paderewski left the United States to return to a free Poland at the end of November 1918. As he was about to depart on the SS *Negantic* he received a cable from Hammerling. He wanted to "present to Poland, through you, as a token of our love and esteem, our land and estates in Brody and Kalwaria Zebrzydowska [both in Galicia] near Kraków, provided that city will be the seat of a free independent Polish government, to be used as a summer palace for its [Poland's] Chief Magistrate. The property is free and clear of indebtedness." Hammerling would literally buy his way into the good graces of the next president of Poland. It was an effort to cultivate the mighty that he had employed since the anthracite years.

After praising Paderewski extensively and wishing him well in combat against the "evil forces arrayed against justice and freedom," Hammerling got down to business: "should you upon arrival decide that I could be of assistance to you in Paris at any time, do not hesitate to cable me at once."[62] He had tried American patriotism to extricate himself from an awkward situation. Now it was time to give Polish patriotism a try. Also, he was about to be sued in New York.

Hammerling had courted Paderewski since the latter's arrival in the United States in 1915. Unfortunately we know nothing about this relationship. The anti-German Polish press in the United States, which normally would have been passionate about exposing a German agent like Hammerling, was also in thrall to Paderewski and never uttered an unkind word about the maestro. Only the insignificant press of the Polish left made an occasional snide comment about Paderewski, and even they were very guarded as he had become *persona ultissima grata* with the Wilson administration.

Hammerling cultivated Paderewski's ne'er-do-well stepson Kazimierz Górski, seeing in him a well-placed link in the economic affairs of newly created Poland. Just before leaving the United States, Hammerling created something called the "Poland Export Corporation." Hammerling made Górski the president, a convenience because of Górski's relationship to Paderewski who had just become premier of Poland. He promised the naïve Górski that the corporation would make $100,000 profit yearly of which Górski would retain a quarter.[63] Hammerling's name did not appear on the letterhead. The Corporation had large ambitions, and they all were based on Górski's relationships; using connections in politics to further business adventures was Hammerling's specialty. He dreamed of the economic reconstruction of large parts of eastern Europe.[64]

In early May 1919, Górski sent his mother a letter that he wanted Prime Minister Paderewski to sign (a high-ranking member of government would be a poor second choice), a letter pledging that the government of Poland was "most sympathetic" to the Corporation and would welcome the cooperation with it by American companies because the Corporation was a "pioneer" in creating Polish-American economic ties. In a conclusion of particular gall for Górski to add, he wanted Paderewski to promise to a prospective American customer that "all available transportation facilities inside of Poland will be granted to your goods as well as your representatives."[65] Górski told his mother that he needed this letter at once as the "success of his whole enterprise may depend on it."[66]

Górski wrote a letter to "Dear Mother" on the 9th of July, 1919, before leaving for Poland with Hammerling. He had just landed a contract to send $1 million worth of cigarettes from the American Tobacco Company to Poland. Details would be effortless "on the strength of Mr. Paderewski's cable." Here we should remember that Hammerling had recommended tobacco magnates to Paderewski when the maestro arrived in 1915. Connections were paying off.

The problem, however, was Górski's business partner, Hammerling. Górski was "a little disappointed" that Hammerling had yet to receive a "cable" asking for him to come to Poland. Hammerling was very anxious to leave, and he "would work for you and could be of tremendous assistance in upbuilding the country." Hammerling was, after all, a "genius" though not a man for details. He was an unrivaled salesman, thus he would travel to Poland at his own expense but, while there, through his unrivaled salesmanship, he would "secure orders for our Corporation." Górski admitted that other Polonia organizations were "fighting" them, but assured Mother that they were prospering. And, he was appreciative of the watch and gloves she had sent.[67]

Apparently, Górski was not satisfied with the speed of his answer, because he cabled Paderewski directly on May16, informing him that American Tobacco had made the arrangement "solely for Paderewski." However, the company wanted interest, prompt payment, and promises of future purchases—on a cash basis. Górski offered to arrange the shipping.[68]

By mid-August Górski had more business for his mother. He had his European director, Michael Kley, ask Mme. Paderewska that the Corporation be registered quickly in Warsaw, as it had already opened an office at a midtown address there. More business was coming. The next day, Górski and Hammerling were trying to negotiate a deal for Poland to purchase American horses![69] In the autumn, Górski and Hammerling tried to buy a vast quantity of shoes from the American Liquidation Commission in Paris. The terms were outrageous and refused. They apparently complained to Warsaw. The young company's business efforts had failed.[70]

The whole enterprise was unsavory at the start. Górski would be Hammerling's pawn, and his mother would get her husband to arrange contracts. Hammerling would be invited by the Polish government to tour around drumming up business: his sponsor being the prime minister. Meanwhile Górski would work "for You" as he said to his mother. Górski's behavior was reprehensible, and we can only wonder what role Hammerling had in urging Górski to write these reprehensible letters.[71]

However, as always with Hammerling, things took a turn. He required a passport and applied for one. He and his attorney were examined by a member of the State Department. Astonishingly, the attorney announced that Hammerling was "an inveterate liar!" The Department examined Hammerling's rather disreputable activities over the last several years, and recommended that he be refused a passport. However, his "affiliation with Górski" who, on account of his connection with Paderewski, was "probably in position to do good business in Poland." The passport was granted.[72]

On August 21, 1919, Hammerling left the United States for Poland; he was not alone. He had his new business partner Górski with him. There were new worlds to conquer. He had strapped $250,000 in a belt around his waist.[73] Górski was the Polish Charles Nagel: another direct conduit to the mighty.

On the next ship was the young Mrs. Hammerling. On February 25, 1915, Hammerling had married a Polish aristocrat of twenty-two; he was then either forty-one or forty-five, probably the latter. She was strikingly beautiful. Her family was wealthy and passionately patriotic. "One of the richest girls in Poland," Hammerling crowed.[74] They had apparently met a few months before their wedding when Hammerling visited Galicia in conjunction with his divorce from Klara. Although there are many moments in his life that would have made conversion convenient for Hammerling, he always claimed that he became a Roman Catholic to marry his wife. They were wed the very day she returned from Europe by Cardinal Farley at a chapel of St. Patrick's Cathedral.[75]

Her name is given in a bewildering variety of ways, and her lineage is rather mysterious. The *New York Times*, which announced the wedding, referred to her as "Countess Sophie von Brzenicka," an unwarranted title. Polish sources usually refer to her as Zofia Janina z Brzezickich, from Lwów in Galicia. Her mother, however, came from the aristocratic Broel-Plater family. She was going home; where Hammerling was going was problematical.

The State Department almost immediately rued its decision to grant Hammerling a passport. Apparently, no sooner did he arrive than he began trading on Paderewski's name. He and Górski were gamboling about "trying to get government contract concessions." Hammerling "demanded" that the American Legation "get him place on train to Paris," as he was bound there "on business for Paderewski." When asked, however, the maestro repudiated Hammerling's claim. It was reported to Washington that, while in Poland, Hammerling engaged in "objectionable and discreditable behavior." The American Minister in Warsaw told Washington that Hammerling's past was so unsavory that he "does us no credit" and found his possession of an American passport "deplorable." He recommended that neither Hammerling nor Górski—"merely a creature of Hammerling"—be given a passport again.[76]

The dubious Corporation was short-lived. In February 1920 a New York court attached Hammerling's property "on an allegation of $39,000 fraud." Since Hammerling had left the United States and presumably "did not intend to return in the near future," the court concluded it had no choice. Eleven banks and trust companies were served; the total of his assets possessed went unreported. The Corporation was the plaintiff asking for the $39,000 from Hammerling because our ever-wily hero got the Corporation to invest that sum to buy stock in one of his businesses. He was attempting to "defraud" and in effect escape the law by going to Poland.[77] A few weeks later an additional $20,033 was attached at Górski's motion.[78]

The Senator from Honolulu

THE POLAND HAMMERLING RETURNED to was radically different from the one he had last visited in 1914. Austrian Poland no longer existed. It was integrated into a new free state, resurrected from partition and destruction in 1795. The Poles had an enormous task to rebuild a functioning country from the wreckage of the world war.

Officially Poland returned to the map of Europe as an entity on November 11, 1918, with the end of the war. But the country existed in name only. Much of it was still occupied by German and Austrian troops who numbered in the hundreds of thousands and all of whom wanted to return, across Polish territory, to their homes. The borders of the country, either reborn or new depending on whether one was a Pole or not, were a complete mystery. The old territories were not simply returned to Poland, but rather it took months of deliberation by the Paris Peace Conference—which met after hostilities to reconstruct Europe—and several wars to carve Poland from the chaos that was eastern Europe. This was a gigantic undertaking and only concluded after the Poles won a major war with Communist Russia in the summer of 1920, a victory whose historical importance is gradually beginning to be recognized.

Initially, power in Poland was in the hands of Józef Piłsudski, a national hero—though a controversial one—who had led Polish military contingents since early in the war and was associated with a martial and bold conception of how Poland was to regain its freedom. In the closing stages of the war, with Russia, Germany, and Austria all in collapse,

Piłsudski simply stepped into a power vacuum at the head of a military force whose ranks he had filled and whose hearts he had captured as early as 1914.

When Paderewski returned in late November, he doubtless thought he would become, by a kind of national draft, the new leader of Poland. Paderewski was, after all, the most famous Pole in the world. He had gained the support of the United States, whose voice in creating a postwar world would be enormous. And he knew Hammerling.

Piłsudski completely outmaneuvered Paderewski: they struck a deal in December 1918 whereby Piłsudski would be chief of state and head of the army and Paderewski would be prime minister. As a result Piłsudski had control of all that mattered, and Paderewski inherited the grueling and thankless task of running the quotidian tasks of government. Paderewski fancied himself a man of destiny and soon proved utterly incompetent. Deals like the Górski tobacco episode were characteristic of a regime in chaos.

The political situation of the country was in flux when Hammerling arrived in 1919. The political right, led by the anti-Semite Roman Dmowski, probably commanded the largest following, but the leftist Piłsudski had the votes and undying loyalty of a considerable proportion of his countrymen. A powerful but enigmatic third faction was the peasant (better called farmers') party, which claimed, accurately, to represent the vast majority of the national population. The leadership of the peasant political movement was notoriously corrupt, fissiparous, and directionless, and was striking for its unwillingness to assert the political power its numbers would make warranted. By 1919 the leading figure in a movement that had many parties and uncountable factions was Wincenty Witos.

Witos is a strange character. To many he epitomized modern Polish populist politics, the most visible and important figure the rural population of Poland has ever produced. To others he was a cunning, unscrupulous, and ambitious rascal without any set principles: in other words, Hammerling's kind of man. Witos, eloquently, described the peasant movement as a "useless plow" needing something to pull it.[1]

Soon after Hammerling returned to Poland he went to call upon Witos. The result was a short-lived but spectacular political career. Hammerling always wanted to run for office in the United States but instead stayed in the background as a manipulator and *éminence grise*. He did not seem to realize this was the role he was predestined to fulfill: when he operated openly his career was a catastrophe.

BUILDING A PEASANT POLITICAL PARTY

While traveling throughout Poland trying to launch the Corporation he finagled poor Górski into, Hammerling had been hatching new plans. By November, only three months after arriving in Poland, Hammerling wanted to travel to Paris, Paderewski lamented to the American Minister, as part of a new scheme: he was going to organize a "foreign news service for Poland"—a sort of AAFLN in reverse. This would require some arrangement with the Associated Press, and he was off to arrange one. It is indicative of Hammerling's interests that he also wanted to found an "important" newspaper in Warsaw.[2] Hammerling acted as though he had a considerable fortune. He later claimed he was founding businesses for patriotic reasons: investing in Poland. No record of these gestures has appeared.

But politics beckoned Hammerling. And here is the nexus between Hammerling and peasant party leader Witos. Poland was in crisis when Hammerling mused over his newspaper adventures: the war with Soviet Russia had begun in earnest in late 1919, a major Polish offensive followed in April of the next year, and the Poles won the decisive battle of Warsaw in August, following it with two important victories in the fall. Meanwhile, the gross incompetence of the Paderewski regime—aided by his own idiosyncrasies—had driven his administration from power. By 1921 Poland had settled to a reasonably stable postwar position. With Paderewski gone, however, Hammerling no longer had any connections to the politically mighty. Witos was his answer. "He came to us to play some political role," said a peasant leader.[3]

It was through the populist leader Jan Bryl that Hammerling met Witos—it was perhaps as late as 1922, though that cannot be proven, and it might have been as early as 1920.[4] Hammerling came to call upon Witos. He emphasized his wealth, business acumen, newly discovered Polish patriotism, and wiliness. Witos and Hammerling soon became close friends. One observer described this process as

Hammerling "attaching himself" to Witos who became his "Godfather" (przyczepił się) and virtually adopted him (kumanie się).[5] Did Hammerling offer Witos anything in particular to gain his favor? Here we must speculate because evidence is extremely scanty.

Although Witos would later try to diminish Hammerling's role in aiding the nascent and rightist Polish Populist Part-Piast [Polskie Stronnictwo Ludowe-Piast], contemporary evidence makes this claim problematical. In the 1922 Polish presidential elections, Witos considered offering his candidacy. At a meeting in Warsaw, other Piast leaders were dubious. At the historic Hotel Europejski, Bryl and Hammerling spoke in favor of Witos. Hammerling asked: "Why do we have to search for other candidates for President, when we have our own Lincoln in the person of president Witos?" Hammerling's nomination was not ardently supported, and Witos probably for that reason decided not to run. Hammerling was a recent figure in Piast circles and already at high party meetings to choose a presidential candidate. He chose his benefactor Witos.[6] The fact that Hammerling's endorsement met with scant approval may well justify the comment by Madejczyk that he rarely spoke; and, when he did, no one was interested.[7]

Witos's PSL-Piast obviously saw Hammerling as a source of ready cash.[8] Hammerling apparently offered to use his money to acquire the nascent Polish press as an agency to promote Witos's political creation: Piast. It had traditionally been associated exclusively with West Galicia, but in 1920 it began to become an all-national party, expanding rapidly.[9] For years Piast was discussing avidly the need to move into eastern Galicia, Hammerling's homeland, where their influence had been practically nil. This would require new people and the infusion of capital. It was essential that a press network be formed. Hammerling was the providential man for Piast's long-cherished hopes.[10]

Buying, or otherwise influencing, small papers to support a political line was Hammerling's specialty: he had done it for the Republicans for years. Witos had found in Hammerling the money and the skills he needed to become the dominant political figure in Poland. Piast rapidly eclipsed the other populist parties. It was, moreover, "rightist," something Hammerling's Republican background would find congenial.

Hammerling was not altruistic in his support for Piast. Early rumors indicated that he wanted to run for the Polish Senate, a fact that was found astonishing by the Polonia press, which was aware of Hammerling's scandalous past. His sordid American years proved not to be an issue in the campaign. It seems that Hammerling cut a deal with the Piast leadership: financial support in exchange for a Senate seat.[11] There is even a rumor that he personally paid off Witos.[12] This type of corruption had been endemic in peasant politics and would not be considered an egregious crime.

Electioneering was frantic in 1921–1922. Eastern Galicia was looked upon as key territory for Witos's Populist Party in the elections of November 1922.[13] It had always voted rightist and that year would prove no exception. Witos logically regarded West Galicia as the base of his party and spoke of a mission to interest the peasantry to the east in public affairs (i.e., a polite way of saying he wanted to win them for Piast). It was only with the 1922 election that Piast expanded its territorial base. When Hammerling arrived it was merely a local party.[14]

Running the election in that part of Poland was Jan Bryl, an engineer by profession and corrupt by preference. Hammerling bribed Bryl into letting him run as a Senate candidate for one of the four seats for the Stanisławów district in eastern Galicia and, once nominated, proceeded to spend what was by Polish standards a fortune on the campaign.[15] He won. A radical paper argued that Hammerling thereafter virtually owned Piast in eastern Galicia.[16] American Polonia papers, aware of Hammerling's wartime shenanigans, were aghast.[17] Hammerling had just become a major figure in Polish populist politics and a very visible one at that. For an expatriate escaping from the clutches of the law, it was quite a second act. There is a fascinating attack launched on Piast by its populist opponent the Peasant Party, Emancipation (PSL-Wyzwolenie), in late 1921. It accused Piast of being bought, a charge not without merit if we consider Hammerling's rapid rise to position in it.

The charges against Hammerling for corruption and influence peddling must be placed in the context of Piast political cynicism. Witos reported to the highest executive authority of Piast on May 15, 1922, that he proposed that in the coming election, Piast should consider forming a bloc with the right in eastern Galicia; however, in West Galicia, "who knows," maybe it would be useful to come to a "quiet compromise" with the socialists."[18]

SENATOR HAMMERLING

The 1922 election results were a major victory for Piast and, within populist ranks, a considerable success for the right. Witos was pleased at Hammerling's election—it is good to keep that much money close by—and regarded Hammerling as one of the better candidates to win election for Piast that year.[19] However, not everyone was pleased with him: there was intraparty gossip that he had bought his victory and that he was a member of a circle of bad advisors who were pushing Witos to the political right.[20] All of this was quite true.

Bryl and Hammerling became close friends, and the populist leader glowingly introduced him to the political world and became his promoter. Witos became quickly convinced that, despite appearances, Hammerling was a political naïf, boastful and rather indiscreet. Rumors, which Hammerling fostered, began to circulate in Poland that he was fabulously rich, with yet more millions in America, where he had access to the highest circles.

Soon after his election, Hammerling made a long rambling apologia to his new Piast Senate colleagues. "Poland is rich," he said, but everyone had to work hard or the country was doomed. This bromide was received with applause. Hammerling next spoke biographically: he emphasized that he was unschooled, yet today "a millionaire." He had founded several businesses in Poland and invested half his fortune in them, but now he would invest everything, because he believed in Poland.[21]

In his first appearances on the Senate floor Hammerling employed a tactic that was to characterize his brief political career: the invocation of the United States as an example for Poland to follow. Thus, he enthusiastically endorsed giving land to veterans in the *kresy* (the eastern borderlands heavily non-Polish) and providing them with credit. This support for agriculture, he said, was characteristic of both the United States and Canada. He criticized land prices. He had much to say about taxes: in the United States the Americans first resented taxation, but with the war gladly paid high taxes, unlike the Poles who despised them. Poland imported too much relative to its wealth; savings must increase. The state is loaning too much to industrialists who are profiting from public funds. Poland has a bright future, but it must change, according to American patterns.[22] A constant refrain for Hammerling. This was actually a very clever tactic for him, though one can only wonder if the Poles appreciated endless invidious comparisons with the Americans. Hammerling was, after all, the personification of what it meant to adopt American business practices. He was now willing to share them with Poland, and perhaps he had something to say.

Hammerling became carried away and began to conduct himself like a celebrity, someone chosen to work great reforms in Poland. His public appearance as a wealthy dandy underscored his unique status. He boasted that his first task would be to bring Poland's finances and treasury in order by gaining major foreign loans at fine rates. However, he linked his spectacular future with the PSL-Piast and made it clear that he wanted to accomplish these feats through its medium.[23]

Nationwide, the 1922 elections were destabilizing. The country's parliament had been dominated by a centrist majority until November; thereafter the center, right, and left all had approximately the same number of seats. This very unstable situation was only made more difficult when the first elected president, Gabriel Narutowicz, was assassinated by a deranged rightist in December. With Poland now in crisis, a temporary non-party government was created under the leadership of General Władysław Sikorski as prime minister. (Later, of course, Sikorski would be the head of the Polish government during much of World War II.) Polish politics seemed to be congealing, when the system was thrown into chaos by a political coup for which Hammerling is often blamed.

THE LANCKORONA PACT

Hammerling lived on the estate of Lanckorona, near a small town of the same name attached to a great lineage, in Galicia. His estate was located between Brody and Kalwaria Zebrzydowska, two villages known for their large Jewish populations.[24] His birthplace of Drohojów was not far from where he married Klara. Lwów, the great metropolis where Janina, his second wife, was raised was midpoint between Kraków and Stanisławów. Hammerling thus left Galicia as an impoverished pseudo-orphan and returned to the region as a magnate. The local boy had indeed made good.[25] Whether Janina could make the same claim was problematical.

On May 17, 1923, after long negotiations, an agreement was signed in Warsaw at the apartment of Julian Zdanowski. Among those present was

Hammerling's devotee Bryl.[26] The pact linked Witos's Piast with the right wing, the Chjeno-Piast coalition ("Chjeno" was the abbreviation for the rightist *Chrześcijański Związek Jedności Narodowej*—Christian Alliance of National Unity). It was widely bruited that the pact was actually negotiated at Hammerling's estate—hence its designation as the Lanckorona Pact (Pakt Lanckoroński)—and that he was a major actor in its creation. The link between these two large political blocs created a solid rightist majority in parliament and paved the way for Witos to become premier. It also linked Piast with the political right, which outraged the other peasant parties who argued that Piast had committed class treason by abandoning the peasants for the mighty.[27] Piast had been pandering for some years to coalesce a majority. Although substantially rightist, Piast had a powerful leftist element and had flirted with alliances with the left.

Hammerling's place in negotiating the pact remains controversial. Initially, he was given the major role. The well-informed American diplomatic representative in Warsaw, Pierre de L. Boal, certainly saw Hammerling as the *spiritus movens*.[28] However, the established historiographical tradition that makes Hammerling the host if not organizer of the pact, was seemingly contradicted by the researches of Witold Stankiewicz who emphasized the Warsaw origins of the agreement in May and largely dismissed the earlier meeting at Lanckorona and any actions there by Hammerling.[29] Nonetheless, Tadeusz Ręk offers a plausible counter to the Stankiewicz proposition. According to Ręk, the go-between for Piast and the Chjeno party was Hammerling. A secret April conference was held at Lanckorona, Hammerling's estate, involving major figures from both parties. Maciej Rataj and Witos were the chief populist representatives. Stanisław Lato states specifically that the initial pact was signed in early April at Hammerling's estate, though he does not attribute any specific role to Hammerling.[30] It was only a month later that the formal pact was signed in Warsaw at Zdanowski's apartment.[31] Hence, Lanckorona was the site of some major developments leading to the pact no matter where the final document was signed. The Ręk version has eerie echoes of the 1902 anthracite negotiations with Hammerling working behind the scenes and not present for the largely ceremonial conclusions.

Witos, for his part, was furious at the attribution of the pact to Hammerling: it was "a vulgar lie" and Hammerling did not know "one letter of the agreement."[32] Witos was very forceful in emphasizing that Hammerling played no real role in Piast politics.[33] Perhaps too forceful. Other sources credit Hammerling with considerable significance in creating the coalition.[34] Witos later claimed that he had no idea where the name of the agreement came from, and he had no idea who initiated the negotiations.[35]

A few things about the pact bear keeping in mind. First, as Stankiewicz pointed out in a letter to the author a few years ago, it cannot be ignored that Hammerling met with Rataj three times in the weeks before the agreement.[36] Rataj was perhaps the second most powerful peasant leader in interwar Poland and was on close terms with Hammerling. Interestingly, at one of these meetings Hammerling told Rataj that he was going to buy the Warsaw daily *Rzeczpospolita*, and at another meeting they discussed transforming the Treasury. These were important meetings at a time when the pact was being negotiated and should give us pause to consider whether Hammerling was as dispensable a figure as Witos has reported.[37] As a matter of fact, there are reports that Hammerling served as Witos's agent during the complex negotiations, a reminder of his service to Quay and Penrose, as well as Mitchell.[38] Finally, Witos was involved in complex political maneuvers in 1922–1923 and could have conceivably formed a coalition with either the left or right. He chose right, the direction Hammerling and his coterie, including Bryl, were pushing him. A small matter perhaps, but not without interest.[39] There is a second strange matter in Rataj's recollections of his meetings with Hammerling. In his published version of the events, he refers to meeting with Hammerling in Kraków on April 3, but in his unpublished notes he describes the meeting as taking place at Hammerling's estate in Lanckorona. Were there two meetings the same day? Did Rataj wish to lessen the intimacy of his relations with Hammerling in the weeks before the pact? Or was Rataj at Lanckorona meeting with Hammerling? Rataj is the key figure linking Hammerling to the pact, and his memoirs provide only scraps.[40]

Whether Hammerling was an inconsequentiality or not, the left in Poland denounced the pact as a rightist coup and blamed Hammerling as its author.[41] Ironically, the anti-Semitic right also attributed the new government to Hammerling and subjected him to vicious criticism because he was a Jew, and, unfortunately for him, they began circulating very damaging reports about his past including that the government created by the Chjeno-Piast coalition was supported by "wealthy Jews and Germans"—one of the occasional anti-Semitic references to Hammerling.[42] The first major attack on Hammerling came days after the new Witos government was installed. He was accused of buying both his Senate seat as well as his influence in the upper chamber: Witos had sold him his position.[43] A charge not wholly without merit.

On the basis of the pact, Witos had the majority to bring him into power, which he assumed on June 1, 1923. Barely seven months later, the government collapsed. It was the first parliamentary government in modern Poland, replacing the authoritarian rule of Piłsudski. The year 1923 was perhaps the worst in interwar Polish history, and the pact had ushered in a totally incompetent administration.[44]

KUCHARSKI: ANOTHER SCANDAL

The new government of Poland, the Chjeno-Piast coalition, faced a catastrophic economic situation: a massive wave of strikes, conscription of workers, and a general strike in Kraków (to which it responded with a cavalry charge), which paralyzed the city. Piłsudski, who had been in power since 1918, departed from all his offices and went into sullen opposition. After a few months, a split in Piast led to the government's downfall. Among the burdens of the doomed government was a dubious if not openly incompetent cabinet. Of all these worthies, however, the most infamous was Władysław Kucharski, who combined inability with corruption. He was, unfortunately, Hammerling's closest friend.

Kucharski was from a humble Kraków family. His involvement with patriotic movements brought him in contact with Roman Dmowski, father of modern Polish nationalism, fanatical anti-Semite, and Kucharski's promoter.[45] In the first months of Poland's reappearance, Kucharski served in a number of local administrative positions and gained the reputation as being a competent manager. In 1919 he aided Dmowski, Poland's representative at the Paris Peace Conference, and so impressed him that Dmowski insisted that he be given a major role in the new Poland.[46] Only thirty-six, he was appointed to an important position in western Poland and, in 1922, was a candidate for parliament on the nationalist ticket. He quickly became one of the parliamentary leaders of one of the rightist parties, and, with the appearance of the Witos government, he was given a cabinet position as Minister of Industry and Commerce (Minister Przemysłu i handlu).[47] Almost immediately Kucharski committed a mammoth error when he allowed the French to purchase a Polish factory at 1 percent of the costs the Warsaw government had just invested to restore it—the so-called "Żyrardów Affair." Kucharski managed to escape serious consequences from this financial mess by a very narrow vote in the parliament.[48] Nonetheless, the scandal weakened the coalition.[49]

Despite this, during Poland's ghastly economic crisis of 1923, it was widely argued that a massive foreign loan could save the situation. No one was more associated with this argument than Hammerling.[50] Using his position as chairman of the Senate Finance Committee—note that this was quite a position for someone whose political career could be measured in months—Hammerling called for negotiating a foreign loan and suggested he would be the ideal candidate to arrange one. An acute American observer concluded that "whoever could secure a 15 million dollar loan to Poland would be given the Finance Ministry on his own conditions."[51] Hammerling was at the center of the most vital concern in 1923 Poland: a major foreign loan. He was again in that whirl of secret meetings, networking, mysterious machinations, and lots of money.

Thus Kucharski and Hammerling came to the same point, but it was not merely a coincidence. The two had met sometime before, although the exact date is unknown, and had become close friends. It was widely rumored that Hammerling was a major financial contributor to Kucharski and that the latter was indebted to him in more ways than one. Reportedly he lent Kucharski the money to buy local papers to control their political line—an echo of Mitchell, and Hammerling's specialty.[52] Kucharski missed cabinet meetings and had to be searched for: he was at Hammerling's house "discussing loans" with his wife.[53]

Kucharski wanted the new Treasury portfolio and campaigned for it in a most dramatic way. Money was the focus of all political circles in Poland, and the Treasury Minister was the central actor in this obsession. Hammerling was his confederate. They conceived the idea of gaining a loan by turning over Polish national assets to foreign hands—something thitherto considered unacceptable.[54]

Without the mandate or even permission of his government, Kucharski and Hammerling went to Paris in August to negotiate a loan.[55] The two met with representatives of Guaranty Trust, and Morgan-Harjes. The bankers told the Poles that they wanted assurances that the government in Poland was politically right and not under Jewish influence. The irony of making this demand to Hammerling needs no comment. It quickly became obvious that it was Hammerling not Kucharski who was leading the talks.[56] He has "been put forward as the principal agent of the Polish Government in carrying out these negotiations."[57] When the talks moved to London—and whether Hammerling played a role here is impossible to determine—the efforts made the worst possible impression: they were conducted with minor banks, held in secret when they were advised to meet only with major houses and do so in the open, and they were angrily objected to by the Polish ambassador in London, Konstanty Skirmunt, who regarded such matters as his special prerogative.[58]

According to the American chargé in Warsaw, since Witos was "thoroughly unscrupulous" he tolerated the Kucharski-Hammerling meanderings: if they gained results he would claim the credit; if they failed he would attribute the blame to them.[59] Witos was notoriously cunning.

They traveled to London and Geneva and offered the Levy and Gordon bank a tobacco monopoly for 250 million francs. Hammerling and Kucharski worked behind the backs of Poland's diplomatic representatives, making the worst possible impression. Warsaw was warned by its representatives in Washington that this desperate loan-seeking was having a deplorable effect on Poland's reputation in financial markets.[60] Reports reached Warsaw that Kucharski was acting incompetently and damaging Poland's image. Witos was furious and called Kucharski's actions "incomprehensible."[61] The Parliament raised charges that the foreign trips of Kucharski and Hammerling were costing the Treasury considerable sums.[62]

They came back in late September empty-handed but full of promises, which Hammerling was tireless in marketing—his favorite boast was that the United States was contemplating a major loan. Given the legend that Hammerling was a powerful figure in the United States, this claim fell on fertile ground.[63] Hope was so high that the incompetent dilettante Kucharski was indeed promoted to Treasury Secretary. Witos, ever open to opportunity, was claiming the loan was possible even when he knew better, to gain support for his floundering regime.[64]

Hammerling met with Montagu Norman, governor of the Bank of England, and proffered a curious project. The first thing to be remembered is that Norman held Poland in absolute contempt and regarded it as incapable of salvation.[65] In 1923 Norman received from an unknown source, possibly Dwight Morrow the businessman and diplomat, this fascinating document, which deserves to be quoted *in extenso*: "Hammerling . . . has called upon me, and, speaking not officially but as one well advised as to Polish conditions, states that he feels the utmost confidence that Poland would see the desirability of accepting the aid, including the control, of the League of Nations if the plan that brought such a result about was accompanied by a substantial loan to the Government for the purpose of putting its financial house in order. He contemplates that the entire proceeds of the loan would be used for bank reserve and not spent on public improvements."

No further reports on this proposal were available, but Norman was being apprised because "of our desire to co-operate heartily with those who look forward to a reconstruction of Poland as a part of the general European problem." He had—the means are not specified—"advised the Polish people . . . that it would be a requisite of any loan that there should be some form of control. We understand that the British American Tobacco Co. and the American Tobacco Co. are working together on this matter."[66]

Hammerling here emerges as a rather more ambitious, and even perhaps more sophisticated, seeker of loans. Turning to the League as guarantor of the loan, however, could not have been considered without close cooperation with the Ministry of Foreign Affairs, and there is no evidence that he sought this cooperation.

Over the next three months Kucharski—and indeed the Witos cabinet in general—fell into political crisis. Hammerling became victim to a virulent press campaign, and his relations with other members of Piast became embittered. The rightist coalition was accused of being, in reality, the creature of rich Jews and Germans who, in effect, ran the party from behind the scenes. This was one of the early, indirect, references to Hammerling as a millionaire Jew using his money to control Piast.[67] This was not made any better by rumors that his wife was having an affair with Kucharski.[68] Witos later claimed that one of the major issues in the campaign to discredit both Hammerling and the Piast party in general was the belief that Hammerling, a wealthy Jew, had in effect bought the party.

The economy continued to deteriorate, the Piast party led by the ruthless Bryl showed signs of disintegration, and, most of all, the *fata morgana* of a foreign loan gradually dissolved. An opposition member in the Sejm (Stanisław Thugutt of PSL-Wyzwolenie) described the Witos administration in these moderate words: "a government of defeat and catastrophe and of national shame and humiliation."[69] Kucharski was widely disparaged, and, most awkwardly, Hammerling was called to stand trial before the Senate.[70]

ON TRIAL

The October 21, 1923, Sunday morning issue of Warsaw's influential *Kurjer Poranny* carried a full-page story entitled "The Senator from Honolulu."[71] It was the third installment of what had become a major series, a continuation of a multipart exposé of Hammerling.[72] The *Kurjer* wanted to bring down the Witos government and found Hammerling an easy target.[73] Previously he had been the subject of nasty gossip and scurrilously attacked by radical publications, but the *Kurjer* was a serious newspaper and widely read.[74]

Installment three began by accusing him of the Lanckorona Pact, which started a "Hammerling path" in Poland.[75] In a later article it referred to Lanckorona as "The Hammerling Pact" and gave him full blame for the Witos government.[76] Soon the press referred to Hammerling as the pact's creator.[77] His guilt was enormous. Kucharski, the paper gloated, had said of Hammerling: he is "the chief expert regarding financial affairs of the Western World."[78] Indeed, it was Hammerling to whom Kucharski was indebted for his cabinet position.[79] Reportedly he had offered to float a personal loan to the Polish government.[80] Subsequent articles mocked the failed loan campaign with which he was intimately associated.[81] A major newspaper was virtually crediting Hammerling with being a central force in contemporary Polish politics.

The accusations and commentary grew increasingly more personal and broadened the ambit. The early parts of Hammerling's biography were recounted with accuracy and fairness. Then, the catalog of accusations poured forth. His citizenship in 1901 was based on a lie; liquor interests in the United States gave him $200,000; he received substantial sums from German and Austrian agents during the war; he was involved in pacifist propaganda—the Appeal—at von Bernstorff's direction from which he earned $209,000; he later lied about the German source of his funds for propaganda.[82] There were other charges, most simply distasteful, but not illegal and certainly not resulting in damage to Poland.[83]

By October 27 the attacks had become personal. Hammerling did not speak Polish well. He once referred to himself as "half-Bohemian"; indeed the first time he ever called himself a Pole was 1919. He lied to Becker when he said Hawaii was a nice place—a damning charge for the *Kurjer* to mention. He was guilty of rampant bribery, and, in what was perhaps the most serious potential charge against him, he had sent those investigators out to survey munitions-manufacturing cities.[84]

The *Kurjer* sustained its attacks on Hammerling, unearthing old charges. Zotti was mentioned on November 1, along with embarrassing details of Hammerling's two marriages.[85] The Van Patten–Pruden issue was aired. Some of Hammerling's more ridiculous claims—that he knew the emperor Charles of Austria, that his father had been Austrian commandant at Przemyśl—were humiliatingly published.[86] Other papers now joined the campaign pouring ridicule on Hammerling and the Piast party.[87] By November 4 they were using the American, not the Polish version of his name: he was being cast off.[88] Perhaps this was the crowning blow for a country as sensitive about its national pride and relations with detested Germany: on November 27 Poland congratulated Hammerling for having close connections to Heinrich Albert, who had just become chancellor of Germany. Albert had been implicated in German subversion in Hammerling's World War I America.[89]

The overwhelming press campaign by *Kurjer Poranny* forced a public airing of the scandal. On December 1, the Minister of Justice convened a "court of honor" in the Hammerling case. On December 6, 1923, Hammerling appeared before the Marshall of the Senate. He was accused of "unethical conduct" while being in the United States. A number of other senators acted as judges; documents were submitted. The Under Secretary of Foreign Affairs was also present because Hammerling's putative wrongs were committed in a foreign country.[90] Derisively, the *Kurjer* noted that the more than 180 pages of evidence would give the jury "moments of deep sadness and shame, but also moments of real merriment."[91]

Hammerling was devastated before the Senate pronounced its verdict. Kucharski resigned in disgrace, a broken man; he would never recover.[92] The government, dominated by Hammerling's Piast, collapsed on December 14. It was accused, in a final damnation, of suffering from "hammerlingism." Hammerling had been the lightning rod for criticism of the Chjeno-Piast administration for the *Kurjer*. The paper carried on a press campaign against him to make its political rival appear corrupt and ridiculous.

On December 21, after three weeks of deliberation, the Senate concluded in extremely convoluted, indeed tortuous, language, that it "did not regard the charges against senator Hammerling as constituting, in so far as is corroborated by the evidence conveyed, behavior, demonstrating, in the extant circumstances which accompanied the deeds charged to senator Hammerling, as sufficiently established to deem to Mr. Hammerling a person unworthy of respect."[93] Hammerling immediately withdrew from Piast (though he kept his Senate seat until 1924) and the budget committee.[94] His political career had lasted scarcely a year.

FINALLY, A DIVORCE

It must have been cold comfort to Hammerling that, while he was being hammered in the Polish press and tried by the Senate, one aspect of his life was moving toward a more positive settlement: the endless quarrel with Klara over their marriage.

Hammerling had divorced Klara by rabbinical decree in Austria in 1914. However, the Imperial Royal Law Court of Austria affirmed the decision just before the conflict. Klara, who spent the war in Britain, returned to the United States in 1920. Conveniently Hammerling had left for Poland in 1919. Klara brought legal action against him in a New York court, claiming they had never been divorced because the United States did not recognize Austrian legal verdicts.[95] Klara then argued that she was twice rendered a common-law wife by living with Hammerling in Pennsylvania between 1897 and 1909, and in New York from 1910 to 1912.[96]

After two years of legal wrangling Hammerling was victorious. Klara admitted that he had given her a 250,000 kronen settlement in 1914, but argued that it was meaningless: the Austrian action had no validity in the United States. Doubtless, the fact that 250,000 kronen had dropped in value to $5 in 1922 must have motivated her. Thus, in 1924, the American court ruled that both of Hammerling's marriages were legal and thus recognized the legality of the Austrian action.[97] This is perhaps the only proceeding that Hammerling ever won.

LAST EFFORTS FOR POLAND

Hammerling did not run for reelection: Piast would never have renominated him. He was ruined not only by the incomprehensible yet damning Senate determination, but by the fact that he was associated, rightly or wrongly, with the Lanckorona Pact that ushered in the wretched Witos government. What Hammerling did for the next few years is another dark spot in his biography.

He made one last bid to resurrect his devastated political career. The Witos government had been replaced by one organized by the competent economist Władysław Grabski. There were rumors, however, that Witos, along with Hammerling, would go to the United States seeking, once more, a major loan.[98] Whether Grabski condoned this was problematical: the economically ignorant Witos would hardly be a credible agent, but Grabski was on the hunt for loans, no matter how small: "he embarked on a course of seeking piecemeal loans to balance his budgets."[99] Hammerling, despite his recent disgrace, was well known in Poland as a man who claimed to have access to American money. Thus a Witos-Hammerling trip to America was bruited about. As it turned out it was only Hammerling who went—traveling on a diplomatic passport—and although there seems to have been little discussed about a loan, Hammerling was nonetheless in the news.[100] We know that he addressed meetings of Polonia leaders, but we do not have the texts of his addresses. Doubtless, they were designed to promote interest in investment in Poland.[101]

In July 1924 Hammerling made an important speech in the Senate. His career was really over and his influence was nil, yet this pronouncement deserves our attention because it is a testimony to what he had hoped to accomplish in Poland on the basis of his long career in American financial circles. If sincere, it shows Hammerling to be a patriot whose advice was worthy of heeding.

Hammerling began by emphasizing that his long experience in international finance moved him to make comments on the Polish economy, which he addressed from a non-Party position. He then moved to a rather unfortunate bit of self-promotion: the 1924 budget had his support because the economy improved, as a result of his travels and contacts abroad. However, these efforts convinced him that international financial circles did not have confidence in Poland to meet its financial responsibilities, the legacy of previous governments. The Americans were suspicious that politics played too large a role in Polish banks and finance. Recently, for example, a representative of the British Overseas Bank had told Senator Aleksander Adelman[102] and Hammerling that the inexperience of the Polish textile industry in Łódź had caused a major British investment to fail.

Hammerling then provided a list of Polish economic failings: the administration of the Treasury; the tax system; the lack of government support for agriculture (this he compared unfavorably to the American government's practice of backing agricultural loans); poor labor productivity due to organizational problems—here again he compares Poland to the United States, something he had done since his first days in the Senate. There was too much currency in circulation: too many banks lending like it was "eggs in a store." He then listed the major foreign banks he negotiated with in 1923, arguing that the negotiations fell through because these banks espied essentially political motives in Polish efforts.

To improve this sorry picture, "it is necessary to act according to American examples." These changes would be necessary before real progress could be made in Polish efforts to obtain foreign loans.[103] If conditions were better: "Then we would see." Poland had possibility: "As I said three years ago and repeat, we shall be a second America in Poland. But we must conclude that work is the honor of everyone," it is everyone's "honor to pay taxes," "do not be jealous if some wear silk stockings and others do not." In conclusion, Poland must convince the world that "we are Poles whether a party is to the right or left, that first of all we are Poles and our first goal is the happiness of Poland."[104]

CHAPTER 8

The Last Chapter
America Again

WE KNOW ONLY SHARDS OF HAMMERLING'S last years. He
repeatedly made visits to the United States. In 1924, while still a member
of the Senate, he visited again. The American consulate in Warsaw had
issued him a diplomatic visa. This is another curious episode in his political career. Despite the quasi-censure, he was still a member of the Polish Senate, and the Witos government was still seeking to borrow out of
desperate straits. Other rumors in Poland already alleged that Witos and
Hammerling were coming together to raise campaign funds for Piast.[1]
Hammerling claimed to have come to New York on vacation, and denied
any plans to negotiate a loan. There were even rumors that he had come
to build a campaign chest to run for reelection in Poland. The only thing
about finances that he said was that in 1923 Poland had needed a loan
for $1 billion, quite a sum then, and vastly more than had been bruited
in 1922.

Senator Lee Overman, who had served on the 1918 Senate investigation of Hammerling, wanted his naturalization revoked and campaigned
for the attorney general to take action when Hammerling arrived.[2] Thus,
Hammerling was met at the pier in New York by agents of the Department of Justice. He was questioned and then released. When he reached
his hotel, he was served. He was charged with making false "representa-
tions" in gaining his 1919 American passport. The American authorities

argued that his original naturalization had been obtained by perjury in 1901 and he had relinquished his citizenship in 1922 in Poland. At the urging of the State Department, the attorney general's office launched a suit seeking to revoke his naturalization.[3] Hammerling dismissed the suit as a mere formality because he had voluntarily surrendered his citizenship in Poland.[4] Why he gained an American visa is another mystery. He agreed to allow his naturalization papers to be canceled if the charges of fraud were dropped against him.[5] His naturalization was duly canceled.[6]

In 1926 Hammerling was again in the United States on another unusual business venture. He recorded his voice into a recording device, the "Deforest machine," regarding Poland. His propaganda would be distributed "with my picture . . . in thirty thousand moving pictures in the United States."[7] He also published articles about Poland—for example, "A Great People Reborn"—in something called *Patches*.[8] Either Hammerling visited the United States more than once in 1926 or his stay lasted almost a year. Coincidently, he was busy ingratiating himself to the people of his home in Brody. In August he was granted "honorary citizenship" in the district. The same year he erected a large, beautiful community center (Dom Ludowy) in Kalwaria Zebrzydowska, which was an event of some local importance. The building bore his name.[9] Thus, in 1926 he was working for Poland but living in the United States: the division that had always been latent. It was about at this time that Hammerling liquidated all his Polish assets.[10]

Hammerling returned to the United States in 1928. He almost immediately became employed in the Foreign Language Press, an advertising agency. Again this company was run according to Hammerling's direction and he controlled all the stock; it had cost him, reportedly, $100,000. It was the AAFLN all over again.[11] "None noted his presence," commented the *New York Times* about Hammerling having successfully inveigled himself once again into the American business world. When Senator Overman protested in 1928 to the Bureau of Immigration and to the public the next year, he was told that Hammerling had been admitted as a "preference quota immigrant"; why this special status was granted is a good question. Overman was quoted as saying that Hammerling's name was associated with liquor interests and German propaganda, and that he was "forced" to leave the United States. He also noted that

Hammerling had started another business.[12] Hammerling was publicly "outraged" by Overman's inquiry, noting that he had been granted a visa in 1928 and was employed, and, moreover, "I intend to become a citizen."[13] He did so only in 1933.[14] By then he ran the "L. N. H. Holding Corporation," with his son Max acting as his attorney.[15]

We know little about the Foreign Language Press, but more is available about the last and most bizarre of all Hammerling's business ventures: spiritualist. This extraordinary tale surrounds Edgar Cayce (1877–1945), "the world's most famous psychic diagnostician," the "sleeping prophet," who did fourteen thousand "psychic" readings during which he would advise his clients regarding their health and, it seems, other issues. Cayce knew nothing of what he said while in this trancelike state and had to be informed later by his secretary.[16] He was a famous man, and he decided to speak of Hammerling.

For some reason Hammerling—and much more frequently, his attorney son Max—was mentioned by the unconscious Cayce. Not always favorably. On October 6, 1928, when Hammerling was still fighting for his American citizenship, Edgar Cayce, or whatever the spirit of Mr. Cayce was called, decided to pronounce a verdict on Hammerling's new business activities. Of all the criticism of Hammerling, this may have been the cruelest because it came from the beyond. The following is an exact quotation with sentence fragments kept intact; "Q" is Cayce's client and "A" is the spirit, speaking through Cayce.

> Q. Recently I was looking under cover of bed, being directed to do so by Schwartz, my employee, I saw a skunk that changed into a man that looked like Louis N. Hammerling.
> A. This, as would be indicated in that seen, that the body that has changed into the skunk has had that in the actions of the life that has caused, and does cause, others to feel and speak unkindly, and are warned against the activities of the body. As is also indicated in that there are and were, physical defects with the body that, through the associations, may be made beneficial. Not that the body Hammerling, as seen is NOT to be watched and studied also. Know many of these conditions that have caused unsavory comment as respecting the body, how the activities of same have brought about various experiences in the life of the body, or as how the body Hammerling has applied that as has been obtained by same,

and take a lesson for self from that understanding as is gained by same. As is seen also respecting the associates and ones who are handling some of the business for the body Hammerling. THIS body watch more closely than either of the two.[17]

What does this mean? It is lost in the ethers surrounding Cayce's somnabulence. It seems to say, watch out for Hammerling, he is, as you have dreamt, a crook.

THE LAST MYSTERIES

The March 11, 1934, issue of the *New York Times* reported with pleasure that the "Lexington Avenue District" in midtown Manhattan was in the midst of a noticeable revival. A twelve-story apartment building worth $890,000 had just been sold, and nearby, at 687 Lexington Avenue, the Hotel Dover had just been purchased by Hammerling, who had lived in the building. The assessed value was almost $800,000 and was the largest transaction in the immediate vicinity in some time.[18] Hammerling, it was rumored, also had a property in Tudor City, and one in Brooklyn.[19] He was, as a Polish journal noted, busy in many things.[20] And he was still a rich man, perhaps very rich. Hammerling's family later recalled that he promised to buy the Lexington building for his son James (Klara's son) and may have done so. All these properties, however, seem to have disappeared by the time of Hammerling's death. Another mystery.[21]

According to the *Illustrated Daily Courier* (Illustrowany Kurier Codzienny), a very popular gazette in Kraków, on April 27 Hammerling finished breakfast on the nineteenth floor of his apartment building on Prospect Place in Manhattan. He had to rush because he had a dental appointment. Walking close to the window, he suddenly became dizzy—something that had been troubling him of late. He lost his balance, and fell from the window.[22] He was killed by the fall.[23]

The *Times* noted that he had been unwell recently and either fell or suffered a heart attack. He was alone. His wife was in France on vacation, their son Louis at school in New Jersey. His sons with Klara—Max, Emanuel, and James—all lived in the city. On his table lay autographed photographs of President Taft and RNC Chairman Frank Hitchcock.

Letters from Teddy Roosevelt and, unexpectedly, General John Pershing, as well as many other famous men, lay upon his bureau.[24] Hammerling left half of all he had to his wife; the remainder went to their son. It was not much: his assets were found to be a mere $26,135 net. What had happened to all the money and appurtenances of wealth?[25] Another enigma.[26] Hammerling died of "a fractured skull and lacerated brain." On the death certificate there is a dash by the question of suicide. The form indicates he died from a "fall or jump from 19th story window" thus leaving open the suicide question. In what is perhaps a final mystery, he is listed as living in the United States for three years, but in New York City for seven.[27]

On April 30, a funeral Mass was celebrated for him at a Polish church, by a Polish priest, in a Polish neighborhood in Brooklyn.[28] For Rome he had died in the bosom of the Church; there was no talk of suicide. His body was taken to Calvary Cemetery in Queens. In a crowded corner of a treeless area near an elevated highway is a modest marker that bears the words: "Robert B. Hammerling, Beloved Son of Louis N. and Sophie Jeane Hammerling, born in New York City, January 15, 1916, died September 12, 1916." Our Hammerling remains, for eternity, a shadowy figure behind someone else.[29]

EPITAPH: THE SORRY END OF THE PUTATIVE COUNTESS

When Hammerling returned to Poland, he had an equestrian portrait of his wife Zofia painted by perhaps Poland's best-known artist, Wojciech Kossak. She was still very young and very handsome.[30] By the time Hammerling left Poland they had obviously become estranged. She did not follow him. Four years after his death, war found her in Kraków. She, like so many other Poles, lived through nightmarish years. On October 2, 1945, she knew she was dying and prepared her last will. She did not know what awaited her—and Poland. It is a touching and pathetic document.

She left half of her estate to her only son, Louis Jr., and it was considerable. She owned a house on Floriańska Street in the center of Kraków; the boutique Hotel pod Różą downtown; seventeen "morgs" (an obsolete term of measurement equaling 95,200 square meters of land) in Płaszów south of Kraków,[31] which she inherited from her husband; the villa

"Zofia" in Nice; and $300 in a French bank. There were also a number of financial institutions in New York City that held unspecified assets of her late husband.

She wanted to die in New York and be buried next to her son and husband, but if she did not survive long enough, she wished the most humble funereal circumstances possible. She ended with a profoundly sad summation. She thanked those who took care of her son when her husband died and noted: "It was the greatest mistake I ever made to desert my new fatherland—America, the country I admire and love. I would have avoided many unpleasant things, blackmailers, and foul people." She died not long after, in Kraków.[32]

Conclusions

Hammerling was one of many assimilated Jews who arrived in the United States at the turn of the century. Whether he was a Pole or not was a matter of choice; he seems, eventually, to have chosen to be one. There is nothing in his early life to indicate that he considered himself anything other than a Pole. The claim that his family spoke only Yiddish must be wrong: Hammerling functioned within a Polish anthracite community from before 1900. In addition he was accepted as a Pole, and someone who was not at least partially fluent in Polish could not have founded the Lithuanian-Polish Club.

In America he had a spectacular career. From the meanest mine worker he became, with astonishing rapidity, a newspaperman, a community organizer, a union leader, a friend and confidant of national figures, an important person in national Republican politics, a wealthy businessman, an advisor to cabinet officials, a correspondent of two presidents, and many other things. He accomplished this despite the fact that he supposedly had no education, was virtually illiterate, and, by several accounts, was not particularly bright—which, given his exploits, is not to be believed.

His role in the 1902 anthracite strike still awaits its elucidation, but almost certainly its evidence died with Hammerling. He was variously described as an agent of Mitchell in negotiations with business and political leaders. He was also, we know definitively, a paid agent of powerful Republican officials. There are even suggestions that his ability to arrange meetings and deals was due to the fact that he was the agent of none other than President Roosevelt. Hammerling, however, always worked behind the scenes. This was not the result of any innate modesty, but rather it reflected a shortcoming he was never able to overcome: the ability to make an impressive public impression. He could neither write nor speak well, and whereas this was no impediment in private negotiations, it was a severe handicap in something public like politics.

His biography demonstrates the possibilities for an aggressive, imaginative, and enterprising immigrant in the America of 1900. Had he never left his homeland, it is almost certain he would have lived and died in dire poverty in the obscure villages of southeastern Poland. He was an American success story and the epitome of the American saga of building a life from nothing to the heights: what Mieczysław Szerer called a "specifically American career,"[1] but what Robert Park deems "over-hasty Americanization."[2]

He was also utterly unscrupulous, a pathological liar, shameless, unprincipled, and seemingly without any fixed values. He lived for money and power and acquired it by whatever means were at hand. He was entirely plastic and conformed to whatever circumstances required. He was the definition of the unscrupulous. There is, however, a single constant in Hammerling's intellectual life. His politics were always to the right: the Republicans in the United States, Piast in Poland. There is no indication that he ever worked for the Democrats for whom he seemed to have an abiding dislike. Hammerling may well have been the quintessence of Mark Hanna's ideal worker: an immigrant Republican working in tandem with the business magnates.

Perhaps most important is the aspect of his life that immigration historians have neglected: Hammerling was one of the powerful immigrants in early twentieth-century America, if not the most powerful. His AAFLN united—indeed dominated—perhaps 800 newspapers read by tens of millions. Hammerling presumed to speak for the entire immigrant community when he dealt with state and federal officials. Certainly, among

Polish immigrants, all other figures are merely local celebrities. Hammerling could meet with presidents, bring cabinet officers to his social events, undertake business ventures with national figures—Mitchell comes to mind—and what other American Pole could do that? The other eastern or southern European communities of that era similarly produced no equal. Hammerling was the most powerful recent immigrant of his day.

Was he a traitor to the United States? A German spy? A supporter of the enemy? No. Hammerling took money from the Germans because they offered it to him. He had no strong views about the war, and almost certainly would have taken British or French money had it been available. Indeed, as circumstantial evidence—and a few blustering remarks—suggest, Hammerling did not like Germans. He was no Rumely.

He took money from the Germans at a time when America was still at least nominally neutral: he violated no American law in encouraging support for Germany. Retrospectively, however, Hammerling's activities seem virtually traitorous: he helped a soon-to-be enemy of the United States; he did not admit it; and although he was part of a larger operation that included violence, he cannot be tied to any German acts of sabotage or worse.

By the time Hammerling left the United States, the federal investigative authorities and the public thoroughly despised him. He had lied to gain his naturalization papers; he had lied in both state and federal inquiries; he had lied in the press; he had broken countless laws in the running of his business; he was almost certainly a blackmailer; he was the author of fraud and slander; he was endlessly guilty of influence peddling; he colluded with German and Austrian authorities who were violating neutrality laws; he was involved in insider trading, unethical business practices, and possibly simple robbery. The AAFLN was a monument of petty crime. His business was paid for by German steamship lines and brewing interests, which he did not admit: the *American Leader* was a fraud.

The public first learned of Hammerling in 1915, but he was lost in the welter of the "spy scare" of that year. Then oddly, he disappeared from public view for almost three years before resurfacing as a victim of almost endless investigations. By 1918 he was virtually forced to leave the United States. He may well have been evicted or incarcerated.

What Hammerling did in Poland for the next several years, the fact that he was a public personality of some weight, made no impression on the American public. For Polonia, when they did invoke Hammerling's name it was scornful: he was a scoundrel and a German spy, and his success in Poland was incomprehensible and repulsive.

In the 1920s he came back to the United States, probably through the influence of powerful Republican supporters, though this cannot be proven. The one senator who tried to expose him, Overman, was a Democrat.

He seemed to become a wealthy New York businessman, though circumstantial evidence suggests he left his wife and son in Europe. But, when he died, he was scarcely rich and no explanation can be found for this conundrum.

THE POLISH PERSPECTIVE

Hammerling was one of those very, very rare Poles of that time who were successful in America. The average Polish immigrant to this country worked in backbreaking and dangerous circumstances, lived in squalor, and suffered the shame and desolation of being regarded by the host society as inferior and unwanted. Hammerling met with the president, owned buildings, traveled in elegance, was the friend of the mighty. He was a hero to the immigrant. More, he was a Polish hero: he chose to be Polish. We could be writing of a powerful Jewish immigrant, but Hammerling forswore that. Regardless of his intimate feelings, publicly he chose to be Polish. When he remarried he married into a profoundly patriotic family, and he threw himself recklessly into Polish politics. He wanted to be a successful Pole, not an immigrant from the United States. This is the main reason that his Jewish background was only of interest to the discreditable rags of the anti-Semitic right, and a few political grumblers, as well as American banks. For the great majority of Poles, Hammerling may not have been born a Pole, but he worked to become one: he had, perhaps, earned his membership in Poland. This also raises profound questions about Polish anti-Semitism. Obviously Hammerling downplayed his Jewish origins, but this was never completely hidden. It was no secret in Poland that he was—or rather had been—a Jew. It seems to have made little discernible difference. This raises the question of whether a converted Jew was rarely the target of true anti-Semitic prejudice. Polish anti-Semitism had its own characteristics.

In his memoirs the populist leader Jan Dębski muses over a curious situation.[3] In eastern Galicia there were a large number of Polish Jews who, upon assimilation, chose an extreme form of Polish nationalism. Hammerling was a Jew from eastern Galicia who assimilated not only to polonism but also to the political right. In the United States he was close to the rightist Paderewski. His relations with American Polonia are bizarre. Within Polonia ranks, pro-Austrian and pro-German sympathies were discernible only on the political left, and Hammerling was a man of the right.

The political right in Polonia was pro-Allied, except for Hammerling. Incidentally, Hammerling was not really a member of Polonia. In the United States he functioned outside the Polish community. He was not an officer of any major Polish organization, or any agency created for relief purposes. The galvanizing of Polish ranks in America did not affect Hammerling. The reasons for this are not entirely clear, but I would speculate that Hammerling did not want to be perceived as being too Polish lest he lose influence among the many immigrant groups that made up the AAFLN. Most American Poles voted Democrat; Hammerling was devoted to the Republicans. His closest friend in the American Polish community was the rightist Jan F. Smulski, a Republican activist.[4]

In Poland he joined the right-wing Piast Party and became very close to Kucharski, who was on the political right within Piast. And, of course, the greatest irony of all, the arch anti-Semite Dmowski was devoted to Kucharski. He must have known Hammerling was a Jew: it seemingly did not affect their relationship.[5] Hammerling was thus a part of a brief political and psychological moment in Poland: the Jew seeking to be more Polish than the Poles, the ultimate act of assimilation.

Hammerling epitomized the Americanized Pole making an awkward return to his native land, now recently independent. Many sources commented on his "American" looks and actions. Hammerling played upon this: he gave speeches urging the Poles to adopt American practices and values and once spoke of Poland becoming a "second America." Here we may wonder whether Hammerling was trying to recapitulate his American successes all over again—at least before things took an ill turn in 1918. Such perfervid celebration of America came to Poland at a critical moment. Prime Minister Paderewski virtually worshipped the United States and employed Americans in key roles in the Polish economy almost at random, so great was his conviction of superior American abilities. Between Wilson's Fourteen Points in 1918 and Hoover's food aid for Poland in 1922, the Americans had gained the affection of the Polish population, as was the case with no other country. Hammerling thus was the right symbol at the right time. He represented the Americanization of Poland. And that had to be good. Whether he was a Pole playing an American to a Polish audience is a good question.

Hammerling symbolizes a significant theme in Poland's relationship with the Poles abroad, especially American Polonia. Polonia was speechless when Hammerling emerged as a Polish senator. Rumors about his scandalous past in America were sometimes alluded to in Polish political circles and the press, but were always very minor matters. Poland simply did not care what Polonia was saying, or had said, about Hammerling. He really only became notable once he had returned home. It is a revealing and, for Polonia, embittering demonstration that the Poles in America were of very little import to Poland and the politics of Polonia were completely without interest.

CARITAS

Hammerling was a failure. He knew it and could not go on. He was old, unwell, and facing increasingly serious financial circumstances. He had been rich and powerful since he was a young man; now he was neither, and the likelihood of a reversal of fortunes must have seemed impossible. He was at the end. His life had been an extraordinary adventure, but now the resources for another chapter of the autobiography were exhausted.

He must have asked himself the hauntingly fundamental questions: Who am I? A Pole? A Jew? An American? Some sort of hybrid? Where does my identity lie? What do I love?[6] Have I been a good man? Hammerling had spent the last twenty years of his life—and possibly much more—as a Roman Catholic. Have I done too much to make recompense? Have I sought the things of this world so devotedly that I have lost sight of the next? Do I face the death of a sinner? I treated my first wife shabbily; my second has left me. When, during our happy early marriage, we had a son, he died in his helpless infancy. His brother does not live with me. I am alone. Perhaps it is time to go home.

NOTES

PROLOGUE

1. Hammerling was recorded as "retired." See "Certificate of Death," New York State Department of Health, NYC Department of Records/Municipal Archives, 1–2 (hereafter cited as Certificate of Death).

2. The death certificate does not make his suicide certain. See ibid.

3. For Hammerling's description as a Bolshevik, see M. Churchill to W. L. Hurley, March 30, 1920, Record Group 165 (hereafter RG 165), folder 10175–110, United States National Archives at College Park (hereafter USNA).

4. See the Military Intelligence Division (MID) document entitled "Re Louis Hammerling," January 3, 1918, in RG 165, folder 10175–110, 2, USNA (hereafter Re Louis Hammerling).

5. For this characterization of Hammerling, endlessly repeated, see, e.g., the "secret" M. I. 5. B.L. rev. vol., nos. 1–1857, RG 165, folder 9140–815/1, nos. 698, 208, USNA.

1: WANDERINGS

1. "Re Louis Hammerling," 2. Hammerling only once made reference to the YMCA; to which YMCA he was referring, and which time period, is unknown. This also contradicts his repeated statement that he never went to school.

2. "Louis N. Hammerling," interrogation by N. H. White, March 9, 1918, RG 165, folder 10175–110, 8, USNA (hereafter White interrogation).

3. Czesław Lechicki, "Hammerling, Ludwik Mikołaj," *Polski Słownik Biograficzny*, vol. 9/2, zeszyt 41, p. 263 (Wrocław: Ossolineum, 1960–1961). For the German reference see Hammerling's marriage certificate of 1915 reproduced in *A Menace to Americanization* (New York: Národni List, 1919), unpaginated. Hammerling told the census taker in 1900 that both his parents were born in Germany; see US Census Bureau, *12th Census of Population, Schedule 1*, vol. 127.

4. In 1918 Hammerling affirmed that he was born in a different town; such inconsistencies are typical. See *Brewing and Liquor Interests and German and Bolshevik Propaganda. Report and Hearings of the Subcommittee on the Judiciary. United States Senate* (Washington, DC: Government Printing Office, 1919), 3 vols., 1:620 (hereafter *Brewing and Liquor Interests*).

5. One source gives his father's name as "August S." and his mother's as "Anna" née Müller. This source also says that the then illiterate Hammerling was an 1893 graduate of the Jan Kazimierz University in Lwów. See *Who Was Who in America, vol. 1, 1897–1942* (Chicago: Marquis Who's Who, 1966), 513; cf. "Dokumenty do historji życia i działań senator z Honolulu," *Kurjer Poranny*, November 1, 1923, 3. Hammerling's mother was recorded on his death certificate as "Esther Miller"; see Certificate of Death, 2.

6. In 1902 he spoke affectionately of his father and indicated they were in regular correspondence; see Hammerling to Mitchell, December 1, 1902, John Mitchell Papers, Department of Archives and Manuscripts, Catholic University of America, Washington, DC (hereafter Mitchell Papers).

7. *Brewing and Liquor Interests*, 1:535–47. Hammerling told a colleague that his father was a senior officer in the Austrian military service and that he was so severe that he had to be raised by servants. See ibid., 639.

8. Additional details are found in "Statement of Louis N. Hammerling," made before the Office of the Attorney General, New York City, July 27, 1918, RG 165, folders 10175–110/36 to 10175/47, USNA (hereafter Statement).

9. Statement, 32–33. See "Inicjator obecnego gabinetu i 'lewa ręka' obecnego ministra skarbu," *Kurjer Poranny*, October 19, 1923, 2.

10. An unsigned printed sheet, probably from 1923, was afloat in Poland. It was titled "Feine Kepele der Louis Nuchim Hammerling."

11. *Brewing and Liquor Interests*, 1:624.

12. Julia Namier, *Lewis Namier: A Biography* (London: Oxford University Press, 1971), 112–13.

13. Ibid., 108.

14. *Brewing and Liquor Interests*, 1:536.

15. "Louis N. Hammerling," *American Courier* (Milwaukee), July 25, 1918, in RG 165, folder 10175–110, USNA. One flawed account lists the date of Hammerling's arrival as 1884; this would comport with his mule-driving work at ten; see *Who Was Who in America*, 513.

16. See the comments regarding "The Setting" in Robert A. Janosov, "Beyond the 'Great Coal Strike': The Anthracite Coal Region in 1902," in Kenneth C. Wolensky, ed., *The "Great Strike": Perspectives on the 1902 Anthracite Coal Strike* (Easton, PA: Canal History and Technology Press, 2002), 6–10, 19. The Polish parishes in the region only predated Hammerling's arrival by a few years; see the discussion in Waclaw Kruszka, *A History of the Poles in America to 1908: Part III. Poles in the Eastern and Southern States* (Washington, DC: The Catholic University of America Press, 1998), 109ff.

17. Philip Shriver Klein and Ari Arthur Hoogenboom, *A History of Pennsylvania* (New York: McGraw, 1973), 282.

18. As a matter of fact, Szechter's statement is also replete with errors; see "Memorandum for Mr. William R. Benham," November 25, 1918, RG 165, file 10175–110, 2, USNA (hereafter Benham memorandum).

19. *Brewing and Liquor Interests*, 1:582. In Lichicki's "Hammerling" (263), he argues that Hammerling left Galicia in 1891, and he may well be right. That Hammerling was drafted is corroborated in Karczewski and Szaflik's *Witos*, 555.

20. *Brewing and Liquor Interests*, 1:582.

21. Benham memorandum, 2.

22. Cf. Statement, 33; *Brewing and Liquor Interests*, 1:538.

23. Statement, 33.

24. US Census Bureau, *12th Census of Population, Schedule 1, Pennsylvania, Luzerne County*, 2. This corresponds to *Who Was Who*, 513.

25. *Brewing and Liquor Interests*, 1:537. Lechicki claims he was a mule driver in his "Hammerling," 263.

26. "Deposition of Louis M. Hammerling," October 30, 1905, folder 10175, MID, RG 165, 1–3, USNA (hereafter Deposition).

27. Janosov, "Beyond," 10–17.

28. See Michael Novak, *The Guns of Lattimer* (New York: Transaction Publishers, 1996).

29. *Brewing and Liquor Interests*, 1:538. For the original of Hammerling's naturalization papers witnessed by Shea, see Luzerne County Court House Prothonotary's Office, Naturalization Docket, 1897–1906, Naturalization File 744.

30. Hammerling's 1915 marriage license, in *A Menace to Americanization*. As late as 1913 Hammerling referred to himself as single; this information is from the Drs. James Solomon and Anne Linder Hammerling Collection.

31. Victoria Hammerling Rosenberg to author, January 22, 2014.

32. I am indebted to Judith Gold, Klara's granddaughter, for this information. It is contained in Judith Gold to author, March 1, 2006. The fact that Klara spoke Polish as a first language is confirmed in "Database: 1930 United States Federal Census," at http://search.ancestry.com/cgi-bin/sse.dll?gsfn=&gsln=hammerling&sx=&f5=&f4=&f7=&f13=&f. Accessed July 10, 2004.

33. Victoria Hammerling Rosenberg to author, January 22, 2014.

34. See "Theodore" to Louis Marshall, August 29, 1913, Louis Marshall Papers, Jacob Rader Marcus Center of the American Jewish Archives, Cincinnati, box 377, folder H (hereafter Marshall Papers).

35. Ibid.

36. Hammerling's anonymous legal queries were handled by Louis Namier.

37. *Brewing and Liquor Interests*, 1:542–43.

38. See The Statue Of Liberty-Ellis Island Foundation, Inc., *Passenger Record*, http://www.ellisislandrecords.org/search/passRecord.asp?MID=108601963700076 12736&FNM=. Accessed October 2, 2004.

39. Lechicki, "Hammerling," 263. Karczewski and Szaflik state unequivocally that Hammerling worked as an agent (akwizytor) for Hearst from 1899 to 1908; see their *Witos*, 555.

40. See Victor R. Greene, *The Slavic Community on Strike: Immigrant Labor in Pennsylvania Anthracite* (University of Notre Dame Press, 1968), 246.

41. Joseph P. McKerns, "The 'Faces' of John Mitchell: News Coverage of the Great Anthracite Strike of 1902 in the Regional and National Press," in Wolensky, *Great Strike*, 29–33.

42. Statement, 34.

43. Ibid.

44. See "Petition without Previous Written Declaration of Intention," Luzerne County Court House Prothonotary's Office, Naturalization File 744.

45. *Brewing and Liquor Interests*, 1:544, 608–9.

46. Statement, 34.

47. *Brewing and Liquor Interests*, 1:539.

48. Earl W. Mayo, "On Strike," reprinted from *Frank Leslie's Popular Monthly*, November 1900; see http://ehistory.osu.edu/exhibitions/LaborConflict/OnStrike/default.

49. See the vertical file marked "Galicia" in Lackawanna County Historical Society, Scranton, PA.

2: BUSINESS, POLITICS, AND COAL

1. A source hostile to Hammerling claims that before 1900 he was already involved in rounding up immigrant votes for the GOP. See Arthur Koppell to Taft, January 29, 1912, Taft Papers, reel 384.

2. "Slander, Cries Hammerling," *New York Times*, October 3, 1912.

3. Hammerling to Mitchell, December 26, 1902, Mitchell Papers.

4. Benham memorandum, 2.

5. US Census Bureau, *12th Census of Population, 1900*, vol. 127.

6. Greene, *The Slavic Community on Strike*, 86–87.

7. See the untitled typescript by Michael J. Kosik, folder 8, box 5, Michael J. Kosik Collection, Pennsylvania State University Special Collections Library, Historical Collections and Labor Archives, State College, PA (hereafter Kosik Collection). This reference is probably taken from the Elsie Glück work on Mitchell, but the referencing is unclear. About the UMWA success with immigrants, see Blatz, *Democratic Miners*, 171–72.

8. Mitchell to Hammerling, September 19, 1902, Mitchell Papers.

9. Lechicki, "Hammerling," 263.

10. Robert H. Wiebe, "The Anthracite Strike of 1902: A Record of Confusion," *The Mississippi Valley Historical Review* 48, no. 2 (September 1961): 229.

11. Republican pressure on the operators played a significant role. See E. Dana Durand, "The Anthracite Coal Strike and Its Settlement," *Political Science Quarterly*, vol. 18 (September 1903): 386. See also Craig Phelan, "The Making of a Labor Leader: John Mitchell and the Anthracite Strike of 1900," *Pennsylvania History*, vol. 63 (Winter 1996), 53–77.

12. "Miners Discussing Operators' Offer"; "Nearing the End!" *Scranton Times*, October 12 and 13, 1900; "Scranton Meeting," *United Mine Workers Journal*, October 18, 1900, 1. His name appears here as "Lewis Hammersly."

13. "Labor Monument," February 27, 1902; "A Monument for Martyred Heroes," in ibid., February 27, 1902, 7 and March 13, 1902, 2.

14. See *Pittsburgh Dispatch*, September 20, 1902, 65 and 125, and other clippings in John Markle, "Newsbooks: Newspaper History of Pennsylvania. Anthracite Coal Strike, 1900," Hazelton Public Library.

15. This argument is drawn, in part, from Wiebe's "Anthracite Strike" (232–34).

16. Ibid.

17. Craig Phelan, "The Making of a Labor Leader," 60–61.

18. See Robert F. Zeidel, "Hayseed Immigration Policy: 'Uncle Joe' Cannon and the Immigration Question," *Illinois Historical Journal*, vol. 88 (Autumn 1995): 183.

19. There are some worthwhile comments on this Republican attitude in Sister Mary Annunciate Merrick, "A Case of Practical Democracy: The Settlement of the Anthracite Coal Strike of 1902," (PhD diss., Notre Dame University, 1942), 48ff; cf. Koppell to Taft, January 29, 1912.

20. Albert Jaudon statement, March 9, 1918, RG 165, folder 10175, 3, USNA (hereafter Jaudon statement).

21. In the fall of 1901 Hammerling's name appears in a myriad of issues of the *Journal.*

22. "Mining Notes," *Journal,* January 16, 1902, 2; "Roll of Honor," *Journal,* February 27, 1902, 4.

23. This story is recounted in Lance E. Metz, "The Role of Intimidation and Violence in the Great Anthracite Strike of 1902," in Wolensky, *Great Strike,* 54.

24. Hammerling is a bit vague about when he abandoned mine work; see *Brewing and Liquor Interests,* 1:537.

25. Deposition, 2.

26. Hammerling to Mitchell, January 15, 1902, Mitchell Papers.

27. Regarding Mitchell's activities, see Craig Phelan, *Divided Loyalties: The Public and Private Life of Labor Leader John Mitchell* (Albany: State University of New York Press, 1994). Hammerling, like Mitchell, "knew he had to court the lords." See Jack McDonough, *The Fire Down Below: The Great Anthracite Strike of 1902 and the People Who Made the Decisions* (Scranton: Avocado Productions, 1902), 101.

28. Deposition, 6, 10. See also the telegrams appended to Deposition paginated 1–8.

29. Deposition, 45, 52.

30. Deposition, 20.

31. "John Mitchell Sees Quay and Penrose," *New York Times,* October 9, 1902, 1.

32. Deposition, 31, 34.

33. Deposition, 33.

34. "Negotiations of the Day," *Brooklyn Eagle,* October 9, 1902, 1; "Meet in New York," *Sandusky Evening Star,* October 9, 1902, 1.

35. "Miners must decide; Mitchell is silent," *Brooklyn Eagle,* October 14, 1902.

36. "Acceptance is urged," *Democrat and Standard* (Coshocton, Ohio), October 21, 1902, 8.

37. Greene, *The Slavic Community on Strike,* 246.

38. "Numerous Conferences," *Lima Times-Democrat,* June 15, 1903, 1.

39. Hammerling to Quay, November 29, 1902, Mitchell Papers.

40. Hammerling's interview is quoted in "The Great Anthracite Strike is Settled Today; the Miners will return to work Thursday," *Marion Daily Star,* October 21, 1902, 1.

41. We see reports of Hammerling as Roosevelt's agent scattered about, such as "Denies Germany Paid for 'Appeal' to stop Munitions," *New York World,* April 7, 1915.

42. "Memorandum for Mr. Creel," n.d., RG 165, folder 10175–110, USNA. Creel later reported this to President Wilson (he offered no evidence). See Creel, "Memorandum to the President," n.d., Woodrow Wilson Papers. Unless otherwise

noted all references to the Wilson Papers come from Series 4, reel 474, Library of Congress (hereafter LC).

43. Hammerling to Mitchell, January 2 and 8, and March 14, 1904, Mitchell Papers; "Hammerling is Ready to Talk," *Wilkes-Barre Leader*, March 14, 1905, Mitchell Papers. There are even those who argue that Hammerling acted as Roosevelt's representative during the negotiations. The only supporting evidence we have for that, and it is slender indeed, was that Courtelyou was a key Roosevelt advisor during the negotiations. See McDonough, *The Fire Down Below*, 17. He was to be a very close friend of Hammerling.

44. "Translated Mine Laws"; "A Wise Move," *Journal*, January 9, 1902, 1.

45. Hammerling to Mitchell, January 4 and 8, 1902, Mitchell Papers.

46. Hammerling to Mitchell, October 17, 1903, Mitchell Papers.

47. Hammerling to Mitchell, December 27, 1902; Hammerling to Mitchell, August 15, 1903, Mitchell Papers.

48. Hammerling to Mitchell, November 24, 1902; Mitchell to Quay and Penrose, and Governor-elect Pennypacker, December 3, 1902; Hammerling to Mitchell, January 31, 1903; Hammerling to Mitchell, March 6, 1913; Quay to Mitchell, December 2, 1902; Hammerling to Mitchell, March 16, 1903; Hammerling to Mitchell, August 17, 1903, Mitchell Papers. In all Mitchell's endorsements he mentioned Hammerling's outstanding service to the Republican Party; see, e.g., Mitchell's December 1, 1902, letters to Quay, Penrose, and Pennypacker, Mitchell Papers.

49. Ellis W. Roberts, *The Breaker Whistle Blows: Mining Disasters and Labor Leaders in the Anthracite Region* (Scranton: Anthracite Museum Press, 1984), 76.

50. Joseph M. Gowaskie, "John Mitchell and the Anthracite Coal Strike of 1902: A Century Later," in Wolensky, *Great Strike*, 125, 135. Mitchell, like Hammerling, was constantly involved in "get-rich schemes"; see the remarks in Joseph A. McCartin's review of Craig Phelan, *Divided Loyalties: The Public and Private Life of Labor Leader John Mitchell* in *Industrial and Labor Relations Review* (Cornell University, ILR Review, October 1996), 182.

51. Victoria Hammerling Rosenberg to author, January 20, 2014.

52. *Brewing and Liquor Interests*, 1:472.

53. Ibid., 471.

54. Ibid., 584.

55. Hammerling's business and home addresses can be traced in *Thompson's Wilkes-Barre Directory for 1902* (Wilkes-Barre, 1902); *Williams' Wilkes-Barre City Directory* (Scranton, 1903); R. L. Polk & Co's' *Wilkes-Barre Directory, 1904* (Wilkes-Barre, 1904); R. L. Polk & Co.'s *Wilkes-Barre Directory, 1908* (n.p., n.d.). All of these rare volumes are on file at the Wyoming Historical & Geological Society, Wyoming, PA.

56. Briefly, in 1904, Hammerling owned something called the "Fiftieth Anniversary Button Company" designed to celebrate the GOP; see the stationery in Hammerling to Taft, May 13, 1904, Taft Papers, reel 44.

57. Hammerling to Mitchell, April 29, 1905; Hammerling to Mitchell, May 17, 1906; Hammerling to Mitchell, July 3, 1905, Mitchell Papers.

58. Mitchell to Hammerling, December 20 and 22, 1906; January 28, 1907, Mitchell Papers.

59. Hammerling to Mitchell, January 30, 1907; Mitchell to Hammerling, January 29, 1907; Mitchell to Hammerling, August 15, 1908, Mitchell Papers. There is a wealth of additional correspondence regarding the "grease business" in the Hammerling-Mitchell correspondence in the Mitchell Papers.

60. See "Notes from Newspaper Clippings from the 'New York World' on the Activities of Louis N. Hammerling" (hereafter Notes from Newspaper Clippings), March 12, 1918, MID document, RG 165, folder 10175, USNA. The suit against Hammerling allegedly was for over $1 million. See also Crosby v. Hammerling and Same v. General Lubricating Co., June 6, 1909, Federal and State Cases Combined, http://www.lexis.com/research/retrieve?_m=b1b6025848401467e2b8dbb0ee2567&docnum=2&. Accessed August 7, 2004.

61. B. Leffler to H. O. Weaver, April 3, 1905, George B. Courtelyou Papers, Washington, DC, container 10; file "H-Harris," LC.

62. Hammerling to Mitchell, January 9, 1906, Mitchell Papers.

63. Hammerling to Mitchell, April 27, 1905, Mitchell Papers. Hammerling had paid $12,500 in 1903 for his share of the company.

64. Hammerling to Mitchell, February 19, 1906, Mitchell Papers.

65. Hammerling to Mitchell, August 12, 1908, Mitchell Papers.

66. "Incorporated in New Jersey," New York Times, December 31, 1903.

67. Hammerling to Mitchell, February 13, 1908, Mitchell Papers.

68. Hammerling to Mitchell, April 25, 1910, Mitchell Papers. This seems, prima facie, a bribe, but it is possible that the money and the letter were not connected. Nonetheless it does indicate that Hammerling still found Mitchell enormously useful, and for some reason not inconsiderable amounts of money were flowing from Hammerling to the labor leader. There is no record of Mitchell sending funds to Hammerling.

69. NN to Hammerling, May 12, 1910, Mitchell Papers.

70. Mitchell met with President Roosevelt for the sole purpose of getting Hammerling the position; see "Mitchell Sees President," News (Frederick), October 5, 1905, 2. Cf. Mitchell to Hammerling, December 20, 1905, and Hammerling to Mitchell, December 2, 1905; Mitchell to Hammerling, December 18, 1905; Hammerling to Mitchell (twice), December 18, 1905, Mitchell Papers.

71. Hammerling to Mitchell, February 8 and 27, and March 24, 1905, Mitchell Papers.

72. "Hammerling for Panama," New York Times, April 5, 1908; "Hammerling Offered a Job," Fort Wayne Daily News, April 4, 1908, 11; "Hammerling is Offered a Place," Marion Daily Star, April 6, 1908, 1. "Henry B. Needham Accepts," Washington Post, May 3, 1908, 2.

73. Hammerling to Mitchell, February 8, 1905, Mitchell Papers.

74. Hammerling to Mitchell, February 27, 1905, Mitchell Papers.

75. President's secretary to Pennypacker, February 24, 1905, Samuel W. Pennypacker Papers, box 26, Pennsylvania State Archives, Harrisburg (hereafter PSA).

76. There is substantial correspondence in this regard; see, e.g., Hammerling to Mitchell, August 25, 1906, Mitchell Papers.

77. "Mine Workers of Anthracite District in Session," *Lima Times-Democrat*, December 14, 1905, 1.

78. See the unattributed clipping from a Wilkes-Barre paper entitled "Translated Mine Laws," dated 1902, attached to Hammerling to Mitchell, January 4, 1902, Mitchell Papers.

79. "A Journal Agent," *United Mine Workers Journal*, January 1, 1903, 1.

80. The *United Mine Workers Journal* reported on Hammerling in a fascinating manner: In the period 1898 to 1901 he is never mentioned in reports concerning the anthracite region. Beginning in the autumn of 1901 he is frequently mentioned, only to disappear after May 1902, and then resurface again in 1903. His disappearance coincides with the strike. Perhaps a coincidence, or perhaps his activities in this period were restricted to behind the scenes.

81. Victoria Hammerling Rosenberg to author, January 20, 2014.

82. See Hammerling's letter to Mitchell of January 25, 1902, Mitchell Papers. The inability, or more likely, unconcern, of the resident population to differentiate among various immigrant communities is striking.

83. "Louis Hammerling, Advertising Agent for Foreign Language Papers in New York." MID memorandum, October 29, 1917, RG 165, folder 10175–231, 1, USNA.

84. He met with New York's Republican leader Lauterbach at the time of McKinley's nomination in 1900; see Deposition, 36.

85. "Re Louis Hammerling. Possible German Propagandist," May 8, 1918, RG 165, folder 10175–110, 3 (hereafter Propagandist).

86. See the stationery used in Hammerling to Mitchell, January 4, 1902, in Mitchell Papers. The club was quite large: at its annual meeting in 1902 it had six hundred delegates representing ten thousand members. Hammerling was listed first as "general manager." The figure for membership seems much inflated.

87. See "A Notable Gathering," *United Mine Workers Journal*, January 2, 1902, 1; Roberts, *The Breaker Whistle Blows*, 79–80.

88. Based on the work of Victor Greene, Robert P. Wolensky asserts that 46 percent of the local population consisted of "Slavs" by 1900. See his "The Subcontracting System and Industrial Conflict in the Northern Anthracite Coal Field," in Wolensky, *Great Strike*, 69. Ray Ginger puts the Italian and eastern European anthracite workers at 33 percent of the total by 1902. See his "Managerial Employees in Anthracite, 1902: A Study in Occupational Mobility," *Journal of Economic History* (Spring 1954): 148.

89. Ben Marsh, "Continuity and Decline in the Anthracite Towns of Pennsylvania," *Annals of the Association of American Geographers*, vol. 77, no. 3 (September 1987), 344; cf. "Depends on Foreigners," *Northern Budget*, September 16, 1902.

90. See Harry Graham, review of Harold W. Aurand, *From the Molly Maquires to the United Mine Workers: The Social Ecology of an Industrial Union, 1869–1897*, in *Industrial and Labor Relations Review* (April 1973), 1045. For an important study regarding the propensity of Polish and other Slavic miners to organize and strike, see Greene, *The Slavic Community on Strike*, and the comments in Oliver Carsten, "Ethnic particularism

and class solidarity," *Theory and Society*, vol. 17 (1988): 434–35.

91. "May Visit Anthracite Region, *Altoona Mirror*, August 15, 1903, 3. For Hammerling's continued close relations with Penrose, see the clippings in Martin E. Olmsted Papers, MG 153, box 5, "scrapbooks, 1874–1913," PSA.

92. Quoted in Wiebe, "Anthracite Strike," 235. Cf. Phelan, "Labor Leader," 54–55, 59. Blatz thinks Wiebe exaggerates Mitchell's dislike of immigrants. I am grateful for this information contained in Blatz's letter to the author, August 26, 2011.

93. *Brewing and Liquor Interests*, 1:544.

94. Ibid.

95. Ibid., 466–67.

96. Hammerling to William Loeb, July 14, 1904, Theodore Roosevelt Papers, reel 45, LC (hereafter Roosevelt Papers).

97. Hammerling to Roosevelt, February 12, 1904, Roosevelt Papers, reel 41.

98. Hammerling to Taft, May 13, 1904, William Howard Taft Papers, reel 44, LC.

99. Hammerling to Mitchell, February 16, 1905, Mitchell Papers. Mitchell met with Labor Secretary Wilson and Vice President Lewis regarding using the foreign language press; Mitchell to Hammerling, February 13, 1905, Mitchell Papers.

100. *Inauguration of Theodore Roosevelt as President of the United States, March 4, 1905* (Washington: Headquarters of the Inaugural Committee, n.d.), 11; "Inaugural Day Music," *Washington Post*, January 26, 1905, 2; "Committees in Charge of Inauguration Ceremonies," *Washington Post*, March 4, 1905, 17.

101. Victoria Hammerling Rosenberg to author, January 20, 2014, Hammerling Collection. Curiously the invitation is only to Hammerling and does not include a wife.

102. "Inaugural Parade of March 4, 1905," *Washington Post*, March 3, 1905; "Imposing Pageant of the Military and Civic Organizations," *Washington Post*, March 5, 1905, 2.

103. Hammerling to Mitchell, November 17, 1904, Mitchell Papers.

104. *Brewing and Liquor Interests*, 1:585.

105. Ibid; Hammerling also stated that the estate had been "confiscated" by 1919, but why and by whom he never explained; ibid., 555. He also said he bought it for "a summer place"; see ibid., 611, but it was also a "philanthropic enterprise" to show his success to his erstwhile countrymen. One report claimed that Hammerling spent $2 million on improvements; see Martin Egan to Lancelot Smith, March 17, 1915; Foreign Office: General Correspondence, FO 371–2560 (hereafter FO 371), United Kingdom, National Archives (hereafter NA), doc. 43236.

106. *Brewing and Liquor Interests*, 1:639.

3: BUSINESS TYCOON AND REPUBLICAN LEADER

1. The "Italian-American Advertising Agency."

2. Quoted in Berkley Hudson and Karen Boyajy, "The Rise and Fall of an Ethnic Advocate and American Huckster, Louis N. Hammerling and the Immigrant Press," *Media History*, vol. 15, no. 3 (2009): 288.

3. *Brewing and Liquor Interests*, 1:465–68.

4. Ibid., 470–71.

5. Ibid., 471.

6. Hudson and Boyajy, "Rise and Fall," 289.

7. For the Ridder story, see "Re Louis Hammerling," 2. There is a mystery surrounding Hammerling's German connections. On June 12, 1917, Hammerling's wife purchased a very sizeable piece of land (27 acres) in Dutchess County, New York, from a woman named "Schultz" for the sum of $10. Was this another payment to Hammerling by German interests? For details of the sale see Dutchess County Deeds, vol. 398, 434, in Records Room, Dutchess County Clerk's Office, Poughkeepsie, NY.

8. See Propagandist, 3.

9. This is Frank Zotti's conclusion. Zotti hated Hammerling, but his conclusion is consonant with the argument that it was the Republican Party that maneuvered Hammerling into control of the nascent AAFLN. See *Brewing and Liquor Interests*, 1:640.

10. John Higham, *Strangers in the Land: Patterns of American Nativism, 1860–1925* (New Brunswick: Rutgers University Press, 1955), 126; Lechicki, "Hammerling," 263–64; Robert E. Park, *The Immigrant Press and Its Control* (New York: Harper, 1922), 376ff.

11. Given Hammerling's political activities, founding of the AAFLN, and publication of the *Leader*, it is a bizarre aside that in 1909 he made an attempt to become American Minister to Romania; it is part of the mystery of Hammerling. See Hammerling to Philander C. Knox, September 16, 1910, RG 59, entry 764: Applications and Recommendations for Appointment to the Consular and Diplomatic Services, 1901–1924.

12. *Brewing and Liquor Interests*, 1:640.

13. *Brewing and Liquor Interests*, 1:xxvii.

14. Hammerling dismissed the idea that he had influence over the foreign language press in 1918; see ibid., 472.

15. "Campaign Cost $85,000," *Star and Sentinel* (Gettysburg), December 16, 1908, 1.

16. Hammerling to Mitchell, November 20, 1908; NN to Hammerling, November 30, 1908, Mitchell Papers.

17. Hudson and Boyajy, "Rise and Fall," 289.

18. Ibid., 292.

19. Ibid., 290.

20. Hudson and Boyajy, "Rise and Fall," 293.

21. See Propagandist, 1.

22. Carl Wittke, *German-Americans and the World War* (Columbus: Ohio State Archaeological and Historical Society, 1936), 165.

23. *Brewing and Liquor Interests*, 1:785–86.

24. Hudson and Boyajy, "Rise and Fall," 294.

25. [Primrose] to [Grey], April 7, 1915, FO 115/1962/169, NA.

26. Jaudon statement, 3.

27. *Brewing and Liquor Interests*, 1:625; "Somebody Lied but Who Is It?" Fort Wayne *Sentinel*, October 7, 1912, 1, 10.

28. *Brewing and Liquor Interests*, 1:469. It is not clear whether Hammerling was referring only to publishers of the foreign language press.

29. It was advertised that President Taft and the entire cabinet would be present according to Hammerling's nemesis, Franjo Zotti; see *Brewing and Liquor Interests*, 1:641; cf. Hudson and Boyajy, "Rise and Fall," 291–92.

30. "Cortelyou urges simpler lawmaking," *New York Times*, November 13, 1910, 16. Hammerling had endorsed Hitchcock in a letter to Taft to be chairman of the RNC; see Hammerling to Taft, June 29, 1908, Taft Papers, reel 85.

31. *Brewing and Liquor Interests*, 1:470.

32. Much of the following information is based on Benham memorandum.

33. Hammerling quoted in Namier, *Namier*, 112–13.

34. R. L. *Polk & Co., 1915 Trow General Directory of New York City*, vol. 128 (New York, 1915), 229.

35. Jaudon statement.

36. *Brewing and Liquor Interests*, 1:633.

37. See the MID examination of Arthur Gabryel, dated March 8, 1918, RG 165, folder 10175, USNA.

38. Ibid. Jaudon is referred to in another place as "E. H."; see *Brewing and Liquor Interests*, 1:626.

39. Ibid., 553.

40. The articles were entitled "Personal Liberty" and appeared in virtually every issue of the *Leader*.

41. *Brewing and Liquor Interests*, 1:486.

42. Ibid., 1:612–13.

43. Ibid., 631–32.

44. Ibid., 472–532.

45. Ibid., 534–35.

46. Benham memorandum, 4.

47. Hammerling to United States Brewers' Association, November 29, 1913, in *Brewing and Liquor Interests*, 1:765. The majority of the issues of the *American Leader* were purchased by the brewers; see ibid., 485.

48. Namier, *Namier*, 107–8, 112.

49. Ormsby McHarg to J. L. Magnes, September 30, 1909, RG 85, box 127, Immigration and Naturalization Service (hereafter INS), USNA. A packet of documents, marked file 52600/13–13a demonstrates that the legal issues were mostly involving Jewish immigrants.

50. This is an example of Hammerling's ambiguous relationship to his Jewish ancestry. See "Jews Attack Plan to Bar Immigrants," *New York Times*, January 23, 1911, 5. Anyone reading the article would conclude that Hammerling was Jewish.

51. "Editors Meet President," *Sheboygan Daily Press*, May 4, 1910, 2.

52. This argument is based on the material presented in Jeanne D. Petit, *The Men and Women We Want: Gender, Race, and the Progressive Era Literacy Test Debate* (Rochester: University of Rochester Press, 2010), 2–3.

53. Jacob Saphirstein to Nagel, January 10, 1911, RG 85, INS, USNA. Regarding the LIS, which may have had 2,000 members, see *Brewing and Liquor Interests*, 1:563–64. It was created to oppose the literacy test; cf. Hudson and Boyajy, "Rise and Fall," 295.

54. Petit, *Men and Women*, 59.

55. Hammerling and the AAFLN are mentioned repeatedly in Petit, *Men and Women*, as campaigning against restriction; see 2–3, 12–13, 59–61, 81–82, 103, 110, 115.

56. "Taft to hear Alien Plea," *Washington Post*, February 6, 1913, 4.

57. "Taft sits as judge on Immigration Bill," *New York Times*, February 7, 1913, 4.

58. "Holds up Alien Bill," *Washington Post*, February 7, 1913, 4.

59. Hammerling to Tumulty, April 28, 1913, Wilson Papers.

60. "Washington News," *Wellsboro Gazette*, January 11, 1911, 1; "Wilson Gives Hearing on Immigration Bill," *Atlanta Constitution*, January 22, 1915, 9. Hammerling acted in the capacity of president of the AAFLN.

61. See the White House secretary's note of March 31, 1916, in Wilson Papers.

62. Louis Makulec, *Church of St. Stanislaus, Bishop and Martyr* (New York: The Roman Catholic Church of St. Stanislaus, B.M., 1954), 56.

63. Ibid., 56, 62.

64. Max Strauss to M. Oustinoff, January 4 and 14, 1916, RG 261, Records of the Russian Consulates, USNA.

65. See Louis Marshall to Hammerling, March 6 and 13, 1914, Marshall Papers, box 1583; Marshall to Hammerling, January 21 and May 21, 1916, Marshall Papers, box 1585.

66. "The Ritual Murder Charge," *New York Times*, October 16, 1913.

67. McHarg to Magnes, September 30, 1909, and associated documents, RG 85, Central Office, folder 52600/13, INS, USNA.

68. "Hearing in the Commissioner's Office," September 27, 1909, RG 85, folder 52600/13A, INS, USNA.

69. Ibid., 24.

70. Ibid., 43–44.

71. Rivka Shpak Lissak, "The National Liberal Immigration League and Immigration Restriction, 1906–1917," *American Jewish Archives*, vol. 46, no. 2 (1994): 221.

72. Ibid., 213.

73. For Hammerling's negotiations with the INS, see Hammerling to McHarg, September 2 and 8, 1909; Dushkind to McHarg, September 18, 1909; Williams to Hammerling, December 29, 1910; Cable to Williams, December 29 and 30, 1910, INS, box 127. Interestingly, Hammerling was not counted among the Jewish leaders present.

74. *Restriction of Immigration: Hearings before the House Committee on Immigration and Naturalization*, 64th Cong., H. R. Doc. 558, 3–5 (January 21, 1916) (statements of Mr. Louis N. Hammerling and Hon. Bourke Cockran of New York City).

75. Almost certainly a garbled version of the committee's secretary "J. S. Momand."

76. Ibid., 4.

77. Lissak, "National Liberal Immigration League," 201.

78. Ibid., 6.

79. See "Editorial," *American Leader* 9 (1916): 69. The Bill was vetoed by President Taft, though the GOP favored it. The same was true of Wilson and the Democrats.

The Progressives were pro-immigration, but were loudly silent about the Bill. See Lissak, "National Liberal Immigration League," 228–29.

80. Lissak, "National Liberal Immigration League," 233–34. By 1914 the League was in a state of decomposition. Hammerling again tried to see the president in 1917; see White House secretary's note of January 3, 1917, Wilson Papers.

81. "Indict Reichmann for Hiding a Loan," New York Times, March 29, 1911, 1.

82. Ibid.; "Got City Deposit to lend to Cummins," New York Times, March 30, 1911, 1.

83. "Hyde Sees Plot to Discredit Him," New York Times, April 10, 1911, 1. This article reproduces Hammerling's dunning letters to Hyde of March 11, March 16, March 25, and June 6, 1910.

84. Ibid.

85. Brewing and Liquor Interests, 1:645.

86. "Dictated by Clarence E. Root," November 1, 1917, RG 165, folder 10175–110, USNA.

87. Statement by Gabryel dated August 10, 1917, RG 165, folder 10175–110, USNA. It should be remembered that Gabryel and Hammerling had a falling out and their relations were embittered by the time he made this statement.

88. G. H. Berg Deposition, March 13, 1918, RG 165, folder 10175–110, USNA (hereafter Berg deposition).

89. "Telegraph News Notes," Chillicothe Constitution, January 22, 1918. Hammerling recalled this episode while addressing the Advertising Club in St. Louis.

90. Brewing and Liquor Interests, 1:616; "Admits Dernburg Tried to Buy Paper," New York Times, December 5, 1918.

91. For the diamond smuggling story, see "Notes from Newspaper Clippings," 1.

92. White interrogation, 1.

93. White interrogation, 1.

94. He repeated that the next day; see Norman H. White Examination of Louis N. Hammerling, March 10, 1918, 3 (hereafter White examination).

95. Ibid.

96. Unless otherwise noted, the discussion of Samuel Weiss's testimony is drawn from the MID investigation titled "Sam Hammerling—alias—Sam Weiss," March 9, 1918, RG 165, folder 10175–110, USNA.

97. MID investigation document entitled "Mr. Dattner," n.d., RG 165, folder 10175, 4, USNA (hereafter Dattner report).

98. The federal authorities apparently concluded that Samuel was Hammerling's brother; see the minute on George Broderick to Nicholas Biddle, March 9, 1918, by White, RG 165, folder 10175, USNA.

99. Judith M. Gold to author, February 23, 2006.

100. Dattner report, 4.

101. This information is drawn substantially from the MID investigation titled "Miss Bertha Leffler," March 9, 1918, RG 165, folder 10175, 1, USNA.

102. Ibid., 2.

103. Memorandum by B. Moran to Department of Justice, November 11, 1917, RG 165, folder 10175, 1, USNA (hereafter Moran memorandum).

104. Dattner report, 4.

105. Ibid.

106. See MID investigation entitled "Arthur Gabryel," March 8, 1918, RG 165, folder 10175, USNA. The Leffler information, along with many other unappetizing tidbits, was supplied to authorities by Gabryel. Of course, we should remember that Hammerling despised Gabryel and noted he would "say anything for a drink." He was one of Hammerling's key employees. Dattner, Margaret Leffler, and Wazeter were critical of Gabryel and tended to support Hammerling; see *Brewing and Liquor Interests*, 2:2472–76.

107. White examination, 2.

108. Moran memorandum, 2; NN to Justice Department, November 17, 1917, RG 165, folder 10175–110, USNA.

4: NATIONAL POLITICS

1. This despite the fact that in the GOP primary campaign he seemingly worked for both Roosevelt and Taft; see "Somebody," 10; "Hooker was Trifle High," *Fort Wayne Sentinel,* October 7, 1912, 1.

2. "Admits Dernburg Tried to Buy Paper," *New York Times,* December 5, 1918.

3. The following account relies heavily on M. B. B. Biskupski, *The United States and the Rebirth of Poland, 1914–1918* (Dordrecht, NL: Republic of Letters, 2012).

4. In his multivolume *History of the American People,* Wilson spoke flatteringly of the Germans and Irish, while of course maintaining the primacy of the "British stock": English, Scottish, and Scotch-Irish. Regarding the more recent immigration from eastern and southern Europe, his verdict was far from favorable. In a striking paragraph, Wilson noted with disdain that in the twentieth century the "sturdy stock" of northern Europe had been supplanted by an immigration composed of "multitudes of men of the lowest class from the south of Italy and men of the meaner sort out of Hungary and Poland, men out of the ranks where there was neither skill nor energy nor any initiative of quick intelligence.... The Chinese were more to be desired, as workmen if not as citizens, than most of the coarse crew that came crowding in." See Woodrow Wilson, *A History of the American People,* 5 vols. (New York: Harper and Brothers, 1902), 4:132–33.

5. Higham, *Strangers,* 190.

6. For Hammerling's work in the 1912 campaign, see his letters to the Republican National Committee from July 22 and 24, August 26 and 28, September 5, 13, 18, 19, and 24; Hammerling to Hilles, September 4, 5, 6, 7, and 11, 1912; Taft to Hammerling, n.d. (ca. March 14, 1912) and September 7, 1912; Taft to A. V. Eilert, June 13, 1912; Hammerling to Wagner, September 11, 1912; Hammerling to NN, September 21, 1912, all in Charles Dewey Hilles Papers (hereafter Hilles Papers), Manuscripts and Archives, Yale University Library, Sterling Memorial Library (hereafter YSML), boxes 118, 122–24.

7. Hammerling to Hilles, September 21, 1912, et seq., Hilles Papers, box 124.

8. "Statement of Leroy Anderson Van Patten, President Van Patten, Inc." to Nicholas Biddle, MID, April 19, 1918 (hereafter Van Patten statement), RG 165, folder 10175/110, USNA.

9. Undated, unsigned memorandum "#8," Hilles Papers, box 149, folder 2032.

10. J. C. Delaney to Hilles, January 11, 1912, Taft Papers, reel 384.

11. Regarding the *American Leader*'s partisan activities, see the following issues: vol. 1, no. 3 (March 28, 1912), 35–37; vol. 1, no. 9 (June 27, 1912), 20–23; vol. 2, no. 3 (August 8, 1912), 165–69; vol. 2, no. 4 (August 22, 1912), 224–28; vol. 2, no. 6 (September 26, 1912), 335–39. Taft published remarks in vol. 1, no. 3 (March 28, 1912), 49–50; vol. 2, no. 8 (October 24, 1912), 471–73; vol. 1, no. 2 (March 14, 1912), 22–23; vol. 1, no. 9 (June 27, 1912), 31; vol. 2, no. 6 (September 26, 1912), 334.

12. Hammerling to Hilles, September 6, 1912, Hilles Papers, box 122.

13. "Ważne dla Obywateli Polaków," issued by a "Committee" of foreign language editors, n.d. The appended list of editors is essentially Hammerling's AAFLN.

14. *Brewing and Liquor Interests*, 1:469.

15. Ibid.

16. See Jaudon statement, 3. The possibility that Hammerling was involved in advertising as early as the 1896 McKinley election would make the Hammerling link to the Hanna-McKinley cultivation of ethnic voters more obvious.

17. Hammerling to M. K. Yoakum, July 22, 1912, Hilles Papers, box 118.

18. Hammerling to Hilles, September 6, 1912, and Hammerling to Hilles, September 11, 1912, Hilles Papers, boxes 122 and 123.

19. Hammerling to Hilles, September 4 and 5, 1912, Hilles Papers, boxes 122 and 123.

20. Hammerling to Hilles, September 11, 1912, Hilles Papers, box 123.

21. W. S. Rylski to Hammerling, September 20 and 23, 1912; Hammerling to Rylski, September 23, 1912, Hilles Papers, box 123.

22. Hammerling to Hilles, August 2, 1912, Hilles Papers, box 73.

23. The correspondence regarding Hammerling's negotiations with various ethnic journals is voluminous and can be found scattered about in Hilles Papers, boxes 118, 122, 123, and 124.

24. This episode is quite unclear, and most of the evidence comes from anti-Alliance partisans; see "Sprawozdanie z działalności Komitetu Obrony Narodowej w Stanach Zjednoczonych" (hereafter "Sprawozdanie z działalności"), October 23, 1919, Akta Adiutantury Generalnej Naczelnego Dowództwa, 1918–1922 (hereafter AAGND), Joseph Piłsudski Institute of America (hereafter JPIA), m. 21, document 1998/T5, 1–2; Stanisław Osada and Adam Olszewski, *Historia Związku Narodowego Polskiego*, 4 vols. (Chicago: Polish National Alliance, 1957–1963) (hereafter *Historia ZNP*), 2:370–72; 3:73. See the discussion, closely followed here, in Biskupski, *The United States and the Rebirth of Poland*.

25. "Dixon loaded for Senate Committee," *New York Times*, October 12, 1912, 2.

26. Ibid.

27. Egan to Spring Rice, April 7, 1915, FO 115/1962/175, NA; Spring Rice to Grey, April 9, 1915, FO 115/1962/178, NA.

28. All of these many letters are scattered throughout reel 384 of the Taft Papers as well as letters of July 19, 1912 (Hammerling to Forester), and Hammerling to Taft of July 23, 1912, reel 444.

29. This discussion of the 1912 vote relies heavily on Biskupski, *The United States and the Rebirth of Poland.*

30. Edward R. Kantowicz, *Polish-American Politics in Chicago, 1888–1940* (Chicago: University of Chicago Press, 1975), 107–8.

31. Donald E. Pienkos, "Polish Americans in Milwaukee Politics," in *Ethnic Politics in Urban America,* ed. Angela T. Pienkos (Chicago: Polish American Historical Association, 1978), 71.

32. Norman E. Mack to Joseph E. Davies, November 5, 1912, Josephus Daniels Papers, container 670, LC.

33. Francis G. Couvares, *The Remaking of Pittsburgh: Class and Culture in an Industrializing City, 1877–1919* (Albany: SUNY Press, 1984), 129.

34. Louis Gerson, *Woodrow Wilson and the Rebirth of Poland, 1914–1920: A Study in the Influence on American Policy of Minority Groups of Foreign Origin* (New Haven: Yale University Press, 1953), 59–60.

35. See Biskupski, *The United States and the Rebirth of Poland.*

36. John B. Duff, "The Italians," in *The Immigrants' Influence on Wilson's Peace Policies,* ed. Joseph P. O'Grady (Lexington: University of Kentucky Press, 1967), 113.

37. Higham, *Strangers,* 190.

38. Morawski-Nałęcz to House, September 15, 1918, Edward M. House Papers, box 157, folder 7524, 1, YSML.

39. Hammerling to Rudolph Forster (assistant secretary to the president), November 4, 1912, Taft Papers, reel 384.

40. Nagel to Hammerling, February 25, and March 9 and 10, 1914, Charles Nagel Papers, reel 24, 234ff., YSML.

41. Nagel to Hammerling, March 11, October 14, November 3, and November 7,1914; Nagel Papers, reel 24, folders 90, 661a, 719, 735, and 815.

42. For Nagel's requesting advice on immigration issues, see his letters to Hammerling of January 4, January 19, and January 31, 1912, Nagel Papers, reel 21, folders 28, 131, and 220. Nagel asked Hammerling how the "political situation strikes you" on June 1, 1912; Nagel Papers, reel 22, folder 283. See also Nagel to Hilles, February 16, 1912, wherein the former refuses to make a statement until he has spoken to Hammerling; see Nagel Papers, reel 21, folder 396.

43. Regarding the cabinet secretaries see Nagel to Hammerling, January 10, 1912, Nagel Papers, reel 21, folder 28.

44. See Nagel's letters to Hammerling of April 11, April 13, April 15, April 21, and April 29, 1911, in Nagel Papers, reel 19, folders 187, 205, 266, 309, and 404. It was reported that Nagel commissioned Hammerling to travel throughout the world studying immigration and commercial questions. This claim was made in Hammerling's official biographies when he was in Polish politics. American sources are silent; see for example the *Who Was Who in America, vol. 1, 1897–1942* (Chicago: Marquis

Who's Who, 1966), 513. Is this another Hammerling myth? See Tadeusz and Witold Rzepecki, *Sejm i senat, 1922–1927* (Poznań: Wielkopolska księgarnia nakładowa Karola Rzepeckiego, 1923), 412–13; Majchrowski, "Hammerling, Ludwik Mikołaj," 514; Mościcki i Dzwonkowski, *Parlament Rzeczypospolitej Polskiej, 1919–1927*. Lechicki repeats this claim (Lechicki, "Hammerling," 264) and lists the Far East, India, Australia, Africa, and South America; he seemingly has relied on the Rzepecki and other brief Polish biographical entries. There is no solid evidence for the claim of a world mission for Hammerling. There is another scrap in S. J. Brzeziński's memoirs where the populist leader claims Hammerling was sent to Europe in 1912, by the secretary of state, to study emigration issues. This seems more possible, but still lacks corroboration. See Zbiory S. J. Brzezińskiego: "Z mego notatnika," s. IV 7a, Zakład Historii Ruchu Ludowego, 141. Hammerling seems never to have referred to the missions abroad while in the United States.

45. White examination, 5.

46. For Hammerling's correspondence with Taft we may note, merely as examples, the following: Hammerling to Taft, September 16, 1910; Hammerling to Taft, December 14, 1910; Hammerling to Charles Norton (Taft's secretary), December 22, 1910; Nagel to Norton, December 23, 1910; Hammerling to Norton, December 27, 1910; Hammerling to Hilles, January 6, 1911; Hammerling to Hilles, January 9, 1911; all in Taft Papers, reel 384. We are leaving aside 1912, an election year when the Taft-Hammerling correspondence increased.

47. "Surplus Remains of Republican Funds," *Reno Evening Gazette*, November 27, 1916, 1.

48. The evidence for the Czechs comes from "Statement of Vaclave A. Hajek," August 15, 1918, RG 165, folder 9140, 20, USNA.

49. See the report of Michael Kruszka, April 5, 1917, General Records of the Department of Justice, Record Group 65 (hereafter RG 65), folder 1105, USNA. This report is not reliable.

50. M. Roberts to Harry A. Taylor, February 28, 1918, RG 165, folder 10175–110, USNA.

51. Rene Carrillo, APL, "Final Report," October 18, 1917; ibid. Both sources are from RG 165, folder 10175–110, USNA.

5: ONE OF THE MOST DANGEROUS GERMAN AGENTS IN AMERICA

1. For the Rumely-Hammerling connect, see the correspondence between the two from spring 1913 through the following spring in E. A. Rumely Collection, Lilly Library, Indiana University at Bloomington, files 62 and 63.

2. "Statement by Mr. Louis Hammerling," March 13, 1918 (hereafter Hammerling statement), RG 165, folder 10175–110, 1–2, USNA; cf. *Brewing and Liquor Interests*, 1:548. See Statement, 22.

3. Reinhard R. Doerries, *Imperial Challenge: Ambassador Count Bernstorff and German-American Relations, 1908–1917* (Chapel Hill: University of North Carolina Press, 1989), 16–17.

4. For the decision to buy the *Mail,* which was reportedly for sale for $1 million, see *Brewing and Liquor Interests,* 1:10–12, a letter dated March 12, 1915, from Alexander Konta to Bernhard Dernburg.

5. Hudson and Boyajy, "Rise and Fall," 296.

6. This description of the decision to acquire the *Evening Mail* is based largely on Doerries, *Imperial Challenge,* 53–55, except where otherwise noted.

7. See, for example, MID to George Creel, July 25, 1918, RG 165, folder 10175–110, USNA; the MID report, August 1, 1918, implicates Hale and Viereck, but does not mention Hammerling; see Biddle report, August 1, 1918, RG 165, 9140, folder 1007, USNA.

8. The German government was subventing other American papers at the time; see Moran memorandum, 3. Rumely vehemently denied that he was acting in behalf of German interests in owning the paper; see "Statement by Dr. Edward A. Rumely" [1918], E. A. Rumely Collection, Lilly Library, Indiana University at Bloomington, file 63.

9. "Louis Hammerling, Advertising Agent for Foreign Language Papers in New York," 1.

10. "The Department Intelligence Office–Chicago," RG 165, folder 10175–110, USNA.

11. See the Nicholas Biddle report in RG 165, folder 10175–231, November 2, 1917, USNA.

12. A useful reconstruction, which mentions Hammerling only in passing, is Rumely et al. v. United States, July 27, 1923, at http//www.lexis.com/research/retrieve?_m=b1b6025848401467e2b8dbb0eel2567&docnum=1&. Accessed August 7, 2004. Hammerling denied any involvement; Statement, 25.

13. *Brewing and Liquor Interests,* 1:559, 561, 638.

14. Statement, 2–3, 18–19.

15. There is a report that Hammerling tried to convince the foreign language editors to appeal to the White House regarding arms manufacturing, but the effort died aborning; see M. F. Pupin to Spring Rice, March 31, 1915, FO 371–2450, NA. If this is so, it may well place Hammerling's contacts with German agents slightly earlier than we assume.

16. Statement, 24.

17. Doerries, *Imperial Challenge,* 105–6.

18. Hammerling statement, 4.

19. *Brewing and Liquor Interests,* 1:549–51.

20. Statement, 3.

21. White examination, 6.

22. Statement, 19. The Senate concluded its investigation by determining that Hammerling "knew at the time the purpose for which he was being employed." See *Brewing and Liquor Interests,* 2:xxvii.

23. Hammerling denied ever meeting von Bernstorff. In his colorful English, Hammerling testified: "If you can prove it, I will be dead right here." Ibid., 551. Gabryel and Dattner claimed they saw von Bernstorff there; see NN to Justice Department,

November 17, 1917, RG 165, folder 10175-110, USNA; *Brewing and Liquor Interests*, 1:627-28. Pruden says the same thing and claimed Hammerling was the source of the information. Ibid., 638.

24. White memorandum, 3. Hammerling always denied that he knew von Bernstorff. This is contradicted by his employee Jaudon in Jaudon statement, 2; Gabryel, another Hammerling employee, claims he saw von Bernstorff in Hammerling's office "a long time"; that he knew that Hammerling had many phone calls with Boy-Ed, which were in German (remember, Hammerling spoke Yiddish fluently); and that he saw letters to Hammerling from Boy-Ed. See Perkins to Department of Justice (referring to an interview with Gabryel), June 30, 1917, RG 65, reel 281, folder OG 1024, USNA; cf. *Brewing and Liquor Interests*, 1:634.

25. Jaudon statement, 2. Jaudon mentions that Hammerling knew the Austrian consul in New York, the Pole Eugeniusz Rozwadowski. One of Hammerling's employees once spoke openly of Austrian money being given to the AAFLN, and Hammerling immediately handed him $200 in hush money; see M. Roberts to Captain Harry A. Taylor, February 28, 1918, RG 165, box 2887, folder 10175-110/9, USNA. Hammerling supposedly sent envoys to Austria during the war in conjunction with the Austrian consulate; see J. F. Kropidłowski Report, December 28, 1917, RG 165, folder 10175-110, USNA.

26. For a list of the signatories, see *Brewing and Liquor Interests*, 1:569-76. Hammerling, of course, was to pay the papers for carrying the advertising. It turns out that, in many instances, he kept the money; see ibid., 1:595-597. A breakdown of the papers that were signed is, according to a British source: 10 Bohemian, 7 Croatian, 9 Greek, 6 French, 113 Italian, 49 Jewish, 47 Polish, 8 Russian, 3 Serbian, 9 Slovak, and 5 "Slavonic." See Spring Rice to Primrose, April 8, 1915, FO 371-2560-41690, NA.

27. Hammerling handled the English language version through his business partner Rankin; see S. Spolansky, "Original Complaint," December 5, 1918, RG 165, folder 10175-110, USNA.

28. MID to George Creel, July 25, 1918, RG 165, folder 10175-110, USNA.

29. Statement, 3. Hammerling later claimed that he entered this in his books as charged to Rumely; *Brewing and Liquor Interests*, 1:581.

30. "Report #3, New York," September 2, 1917, RG 59, Office of the Counselor (hereafter RG 59: Counselor), box 163, folder 862.2/294, USNA; H. P. Falcke, *Vor dem Eintritt Amerikas in dem Weltkrieg: Deutsche Propaganda in den Vereinigten Staaten von Amerika, 1914-1915* (Dresden: C. Reissner, 1928), 146.

31. The text quoted appears as an exhibit in *Brewing and Liquor Interests*, 1:568-76.

32. "Analysis of the Signatures of the Manifesto," Foreign Office: General Correspondence: News, 115-1962-181,188, NA (hereafter FO 115); Eustace Percy to "Tom," April 23, 1915, FO 115/1962, NA; Spring Rice to Primrose, April 8, 1915, FO 371-2560, NA. For Namier's service to the British government see Calder, *Britain and the Origins of the New Europe, 1914-1918* (Cambridge University Press, 1976), 55ff.; 85ff.

33. Spring Rice "Memorandum," March 25, 1915, FO 371, NA.

34. Jaudon statement, 4.

35. *Brewing and Liquor Interests*, 1:594-95.

36. See, e.g., ibid., 591–92.

37. Ibid., 610.

38. Ibid., 2:1431–32. A. Bruce Bielaski of the Justice Department admitted some uncertainty about the letter.

39. Statement, 8.

40. "Report No. 2," September 1, 1917, Office of the Counselor/Under Secretary and the Chief Special Agent. Central File 1917–1927, RG 59, folder 862.2/294, USNA; "Who Paid for Peace 'Ad'?" *New York Times*, April 6, 1915, 4; "Denies Germany Paid for 'Appeal' to Stop Munitions," *New York World*, April 7, 1915. Vide, e.g., "Wystąpienie senatora Overmana przeciw Ludwikowi Hammerlingowi," *Ameryka-Echo*, August 4, 1929, 1.

41. See the unattributed clipping in the MID files titled "Hold Hammerling on Charge of Libel," RG 165, folder 10175–110, USNA. There was a curious exception. See "Statement of Leroy Andrew Van Patten," April 19, 1918, RG 165, 10175, 3, USNA (hereafter Van Patten statement).

42. "Admits Campaign to Stop Munitions," *New York Times*, December 4, 1918.

43. Percy's memorandum of March 3, 1915, is quoted in Calder, *Britain and the Origins*, 60ff.

44. Vide Robert Borden to George Perley [enclosing Spring Rice to Borden, September 17, 1916], September 20, 1916, Sir George H. Perley Papers, MG 27 II D 12, vol. 6, Public Archives of Canada.

45. Martin Egan to Lancelot Smith, March 15 and 17, 1915; Spring Rice to Grey, March 25, 1915, FO 371–2560, docs. 41805, 43236, NA. Curiously enough there were also reports, alluded to in this correspondence, that Hammerling was in British pay and working against the Germans.

46. [Primrose] to [Grey], April 7, 1915, FO 115/1962/169, NA.

47. Calder, *Britain and the Origins*, 50–51; H. C. Peterson, *Propaganda for the War: The Campaign against American Neutrality, 1914–1917* (Norman: University of Oklahoma Press, 1939), 152–53; Henry Wickham Steed, *Through Thirty Years, 1892–1922: A Personal Narrative*, 2 vols. (London: Heinemann, 1924), 2:2–43, 2:46–47.

48. Peterson, *Propaganda*, 152ff.

49. Egan to Lancelot Smith, March 15 and 17, 1915; FO 371–2560–41805, NA.

50. Spring Rice to Grey, March 25, 1915, FO 371–2560–43236, NA.

51. Doerries, *Imperial Challenge*, 36, 53. Ballin was also in close touch with Roger Casement.

52. Egan to Smith, March 15 and March 17, 1915, FO 371–2560, NA; "Foreign Press of U.S.," April 4, 1915, FO 371–2560, NA. It was noted that the exception was the German press.

53. Spring Rice to "Mr. Primrose," April 8, [1915], FO 371–2560, 41690, NA; Spring Rice to Grey, April 9, 1915, FO 115, 115–1962–43, 44, NA; Spring Rice to Primrose, April 17, 1915, FO 115, 115–1962–72, 73, NA. The FO memorandum of May 12, 1915, FO 371–58412, NA, reiterated Namier's analysis.

54. British Consul General, New York, to Spring Rice, April 6, 1915; Spring Rice to Foreign Office, April 7, 1915; Martin Egan to Spring Rice, April 7, 1915; Fred-

erick Dixon to Spring Rice, April 7, 1915; Spring Rice to Grey, April 9, 1915; Henry Mann to D. G. Osborne, April 5, 1915; Pupin to Spring Rice, April 14, 1915; Spring Rice to Pupin, April 16, 1915; Spring Rice to Grey, April 17, 1915; Spring Rice to Percy, May 10, 1915, FO 115/1962, NA; Egan to Lancelot Smith, March 15 and March 17, 1915, FO 371-2560, 41805, NA.

55. Spring Rice to Primrose, April 17, 1915, FO 115, 115-1962-72, 73, NA.

56. Calder, *Britain and the Origins*, 65-69.

57. Foreign Office [Memorandum], for Grey, April 7, 1915, FO 115/1962, NA; Memorandum of May 12, 1915, FO 58412, NA.

58. Note to "Tom" from E. P[ercy], May 8, 1915, FO 115-1962, 177-80, NA. Namier seems to have been the ultimate source of the information.

59. Spring Rice to Grey, April 9, 1915, FO 115/1962/179, NA. Actually, this is a small window into the vast complexity of international Polish politics. Józef Piłsudski, the founder of the Polish Socialist Party, was a soldier associated with the Austrians, and hence, reluctantly, with the Germans during the war. Thus his allies among American Polonia were drawn from the left, but pro-Austrian. Hammerling was a Republican, but working for the Germans. He, however, had a much clearer linkage: he wanted money. It also reflected the verdict of Mihajlo Pupin, the great Serbian physicist and activist: gullible Americans "will never understand the trickiness of the Austrian Jew" (Pupin to Spring Rice, April 14, 1915, FO 115/1962/176, NA).

60. Spring Rice to Grey, April 17, 1915, FO 115/1962/184, NA.

61. Calder, *Britain and the Origins*, 69.

62. Emmanuel Victor Voska and Will Irwin, *Spy and Counter-Spy* (London: Doubleday, Doran, 1940), 28ff.

63. Peterson, *Propaganda,* 153.

64. See Wilson to Polk, March 16, 1916, Frank L. Polk Papers [Polk Papers], box 14, folder 490, YSML.

65. "Lay Harbor Plot to German Embassy," *New York Times,* April 12, 1915, 1.

66. "Deny Any Share in a Harbor Plot," *New York Times,* April 13, 1915, 3; "Challenges Plot Denial," *New York Times,* April 18, 1915, 4.

67. Arthur S. Link, *Woodrow Wilson and the Progressive Era, 1910–1917* (New York: Harper, 1954), 200n. R. W. Seton-Watson describes Hammerling as "a prominent German-Jewish agent of the German government." See R. W. Seton-Watson, *Masaryk in England* (Cambridge University Press, 1941), 98n.; Park, *Immigrant Press*, 390.

68. Falcke, *Vor der Eintritt,* 146.

69. William G. McAdoo, *Crowded Years* (New York: Houghton Mifflin, 1931), 323–30; cf. Voska and Irwin, *Spy and Counter-Spy,* 90ff.

70. Charles Seymour, *Woodrow Wilson and the World War: A Chronicle of Our Own Times* (New Haven: Yale University Press, 1921), 78; "The country was agog over spy rumors," John M. Blum, *Joe Tumulty and the Wilson Era* (Hamden, CT: Archon, 1969), 98.

71. Wilson's comment was made on August 4, 1915; Link, *Wilson and the Progressive Era,* 200.

72. Patrick Devlin, *Too Proud to Fight: Woodrow Wilson's Neutrality* (New York: Oxford University Press, 1975), 287ff.

73. Gabryel said that he saw the Appeal in Hammerling's office. See Perkins to Department of Justice, June 30, 1917, RG 65, reel 281, folder OG 1024, USNA; cf. *Brewing and Liquor Interests,* 1:627–28.

74. Ibid., 629.

75. Ibid., 567. He also said he wrote it with Momand; Statement, 7.

76. *Brewing and Liquor Interests,* 1:630; Hammerling denied the whole incident; ibid., 555.

77. G. D. Dreheuil (the French Military Attaché) to NN, February 4, 1920; "Report #3, New York," September 2, 1917, RG 59: Counselor. Both sources are from box 163, folder 862.2/294, USNA. A partial list of foreign language papers subsidized by the Austrian consul is in Rozwadowski to NN, November 5, 1915, RG 59: Counselor, folder 861.0–185, USNA. If the Austrians were bribing the press that was part of Hammerling's AAFLN, it is hard to believe that there was not some working relationship between Hammerling and the Austrians.

78. There is considerable evidence in this regard, see, e.g., "Original Complaint," by J. Spolansky (MID), December 5, 1918, RG 165, folder 10175–110, USNA.

79. FO draft memorandum, initialed "EG," May 12, 1915, no. 58412 in FO 371–2586, NA; cf. the minute by Percy on NN to NN, April 14, 1915, FO 371–2450–43258, NA.

80. *Brewing and Liquor Interests,* 1:643. Hammerling denied pressuring Zotti; ibid., 562.

81. Ibid., 643; see Leon Wazeter's deposition of March 11, 1918 (hereafter Wazeter deposition), 2, RG 165, folder 10175–110, 2, USNA.

82. Berg deposition, 3.

83. Hammerling was virtually hysterical about Zotti's persecution of him, justified or not. He made it clear that Gabryel was working with Zotti. See Statement, 26. Zotti was almost certainly blackmailing Hammerling; see Wazeter deposition, 2, and the sworn statements by Momand, March 11, 1919, and G. H. Berg, March 13, 1919; RG 165, 10175–110, USNA.

84. The Zotti blackmailing scheme is very controversial. See his own comments in *Brewing and Liquor Interests,* 1:646.

85. Zotti to Hammerling, April 3, 1918, RG 165, folder 10175–110, USNA.

86. See the MID "Memorandum for Colonel Pakenham," June 26, 1918, RG 165, folder 10175–110, USNA. Hammerling eventually sued Zotti for libel; Zotti won. See Henry Uterhart (MID) to George Creel, July 26, 1918, RG 165, folder 10175–110, USNA.

87. "Louis N. Hammerling," *American Courier* (Milwaukee), July 25, 1918, RG 165, box 2888, folder 10175–110, 1, USNA.

88. "Our Free Alien Press," *New York Times,* September 24, 1915, 14.

89. "Hammerling Exposed!" *New York World,* October 7, 1917.

90. "Viereck Conferred on Buying a Paper," *New York Times,* August 12, 1918.

91. Gabryel quoting Hammerling in *Brewing and Liquor Interests,* 1:628. Cf. Dumba, who would make the same survey in September. See NN to Dumba, September 27, 1915, 897; Liasse Krieg 7b, USA 1915–1916, 205, Haus-, Hof- und Staatsarchiv, Österreichisches Staatsarchiv, Vienna. Gabryel insisted the survey was made for Austrian

not German interest, which seems logical; see the affidavit marked "Arthur Gabryel" (hereafter Gabryel affidavit), March 8, 1918, RG 165, folder 10175–110, 1, USNA.

92. This list is from Gabryel's testimony. See *Brewing and Liquor Interests*, 1:629. Other sources mention Wazeter going to Utica, and a Swede named Burke also being dispatched; see NN to Justice Department, November 17, 1917, RG 165, folder 10175–110, USNA; cf. White's interrogation of Dattner, ND, RG 165, folder 10175–110, 1, USNA.

93. Hammerling claimed there were no written reports; see *Brewing and Liquor Interests*, 1:629; White interrogation of Hammerling, 5. However, Dattner claimed he prepared one; see White's interrogation of Dattner, 2. Gabryel said that they handed written reports to Hammerling; see Gabryel affidavit; *Brewing and Liquor Interests*, 1:629.

94. Statement, 15–18.

95. "Hun Post-War Campaign Set for July, 1917," *New-York Tribune*, July 29, 1918, 14.

96. *Brewing and Liquor Interests*, 1:565.

97. Ibid.

98. Ibid., 566.

99. Ibid., 567.

100. Perkins's Report, September 30, 1917, RG 65, reel 281, folder OG 1024, USNA. Gabryel and Hammerling both note that the investigation was generously financed. This stands in interesting juxtaposition to the claims by Zotti that the whole affair was financed by the German and Austrian embassies. See "Hammerling to the Stand!" *Národni List*, March 10, 1918, 1.

101. Benham memorandum, 5.

102. Henry Landau, *The Enemy Within: The Inside Story of German Sabotage in America* (New York: G. P. Putnam's Sons, 1937), 52.

103. A key document here is the report of the Austrian ambassador to Berlin to the Ballhausplatz, October 8, 1915, Politisches Archiv I (PAI), 897, Österreichisches Staatsarchiv, Vienna; Liasse Krieg 7b, USA 1915–1916, 213–14.

104. *Brewing and Liquor Interests*, 1:9.

105. See the introduction to ibid., xiii.

106. Ibid., xiii–xiv.

107. Jules Witcover, *Sabotage at Black Tom: Imperial Germany's Secret War in America, 1914–1917* (Chapel Hill: Algonquin Books, 1989), 108.

108. Witcover has written a fine volume of the Black Tom affair and also included a discussion of early 1917's Kingsland fire in ibid.

109. "The Department Intelligence Office–Chicago," December 18, 1918, RG 165, folder 10175–110, USNA.

110. Ibid. Hammerling was also linked with Dumba in hostile press reports; see American Protective League report of October 18, 1917, RG 165, folder 10175–110, USNA; cf. "Summary Account," February 8, 1918, RG 165, folder 10175–110, USNA.

111. See "Heil dem Habsburger!" *New-Yorker Staats-Zeitung*, August 19, 1915.

112. See "Passenger Record" for Louis N. Hammerling, at http://www.ellisislandrecords.org/search/passRecord.asp?MID=10860196370007612736& LNM=. Accessed October 2, 2004.

113. We know of them through Polish sources; see Biskupski, *The United States and the Rebirth of Poland*, 114. Even Hammerling admitted that; see Statement, 28–30.

115. White examination, 3.

116. Ibid. 117. Assistant Attorney General to Secretary of State, March 23, 1917, in RG 65, reel 281, folder OG 1024, USNA.

118. See Kropidłowski to MID, December 28, 1917, a memorandum entitled "Austrian Enemy Aliens," RG 165, box 2436, folder 9140–686, USNA. Kropidłowski affirms that earlier reports, some dating from the beginning of the war, confirmed his conclusions. Unfortunately for the Americans, Kropidłowski was not a particularly good spy; see M. B. B. Biskupski, "Socialists, Spies, and Presbyterians: A Case Study of the Poles as Alien Enemies in World War I," in *Ethnicity, Culture, City*, eds. Thomas Gladsky, Adam Walaszek, and Małgorzatka M. Wawrzykiewicz (Warsaw: Oficyna Naukowa, 1998), 265–86.

119. Bureau of Investigation memorandum (February 27, 1917), RG 65, reel 942, folder OG 2500, USNA.

120. Even Arthur Gabryel, who never failed to excoriate Hammerling, noted that he never saw Dumba or any other Austrian official in Hammerling's office; see *Brewing and Liquor Interests*, 1:635.

121. "Statement of Slavomir Kratochvil," n.d., made to the New York Attorney General's office, RG 165, folder 9140–7021, USNA; "Statement of Vaclave A. Hajek," August 15, 1918, RG 165, folder 9140–7021, USNA; cf. *Brewing and Liquor Interests*, 1:560. Gregr's activities are quite mysterious.

122. Vienna's failure to denounce Germany's decision for unrestricted submarine warfare inclined the Wilson administration not to receive its ambassador; vide Angelo Ara, *L'Austria-Ungheria nella politica Americana durante la prima Guerra mondiale* (Rome: Edizioni dell'Ateneo, 1973), 30.

123. See Lansing to Wilson, March 27, 1917; Tarnowski to Lansing, March 26, 1917; Wilson to Lansing, March 27, 1917; Phillips to Lansing, March 28, 1917; Robert Lansing Papers (hereafter Lansing Papers–Mudd), MS 17880, Mudd Library, Princeton University (hereafter PML), boxes 2 and 3.

124. Regarding the Sosnowski-Tarnowski talks, see the unsigned memorandum of March 29, 1917, marked "confidential," and a second "Memorandum of interview with Mr. Sosnowski," dated March 31, 1917, as well as "memorandum of talk between Mr. Sosnowski & Count Tarnowski," April 2, 1917, signed by William LeGendre; William G. McAdoo to Wilson, March 30, 1917; Wilson to Lansing, April 12, 1917, RG 43, Records of United States Participation in International Conferences, Commissions, and Expositions: Records of the Department of State Relating to World War I and Its Termination, RG 59: M367, roll 374, 763.72119/559–1/2— 763.72119/561–1/2, USNA; LeGendre to John Skelton Williams, April 3, 1917, Robert Lansing Papers, vol. 25, LC.

125. That Polish goals were the motivation for the enterprise is clear from LeGendre's memorandum of December 24, 1925, William LeGendre Papers, Hoover Institution, Stanford, CA, f. 1.

126. Regarding Tarnowski's efforts to stay on in Washington, without official status, vide the handwritten note by Tarnowski to Lansing, May 3, 1917, in Lansing Papers–Mudd, box 3, PML; William Phillips Diary, entry for May 4, 1917, William Phillips Papers, Harvard, Houghton Library (HHL).

127. See memorandum to Captain F. P. Adams, February 18, 1918, RG 165, folder 10165–110, USNA.

128. Hammerling to Rudolph Forster, June 17, 1918, Wilson Papers.

129. Hammerling to Wilson, July 6, 1918; undated memorandum entitled "Louis N. Hammerling," probably by a White House secretary; Wilson Papers.

130. Entry for July 7, 1917, Diary vol. 23, Jaworski Papers, Archiwum Polska Akademia Nauk-Warsaw (APAN-W).

131. Wilson to Creel, July 9, 1918, Wilson Papers.

132. Creel to Wilson, n.d., Wilson Papers.

133. Ibid.

134. Wilson to Tumulty, n.d., Wilson Papers.

135. WFJ to Wilson, July 17, 1918; Wilson to Tumulty, July 18, 1918, Wilson Papers.

136. Hammerling to Tumulty, July 22, 1918; Hammerling "Memorandum," July 22, 1918, Wilson Papers.

137. Wilson to Tumulty, July 22, 1918, Wilson Papers.

138. The fact that Tarnowski associated himself with Sosnowski in these efforts certainly indicates he did not always have good judgment when it came to selecting Polish confidants.

139. See M. B. B. Biskupski, "Strategy, Politics and Suffering: The Wartime Relief of Belgium, Serbia, and Poland, 1914–1918," in *Ideology, Politics and Diplomacy in East Central Europe,* ed. M. B. B. Biskupski (Rochester: University of Rochester Press, 2003), 31–57.

140. Polish-American Relief Committee in New York, meeting of November 16, 1914, folder 61.2, Polish Institute of Arts and Sciences in America, New York.

141. See the untitled and undated document that begins, on page 3, "Louis N. Hammerling . . . proposes the following names," folder 597, subfolder 1, Archiwum Ignacego Paderewskiego, Archiwum Akt Nowych (hereafter AAN), Warsaw. Hammerling's list of nine names is dominated by tobacco magnates. He told Paderewski that $50,000 was assured.

142. Ibid.

143. Hammerling claimed to "despise" the Germans, who regarded him as an ardent Pole; see Statement, 35.

144. In all the testimony of Hammerling, and it is voluminous, he once mentioned Paderewski, but only fleetingly: "Mr. Paderewski will tell you . . ." See Statement, 36.

145. In this regard see the scathing, unpublished work—probably by Tytus Filipowicz—"Kim jest Pan Jan Marjan Horodyski," n.d., in Materiay po Tytusie Filipowiczu, Biblioteka, SGH, Zbiory Specjalne, box 62, file 1; cf. Artur Hausner, "Sprawozdanie," Archiwum NKN, Archiwum Państwowe Krakowa i województwa krakowskiego, file 19, 32–33.

6: DREAMS AND RUIN

1. Statement, 9.

2. A report from the APL (American Protective League) puts the date at December 1916–January 1917); see Propagandist, 1.

3. "No German Advertising," *New York Times*, July 30, 1918. These were apparently the Collin Armstrong Advertising Agency, and possibly the Presbrey Advertising Agency. See Propagandist, 1–2.

4. See Van Patten statement, 1; cf. *Brewing and Liquor Interests*, 1:636ff.

5. Propagandist, 1–2.

6. The Van Patten statement says July; the Propagandist memorandum claims June.

7. *Brewing and Liquor Interests*, 1:638.

8. Van Patten statement, 2. In 1932, the British claimed that the Hamburg-America Line had been involved in a "secret service" for Germany since 1914; see H. H. Martin, "Memorandum," June 7, 1932, RG 76, International Claims Commission, box 121.

9. Propagandist, 1.

10. Van Patten statement, 2.

11. Ibid., 3.

12. Propagandist, 1.

13. Ibid., 2.

14. *Brewing and Liquor Interests*, 1:610.

15. See, for example, Hammerling to "publisher," April 24, 1917; Herbert S. Houston to Hammerling, April 24, 1917; Record Group 63 (hereafter RG 63), Records of the Committee on Public Information (hereafter CPI), box 1, USNA.

16. Hammerling to Tumulty [for Wilson], October 21, 1917, Wilson Papers.

17. Wilson to Tumulty (1917), Wilson Papers.

18. Ibid.; McCormick to NN, October 23, 1917, Wilson Papers.

19. "Few German Papers Outspokenly Loyal," *New York Times*, August 20, 1917, 4. Smulski was still convinced that Hammerling had enough influence in Congress to gain equipment for the Polish Army being raised in the United States; Paderewski's pet project. Whether Hammerling took any action in this area is unknown; see Papiery Gąsiorowski, folder 15237/III, Ossolineum, Wrocław.

20. The "Foreign Language Division" of the Liberty Loan Committee, which was organized by Hammerling, was very successful. See Charles H. Schweppe to Hammerling, November 28, 1917, *American Leader* 12 (December 13, 1917): 661.

21. For this list, much abbreviated here, see Hammerling to NN, March 13, 1918, RG 165, folder 10175–110, USNA. The Liberty Loan people were very pleased with Hammerling's work; see Wilbur D. Nesbit to Hammerling, May 8, 1918, RG 165, folder 10175–110, USNA.

22. Hammerling to Byoir, January 7, 1918, RG 165, folder 10175–110, USNA.

23. "Foreign Language Editors Pay Tribute to President," *Official Bulletin*, June 6, 1918, 18.

24. Hammerling to Byoir, May 27, 1918, RG 165, folder 10175–110, USNA.

25. Hammerling to Byoir, February 4, 1918, RG 165, folder 10175–110, USNA. Major U. S. R. [*sic*] to Chief, Military Intelligence Section, February 7, 1918, RG 165, folder 10175–110, USNA. Hammerling became chairman of the Division of Advertising of the CPI. Curiously, he suggested the CPI retain William H. Rankin, a man rumored to have written the infamous Appeal; see Hammerling to Byoir, January 30, 1918, RG 165, folder 10175–110, USNA.

26. "Moves to declare Hammerling an Alien," *New York Times*, January 22, 1919, part 2, 4.

27. "Hold Hammerling on Charge of Libel."

28. Zotti would send materials to Kruszka who would then publish them in the Polish language press; see Kruszka to Zotti, March 28, 1918, RG 165, folder 10175–110, USNA.

29. See, for example, Hammerling to Byoir, April 8, 1918, RG 63, Records of the CPI, box 2, folder 6, USNA.

30. Wazeter deposition, March 11, 1918, RG 165, folder 10175–110, USNA.

31. *New York World*, January 31 and February 8, 1918.

32. Rather than attribute each charge, we shall list the sources of the majority of the accusations: "Impenitent Camouflage," *Il Cittadino*, April 4, 1918; the details of Hammerling's financial manipulations with his clients is detailed in E. H. Jaudon to Zotti, February 8, 1918, RG 165, folder 10175–110, USNA; cf. "Hammerling Exposed," citing Zotti, and "Hammerling to the Stand!"; "Some More of Hammerling's Dirty Work"; "Answer, Mr. Hammerling"; "Hammerling, Author and Great American Patriot?" *Národni List*, February 8, March 21, and May 19, 1918, all on the first page.

33. "$250,000 suit for libel begun by Hammerling," *New-York Commercial Advertiser*, May 7, 1918, 1. The article was written, purportedly, by Hammerling.

34. The *locus classicus* of this is Leon Wazeter to [District Attorney] Edward Swann, April 26, 1918, RG 165, folder 10175–110, USNA.

35. Byoir to Colonel Van Deman (MID), [1918], RG 165, folder 10175–110, USNA.

36. Churchill to Creel, July 26, 1918, RG 63, box 1, USNA; H. A. Taylor to Creel, March 2, 1918, RG 165, folder 10175–110, USNA.

37. M. I. 5. B.L. rev. vol., nos. 1–1857, RG 165, folder 9140–815/1, nos. 698, 208, USNA.

38. This is a very important document concerning Hammerling; see the undated "Memorandum for Mr. Creel," RG 165, folder 10175–110, 2, USNA.

39. Ibid., 1–2.

40. Gabryel affidavit, 1–2.

41. It seems clear that Hammerling sent former President Roosevelt the damning letters written about him by Zotti and Kruszka. They are in Roosevelt's correspondence; unfortunately a covering letter from Hammerling to Roosevelt is not there; see Zotti to Hammerling, April 3, 1918, and Kruszka to Zotti, March 26, 1918, Roosevelt Papers, reel 270. It was about this time that the Secret Service was also charged with investigating Hammerling; see Walter Mearsday to Attorney General, March 15, 1918, Wilson Papers.

42. White examination, 3.

43. Ibid., 4.

44. MID (New York) to MID (Washington), June 5, 1918, RG 165, folder 10175-231, USNA.

45. Document titled "Hammerling," n.d., RG 165, folder 10175-110, USNA.

46. A valuable brief synopsis of the Becker investigation is "Teuton Propaganda Paid for by Rumely," *New York Times*, July 29, 1918, 18. Bolo's involvement with French efforts for a separate peace is very complicated, and takes us far afield.

47. *Brewing and Liquor Interests*, 2:2039ff.; 2104.

48. Memorandum for Colonel Churchill, August 5, 1918, RG 165, folder 10175-110, USNA; cf. the earlier British warning in British List 698, February 2, 1916, RG 165, folder 9140-815, USNA.

49. NN to Colonel Van Deman, March 13, 1918, RG 165, folder 10175-110, USNA.

50. Biddle to Chief, MID, April 20, 1918, RG 165, folder 10175-110, USNA.

51. "Statement by Louis M. Hammerling," August 12, 1918, RG 165, folder 10175-110, USNA; enclosed in Hammerling to Byoir, August 12, 1918. Hammerling characterized himself as the victim of people trying to "put 'mud' on me."

52. Chief, MID, to Biddle, March 21, 1918; Uterhart to Van Dusen, May 15, 1918; "Memorandum for Lieut. Van Dusen," June 18, 1918; Van Dusen to Uterhart, June 13 and 18, 1918, RG 165, folder 10175-110, USNA.

53. Adee to Attorney General, 1919, General Records of the Department of State, RG 59, 860c.00/38, USNA. Division of Passport Control to NN, January 17, 1919, RG 59, 860c.00/37, USNA; Nicholas Biddle, MID, to Director, MID, August 6, 1918, RG 165, folder 10175-110-39, USNA.

54. Byoir to Hammerling, September 6, 1918, RG 63, box 2, folder 6, USNA.

55. Hipolit Gliwic to Minister in Washington, June 8, 1923, Ambasada RP w Waszyngtonie, AAN, Warsaw, folder 2596, 35-36; cf. White's interrogation of Dattner, n.d., RG 165, folder 10175-110, USNA.

56. "Gather data here for Senate Inquiry," *New York Times*, November 29, 1918, 7.

57. "Austria's Crime," *American Leader* 12 (December 13, 1917): 651-53; *Brewing and Liquor Interests*, 1:626-27.

58. MID (New York) to Director, MID, December 5, 1918, RG 165, folder 10175-110, USNA. Hammerling denied to the Senate that he apologized for the article; see *Brewing and Liquor Interests*, 1:600-601.

59. *Brewing and Liquor Interests*, 1:23-25; "Admits Campaign to Stop Munitions," *New York Times*, December 4, 1918, 11; "Admits Dernburg tried to buy Paper," *New York Times*, December 5, 1918, 22.

60. "Seek Hammerling Cash," *New York Times*, February 28, 1920.

61. "Hammerling Resigns," *New York Times*, March 5, 1919, 18.

62. Hammerling to Paderewski, November 22, 1918, Archiwum Paderewskiego, AAN, folder 621, 259-60.

63. Górski referred to Hammerling's having "induced him to become President"; see "Paderewski's Stepson Sues," *New York Times*, March 18, 1920, part II, 4.

64. Namier, *Namier*, 148–49.

65. Górski to Mme. Paderewska, May 19, 1919, Archiwum Paderewskiego, folder 991, 4–5.

66. Ibid., 4.

67. See Górski to Mme. Paderewska, July 9, 1919, Archiwum Paderewskiego, folder 991, 18–19.

68. Górski to Paderewski, July 16, 1919, Archiwum Paderewskiego, folder 991, 23–25.

69. Kley to Mme. Paderewska, August 18, 1919, Archiwum Paderewskiego, folder 992, 14. The Paderewski government's history of foreign purchases for the military is quite unbelievable. See Skarzyński to Paderewski, August 19, 1919, Archiwum Paderewskiego, folder 698, 73.

70. W. I. Shuman to Ciechanowski, October 23, 1919, Archiwum Paderewskiego, t. 988. 64, AAN.

71. It is worth remembering that in Poland Hammerling was regarded as being in Mme. Paderewska's circle, not the maestro's. See for example "Inicjator obecnego gabinetu," 2.

72. Harrison to Winslow, September 19, 1919, RG 59, doc. 862.20211/163, USNA; Zotti to Tumulty, October 20, 1919, Wilson Papers.

73. This at least is Górski's recollection; see "Paderewski's Stepson Sues," *New York Times*, March 18, 1920, part 2, 4.

74. Statement, 34.

75. "His Bride a Countess," *New York Times*, February 26, 1915, 9.

76. Hugh S. Gibson to Secretary of State, November 18, 1919, RG 59, 862.20211/1618, USNA; Alvey A. Adee to Attorney General, December 27, 1919, RG 59, 860c.00/38, USNA.

77. "Seek Hammerling Cash," *New York Times*, February 28, 1919.

78. "Paderewski's Stepson Sues."

7: THE SENATOR FROM HONOLULU

1. Gibson to Secretary of State, April 19, 1922, RG 59, 860c.00/182, USNA.

2. Gibson to Secretary of State, November 25, 1919, RG 59, 860c.00/38, USNA.

3. Jan Madejczyk, *Wspomnienia* (Warsaw: Ludowa Spółdzielnia Wydawnicza, 1965), 152.

4. Wincenty Witos, "Moje otoczenie," Ossolineum, Wrocław, collection 15344/II, 21–22.

5. *Jana Drohojowskiego Wspomnienia dyplomatyczne* (Warsaw: Państwowy Instytut Wydawniczy, 1959), 22.

6. Aleksander Bogusławski, "Wspomnienia," (1922–1929), P-33/IV, vol. 4, (Warsaw: Zakład historii ruchu ludowego [ZHRL]).

7. Madejczyk, another Piast leader, has disparaging remarks about Hammerling: "he looked like an American." See Madejczyk, *Wspomnienia*, 152.

8. Karczewski and Szaflik, *Witos*, 555.

9. Jerzy Holzer, *Mozaika polityczna Drugiej Rzeczypospolitej* (Warsaw: Książka i Wiedza, 1974), 156–57. Piast leftist opponents were well aware of Piast's ambitious plans; see Jan Smola, "Różne partje polityczne a Wyzwolenie" (Warsaw, September 1927), s. 19, 47–48; an unpublished pamphlet in PSL-Wyzwolenie, ZHRL.

10. The primary literature on Piast's political plans is quite considerable. In rough order of importance we may cite: "Protokół z XIII posiedzenia Oddziału organizacyjnego," July 12, 1919; "Posiedzenia Zarządu PSL," September 29, 1919; "Protokół z XIX posiedzenia Oddziału organizacyjnego," November 17, 1919; "Protokół z posiedzenia Zarządu okręgowego PSL," January 20, 1923; all in PSL-Piast, s. 13; Zofia Dąbska, "Pamiętniki, 1912–1927," s. P-225, 79, ZHRL. Specifically regarding the need for a PSL-Piast press network see Andrzej Bogusławski, "Wspomnienia," s. P189/IIb t.III, ZHRL, 194–95.

11. "Raport Biura prasowego z dnia 29 I 30 czerwca 1920," Ambasada w Waszyngtonie, AAN, folder 1137, 1. While Andrzej Waleron supports this argument, it is rejected by Stanisław Lato who argues that Hammerling only contributed money for the election in one district, Stanisławów. Thus the argument remains open, but all admit the fact that Hammerling made cash contributions to Piasts's election efforts, and it is their extent that is at issue; see Stanisław Lato, *Ruch Ludowy a Centrolew* (Warsaw: Ludowa Spółdzielnia Wydawnicza, 1965), 74n.

12. Andrzej Zakrzewski, *Wincenty Witos: Chłopski polityk i mąż stanu* (Warsaw: Ludowa Spółdzielnia Wydawnicza, 1977), 311.

13. "Sukces PSL w Małopolsce," *Dziennik Narodowy* [Piotrków], November 9, 1922, 1.

14. "Pamiętniki W. Witosa oraz suplementy," a subfile of his "Pamiętniki," s. 7, ZHRL, 19, 24.

15. Wincenty Witos, *Moje Wspomnienia*, vol. 3 (Paris: Instytut Literacki, 1965), 27. Witos's reflections on Bryl were absolutely vile, even if deserved: it was characteristic of him. For Hammerling's ability to buy a seat see Andrzej Zakrzewski, in his edited collection *Sejmy Drugiej Rzeczypospolitej* (Warsaw: Ludowa Spółdzielnia Wydawnicza, 1990), 194. Bryl apparently borrowed $5,000 from Hammerling for his own campaign; see the poster "Czy tacy mogą być naszymi przywodcami," PSL-Piast, s. 7, ZHRL.

16. A viciously anti-Semitic paper, *Głos*, published a nasty but insightful article, "Feine Kepele der Louis Nuchim Hammerling," which discussed his position in Piast politics in eastern Galicia in a convincing manner. See the issue for June 16, 1923.

17. See, e.g., "W ostatnich czasach," *Telegram* [Buffalo], April 27, 1923; "Raport biura prasowego z dnia 29 I 30 czerwca 1920," report from *Kuryer Narodowy* (New York).

18. "Protokół z nadzwyczajnego pelnego posiedzenia Zarządu Okręgu PSL," May 15, 1922, 71–76, ZHRL. See also Witos's comments in "Protokół z posiedzenia Ludowych Rad Powiatowych," August 5, 1922, 78, ZHRL.

19. Wincenty Witos, "Moje otoczenie," Ossolineum, collection 15344/II, 21.

20. Jan Dębski, "Wspomnienia z lat 1889–1973," vol. 2, collection 15354/II Ossolineum, 307.

21. "Z Pamiętników Jakuba Bojki," s. P-6, ZHRL, 13.

22. *Senat Rzeczypospolitej Polskiej. Okres I. Sprawozdanie Stenograficzne z 18 po-siedzenia Senata Rzeczypospolitej z dnia 19 kwietnia 1923r.* (Warsaw: Senat RP, 1923), 22–26; *Senat Rzeczypospolitej Polskiej. Okres I. Sprawozdanie Stenograficzne z 23 posiedze-nia Senata Rzeczypospolitej z dnia 15 czerwca 1923r.* (Warsaw: Senat RP, 1923), 52–53.

23. This discussion of Hammerling by Witos does not appear in the published version of his memoirs [*Wspomnienia,* q.v.], but can be found in the original unedited typescript entitled "Działalność polityczna w latach 1919–1926," Ossolineum, Collection 13153/II, vol. 4, 22–23.

24. Drohojów is near the present Ukrainian border on the Polish side. It was in Austrian Galicia when Hammerling was born and within Poland when Hammerling was in the Senate. Lanckorona, the site of Hammerling's estate, was farther to the west, near Kraków as was Kalwaria Zebrzydowska and Brody. Stanisławów, the district he represented in the Senate, was the town farthest to the east. The Lanckorona estate was situated between Kalwaria Zebrzydowska and Lanckorona. All were historically Polish towns.

25. It is unclear whether this is the property he purchased in 1911 or another he acquired after returning to Poland. Most likely it is the former.

26. Bryl was in Hammerling's pay by this time; Witold Stankiewicz to author, January 8, 1996, 1–2.

27. See the handbill "Polskie Stronnictwo Ludowe-Wyzwolenie: Wielki Zjazd Chłopski," October 23, 1923, PSL-Wyzwolenie, s. 9, ZHRL.

28. De L. Boal, to Secretary of State, February 6, 1925, RG 59, 860c.00/275, USNA.

29. Witold Stankiewicz, "Pakt Lanckoroński," *Roczniki dziejowa ruchu ludowego,* vol. 1 (1959), 196–216. For a brief statement of the former view, see Tadeusz Ręk, *Chjeno-Piast, 1922–1926: W świetle obrad sejmu i senatu* (Warsaw: Ludowa Spółdzielnia Wydawnicza, 1955), 26, 68.

30. Lato, *Ruch Ludowy,* 79.

31. Tadeusz Ręk, "Lekcja historii," *Dziennik Ludowy,* June 15, 1947, 3. This version is repeated in the memoirs of the populist leader Bogusławki, "Wspomnienia," 44–45.

32. "Działalność polityczna," 267–68.

33. "Moje otoczenie," 22–23.

34. See the anonymous pamphlet "Poseł Wincenty Witos w odpowiedzi na 'man-ifest' senator Jakoba Bojki," n.d. (probably 1927), Piast, zespół 108/II, microfilm AC KC PZPR, AAN. Hammerling's vital role was the opinion of the American Minister, Alfred J. Pearson: see his dispatch of February 6, 1925, RG 59, 860c.00/275, USNA.

35. See Witos, "Pamiętniki," AHRL, 220, 316. This original unpublished ver-sion was utilized instead of the slightly later published version. Cf. Zygmunt Lasocki, "Z lat niedoli Wincentego Witosa," s. 21, 66, ZHRL.

36. Jan Dębski, ed., *Maciej Rataj. Pamiętniki* (Warsaw: Ludowa Spółdzielnia Wydawnicza, 1965), 154, 157.

37. Witold Stankiewicz to author, January 8, 1996.

38. Lechicki, "Hammerling," 264; Drohojowski, *Wspomnienia,* 22. Hammerling is referred to as the "midwife" (akuszerka), of the pact.

39. Dębski, "Wspomnienia," 307–12. Cf. Gibson to Secretary of State, April 19, 1922, RG 59, 860c.00/182.

40. For the published version of the April 3, 1923, meeting, see Rataj: Pamiętniki, 161, but the older unpublished version mentioning a meeting the same day at Hammerling's home is in "Pamiętniki M. Rataja, 1920–1923," s. 12, 188, Zbiór Macieja Rataj, ZHRL.

41. Witos blamed the left for inventing the whole manufactured scandal of the Lanckorona Pact and denounced them bitterly for their "unprecedented campaign" against him. Of course he also blamed leftist elements within Piast for causing the destruction of the coalition; this latter charge is extremely vague. See his "Pamiętniki: suplementy," 25, 31.

42. "Obywatele!" Piast-Wyzwolenie broadside in PSL-Wyzwolenie, ZHRL, s. 19; see also the remarks by Kiernik in "Tzw. Układ większości parlamentarnej w r. 1923," Archiwum Władysław Kiernika, s. 59, ZHRL, 12–17.

43. See "T.H.," "We własnym dole," Głos, June 16, 1923, 2–4.

44. This characterization of 1923 is by the then Treasury Minister, Jerzy Michalski; see Jerzy Michalski, "Pamiętniki," collection 9820.III, Biblioteka Uniwersyteu Jagiellońskiego [BUJ], Kraków.

45. "Działalność polityczna," 271.

46. Witos, "Pamiętniki," 328, ZHRL.

47. Witos later noted that he was surprised that a man with such early talent would show himself to be so incompetent at the national level; see Wincenty Witos, "Pamiętniki," Cz. II., 112, ZHRL.

48. A reliable brief account of Kucharski's path to power is Zbigniew Landau, "Kucharski, Władysław," in Polski Słownik Biograficzny, vol. 41 (1971), 54–57. For Żyrardów see the printed investigation by the parliament entitled "Wniosek," Archiwum Moraczewskich. Collection 71/1–42, microfilm 2314/4, pages 1–3, AAN; Klaudiusz Hrabyk, "Z drugiej strony barykady. Wspomnienia i dzienniki," vol. 2, collection 15352/II, Ossolineum, 306–7. A pro-Kucharski account is Akta Stanisława Rymara (hereafter Rymar), container 5, AAN, 41–42.

49. See the handbill "Co robili piastowcy w Sejmie?" PSL Wyzwolenia, ZHRL, s. 19.

50. Pierre de L. Boal to Secretary of State, September 21, 1923, RG 59, 860c.00/200, USNA.

51. Ibid.

52. "Wśród ciężkich problemów kryzysu państwowego," Kurjer Poranny, October 12, 1923, 2; Landau, "Kucharski," 56.

53. "Działalność polityczna," 271–72. Of course at other times Hammerling was discovered discussing finances with Mrs. Hammerling, Witos, "Pamiętniki," 328.

54. Ibid.

55. One keen observer, Gen. Władysław Sikorski, regarded the Kucharski negotiations in Paris as very important for Poland. This was thus no mere gambit for Kucharski and Hammerling; see Sikorski to Józef H. Retinger, August 23, 1923, Retinger Papers, kol. 68, Polish Institute and Sikorski Museum, London.

56. Juliusz Zdanowski, "Dziennik," vol. 5, collection 14023.II, Ossolineum; Henryk Dzendzel, "U boku premiera Wincentego Witosa," in *Wspomnienia weteranów ruchu ludowego* (Warsaw: Ludowa Spółdzielnia Wydawnicza, 1968), 99.

57. De L. Boal to Secretary of State, September 20, 1923, RG 59, 860c.00/205, USNA.

58. NN to NN, September 30, 1923, folder 68/9 labeled "Dr. Józef Retinger," and Retinger to MSZ, February 15, 1923; folder 68/7 labeled Korrespondencja z W. Witosem both in the Józef Retinger Papers.

59. De L. Boal to Secretary of State, August 23, 1923, RG 59, 860c.00/200, USNA.

60. Neal Pease, *Poland, the United States and the Stabilization of Europe, 1919–1933* (New York: Oxford University Press, 1986), 17.

61. "Działalność polityczna," 271–72.

62. *Senat Rzeczypospolitej Polskiej. Okres I. Sprawozdanie Stenograficzne z 33 posiedzenia Senata Rzeczypospolitej z dnia 10 października 1923r.* (Warsaw: Senat RP, 1923).

63. De L. Boal to Secretary of State, September 6, 1923, RG 59, 860c.00/202, USNA.

64. De L. Boal to Secretary of State, September 13, 1923, RG 59, 860c.23/204, USNA.

65. See, for example, Pease, *Stabilization of Europe*, 55, 57.

66. This memorandum is found in the Dwight Morrow Papers at Amherst College (box 38, folder 104); it is not signed, but circumstantial evidence suggests it was the work of Morrow. The addressee is listed only as "Norman," but given Morrow's financial involvements, I have assumed it is Montagu Norman, governor of the Bank of England.

67. "Obywatele!" Piast-Wyzwolenie broadside in PSL-Wyzwolenie, February 15, 1921, ZHRL, s. 19; Witos, "Pamiętniki," s. 8, 328.

68. Ibid., 119.

69. Quoted in Zygmunt Hemmerling, *PSL "Wyzwolenie" w parlamentach II Rzeczypospolitej, 1919–1931* (Warsaw: Uniwersytet Warszawski, 1990), 181.

70. De L. Boal to Secretary of State, September 27, 1923; November 15, November 22, December 6, December 13, RG 59, 860c.00/206/207/214/215/218/219, USNA; Gibson to Secretary of State, October 4, October 11, October 18, November 1, November 15, RG 59, 860c.00/27/208/209/212, USNA. Kucharski, almost universally regarded as incompetent, was able to hold his position solely due to the support of Dmowski, who had enormous influence on the political right. The irony, of course, is that Kucharski's two closest supporters were an anti-Semite and a Jew.

71. "Dalszy ciąg historji życia i czynów 'senatora z Honolulu,'" *Kurjer Poranny*, October 21, 1923, 3.

72. The first installment, titled "Inicjator obecnego gabinetu i 'lewa ręka' obecnego Ministra Skarbu," appeared on October 19; part two was the next day and bore the title "Dalszy ciąg historji życia i czynów 'senatora z Honolulu.'"

73. See, for example, "Rząd osiemkowo-piastowy w świetle faktów: do dymisji, do dymisji, do dymisji!!!" *Kurjer Poranny*, October 18, 1923, 3.

74. Kurjer was leftist and Piłsudskiite, a strong opponent of the Chjeno-Piast coalition of Lanckorona.

75. "Inicjator," 2.

76. Ibid., 2–3.

77. "Lanckorońska konstytucja," *Kurjer Poranny*, October 27, 1923, 2; cf. "Konfederacja Lanckorońska w walce o ustrój państwa," *Kurjer Poranny*, December 6, 1923, 2; "Senator Hammerling z Honolulu i niedoszły kanclerz," *Kurjer Poranny*, November 28, 1923, 2.

78. "Dalszy ciąg," *Kurjer Poranny*, October 23, 1923, 2; "Ojd ło owdo," *Kurjer Poranny*, December 4, 1923, 3.

79. "Inicjator," 2.

80. "Ojd ło owdo."

81. *Kurjer Poranny*, October 23, 1923

82. "Dalszy ciąg," October 21, 1923, 3.

83. He even organized an Easter Party for Chjeno-Piast; "Ciąg dalszy," *Kurjer Poranny*, October 23, 1923.

84. "Ciąg dalszy," October 27, 1923, 3.

85. The *Kurjer* repeated the claim that his wife was a countess (hrabianka Zofia de Brzezicka)—perhaps sarcastically. It also noted that Rumely was at their wedding, a curious aside; see "Ciąg dalszy," October 23, 1923.

86. "Dokumenty do historji życia I działań senator z Honolulu," *Kurjer Poranny*, November 1, 1923, 3.

87. "Dokumenty," *Kurjer Warszawski*, November 6, 1923, 4.

88. "Dobra Louisa N. Hammerlinga," *Kurjer Poranny*, November 4, 1923, 3.

89. "Kanclerz Albert i senator Hammerling," *Kurjer Poranny*, November 27, 1923, 3.

90. "Życie politycznie"; "Senator Hammerling pod sądem Marszałkiem," *Kurjer Poranny*, December 6, 1923, 3; "Minister sprawiedliwości zwołuje senaci sąd honorowy w sprawie Hammerlinga," *Kurjer Poranny*, December 2, 1923, 4.

91. "Minister sprawiedliwości."

92. Rymar, 44; De L. Boal to Secretary of State, December 13, 1923, RG 59, 860c.00/219, USNA.

93. "Dyplom 'niepozbawionia' czci Luisa [*sic*] N. Hammerlingu," *Kurjer Poranny*, December 22, 1923, 2.

94. "W klubach sejmowych," *Kurjer Polski*, April 2, 1924, 2; Lechicki, "Hammerling," 264.

95. "Alien Divorce to Go Before High Court," *New York Times*, April 4, 1922, 21.

96. "First Wife Would Alter Divorce Plea," *New York Times*, August 17, 1922, 16.

97. "Rabbinical Divorce Upheld in Suit Here," *New York Times*, March 18, 1924.

98. Whether Grabski approved of this notion is unanswerable.

99. Pease, *Poland, the United States*, 24.

100. As for the rumored Witos-Hammerling mission see Ministry of Foreign Affairs to Mission in Washington, February 15, February 29, and March 18, 1924; Ambasada w Waszyngtonie, folders 1234 and 1235.

101. See *Senat Rzeczypospolitej Polskiej. Okres I. Sprawozdanie Stenograficzne z 67 posiedzenia Senata Rzeczypospolitej z dnia 24 lipca 1924r* (Warsaw: Senat RP, 1924), 94–98.

102. Senator Aleksander Adelman was, like Hammerling, in his first term in the Senate.

103. These remarks are summarized from *Senat Rzeczypospolitej Polskiej. Okres I. Sprawozdanie Stenograficzne z 67 posiedzenia Senata Rzeczypospolitej z dnia 24 lipca 1924r* (Warsaw: Senat RP, 1924), 94–98.

104. Ibid.

8: THE LAST CHAPTER: AMERICA AGAIN

1. "Overman asks facts on Hammerling Case," *New York Times*, February 24, 1924, 5.

2. Ibid.

3. Alvey A. Adee to Attorney General [1919], RG 59, 860c.00/38, USNA.

4. Hammerling sued on his Citizenship," *New York Times*, March 19, 1924, 10.

5. "Hammerling won't Fight," *New York Times*, March 20, 1924.

6. See the notation in red across Hammerling's Naturalization Papers, "Naturalization Docket, 1897–1906.

7. Hammerling to Franciszek Fronczak, February 19, 1926, Frances E. Fronczak Papers [hereafter Fronczak Papers], Buffalo and Erie County Historical Society, box 42.

8. Fronczak to Hammerling, February 20, 1926, Fronczak Papers, box 42.

9. See the postal card showing the building and local dignitaries gathered round it; Hammerling to Fronczak, December 22, 1926, Fronczak Papers, box 42.

10. "Jak zginął Senator Hammerling?" May 1, 1935, *Illustrowany Kurier Codzienny*, 6.

11. "Wystąpienie senator Overmana przeciw Ludwikowi Hammerlingowi," *Ameryka-Echo* [Buffalo], August 4, 1929, 1.

12. Ibid.

13. "Hammerling Plans New Citizenship Plea"; "Replies on Hammerling"; *New York Times*, July 24 and 27, 1929, 14, 4.

14. "Hammerling Funeral Today," *New York Times*, April 30, 1935, 17.

15. "200 Room Hotel Sold on Lexington Avenue," *New York Times*, February 10, 1934.

16. There is a very laudatory entry on Cayce at http://soli.inav.net/~ecprod/edgar.htm. Accessed August 4, 1999.

17. "Reading 900–409," October 6, 1928, http://astrologer.ru/EdgarCayce/readings/0900–409. Accessed August 4, 1999.

18. "Improvement in trading Reported in the Lexington Avenue District," *New York Times*, March 11, 1934, 1; "200 Room Hotel Sold on Lexington Avenue."

19. Fronczak to Hammerling, January 26, 1935, Fronczak Papers, box 42.

20. "Jak zginął Senator Hammerling?" May 1, 1935, *Illustrowany Kurier Codzienny*, 6.

21. Victoria Hammerling Rosenberg to author, January 22, 2014.

22. Ibid. 23. "18-story fall kills Louis N. Hammerling," *New York Times*, April 28, 1935, 2.

24. Ibid. Hammerling's relationship with Pershing cannot be reconstructed. Shortly before his death, Hammerling was among those paying public tribute to the general; see "Pershing's Tribute Tells of Sorrow," *New York Times*, April 11, 1935, 18.

25. "Estates Appraised," *New York Times*, March 17, 1936, 44.

26. Hammerling's granddaughter Victoria Rosenberg suggests that Hammerling may have purchased the property for his son James, a purchase he had promised. This would account for a considerable amount of money. See Victoria Rosenberg to author, January 22, 2014. There is also a family story, probably true, that Hammerling's heirs squandered his monies. See ibid.

27. "Certificate of Death," 1. Whether Hammerling died by accident or by suicide is still being debated in his family generations later; see Victoria Rosenberg to author, February 6, 2014.

28. St. Casimir's Church, 40 Greene St., Brooklyn; see "Hammerling," in the obituary column of the *New York Times*, April 30, 1935, 17.

29. Joseph Giulietti to author, July 13, 2004, and author's personal observations at Calvary Cemetery in Woodside, NY.

30. See "Portret Zofii z Brzezickich Hammerlingowej (1924)," in Kazimierz Olszański, *Wojciech Kossak* (Wrocław: Ossolineum, 1976), illustration 193.

31. Ironically, it was the site of a German concentration camp during the war.

32. For her will see "Testament Zofii Janiny z Brzezickich Hammerling, 1945," in Różne sprawy procesowe prowadzone przez Jana Gwiazdomorskiego. H, Zofia (1945), Archiwum PAN w Krakowie, Kraków.

CONCLUSIONS

1. Mieczysław Szerer, "Szlakami propagandy," *Pregląd dyplomatyczny*, vol. 3 (September-October 1921), 473.

2. Park, *Immigrant Press*, 405–6.

3. See the discussion in Jan Dębski, "Wspomnienia," Ossolineum, vol. 2; vol. 4.

4. See, for example, "Pierwsza kampania o nową pozyczkę wolnościowa podjęta przez prasę obcojęzyczną," *Dziennik Narodowy*, September 26, 1917. Hammerling published Smulski material in the *American Leader*; see FO 371–2450, NA. Smulski was convinced that Hammerling was so influential with Senator Penroes and such a Polish patriot that he would use his connections to get military supplies for any Polish army raised in the United States; see Papiery Gąsiorowskiego, 15237/III, Ossolineum.

5. Dębski contends that Hammerling so successfully denied his being a Jew while in the US that Dmowski did not suspect it. This strains credulity as the political right noted that Hammerling was of Jewish origin, and many of his Piast allies mention it in their recollections; see Dębski, "Wspomnienia," vol. 2, 326–27.

6. Szerer, "Szlakami," 473. Szerer referred to Hammerling's nationality as "complicated."

BIBLIOGRAPHY

PRIMARY SOURCES
Archival Sources

Austria
Vienna
Haus-, Hof- und Staatsarchiv, Österreichisches Staatsarchiv
Liasse Krieg 7b, USA 1915-1916.
Canada
Public Archives of Canada
Sir George H. Perley Papers, MG 27 II D 12.
Poland
Kraków
Archiwum PAN w Krakowie
"Testament Zofii Janiny z Brzezickich Hammerling, 1945," in
Różne sprawy procesowe prowadzone przez Jana Gwiazdomor-
skiego, 1945.
Biblioteka Uniwersyteu Jagiellońskiego
Jerzy Michalski, "Pamiętniki." Collection 9820.III.
Warsaw
Archiwum Akt Nowych
Akta Stanisława Rymara.
Ambasada w Waszyngtonie.
Archiwum Ignacego Paderewskiego.
Archiwum Moraczewskich. Collection 71/1-42.
Piast, zespół 108/II, microfilm AC KC PZPR.
Zakład Historii Ruchu Ludowego
Aleksander Bogusławski, Wspomnienia. Nom IV, 1922-29.
Zofia Dąbska, Pamiętniki, 1912-1927.
Archiwum Władysław Kiernika.
Działalność parlementarna posłów ludowych w sejmie, 1922–1926
Władysław Ostrowski, Drugi Sejm, 1922–1927.
Władysław Ostrowski, Fragment o sejmie.
Władysław Ostrowski, Pamiętniki: Wincenty Witos.
Pamiętniki Wincentego Witosa.
Pluta, Andrzej. Wspomnienia, Zeszyt V.
PSL-Piast.
PSL-Wyzwolenia.
Z Pamiętniki Jakuba Bojki.
Zbiory S. J. Brzezińskiego.

Zbiór Macieja Rataja.

Romuald Wasilewski, Wspomnienia o Andrzeje Bogusławskim.

Ulotki.

Zbiór Wincentego Witosa.

Wrocław

Ossolineum

Jan Dębski, "Wspomnienia z lat 1889-1973." Vol. 2, collection
15354.

Papiery Gąsiorowskiego.

Wincenty Witos, "Działalność polityczna w latach 1919-1926. Vol.
2, collection 13153, folder 4.

Wincenty Witos, "Moje otoczenie."

Juliusz Zdanowski, "Dziennik." Vol. 5, collection 14023.II.

United Kingdom

Kew Gardens

National Archives

Foreign Office 115: General Correspondence: News.

Foreign Office 371: Foreign Office: General Correspondence.

London

Sikorski Institute

Józef Retinger Papers.

United States

Amherst, MA

Amherst College

Dwight W. Morrow Papers.

Bloomington, IN

Lilly Library, Indiana University at Bloomington

E. A. Rumely Collection.

Buffalo, NY

Buffalo and Erie County Historical Society, box 42.

Frances E. Fronczak Papers.

Cambridge. MA

Harvard University, Houghton Library

William Phillips Papers.

Cincinnati, OH

Jacob Rader Marcus Center of the American Jewish Archives

Louis Marshall Papers.

College Park, MD

United States National Archives

Record Group 43: Records of United States Participation in International Conferences, Commissions, and Expositions.

Record Group 59: General Records of the Department of State.

Record Group 59: Office of the Counselor/Under Secretary and
the Chief Special Agent. Central File 1917-1927.

Record Group 63: Records of the Committee on Public Information.

Record Group 65: General Records of the Department of Justice.

Record Group 76: International Claims Commission.

Record Group 85: Immigration and Naturalization Service.

Record Group 165: Administrative Files of the War Department, Military Intelligence Division (MID).

Record Group 261: Records of the Russian Consulates.

Harrisburg, PA
  Pennsylvania State Archives
    Martin E. Olmsted Papers.
    Samuel W. Pennypacker Papers.

Hazelton, PA
  Hazelton Public Library
    Newsbooks: Newspaper History of Pennsylvania: Anthracite Coal Strike, 1900.

New Haven, CT
  Yale University, Sterling Library
    Charles Hilles Papers.
    Colonel Edward M. House Papers.
    Charles Nagel Papers.
    Frank L. Polk Papers.

New York City, NY
  Ellis Island
    Passenger Records.
  Joseph Piłsudski Institute of America.
    Akta Adiutantury Generalnej Naczelnego Dowództwa, 1918–1922.
  New York City Department of Records: Municipal Archives.
  Polish Institute of Arts and Sciences in America
    Polish-American Relief Committee in New York.

Poughkeepsie, NY
  Dutchess County Clerk's Office.

Princeton, NJ
  Mudd Library, Princeton University
    Robert Lansing Papers.

Scranton, PA
  Lackawanna Historical Society
    Galicia.

State College, PA
  Penn State Special Collections Library: Historical and Labor Archives
    Michael J. Kosik Collection.

Washington, DC
  Catholic University of America: Archives
    John Mitchell Papers.

Library of Congress
  George B. Courtelyou Papers.
  Josephus Daniels Papers.
  Robert Lansing Papers.
  Theodore Roosevelt Papers.
  William Howard Taft Papers.
  Woodrow Wilson Papers.
Wilkes-Barre, PA
  Luzerne County Courthouse: Prothonatory's Office.
Wyoming, PA
  Wyoming Historical & Geological Society
    City Directories.

Theses and Dissertations

Sister Mary Annunciate Merrick. "A Case of Practical Democracy: The Settlement of the Anthracite Coal Strike of 1902." PhD diss., Notre Dame University, 1942.

Published Works

A Menace to Americanization. New York: Národni List, 1919.
Brewing and Liquor Interests and German and Bolshevik Propaganda. Report and Hearings of the Subcommittee on the Judiciary. United States Senate. 3 vols. Washington, DC: Government Printing Office, 1919.
Inauguration of Theodore Roosevelt as President of the United States, March 4, 1905. Washington, DC: Headquarters of the Inaugural Committee, n.d.
Lechicki, Czesław. "Hammerling, Ludwik Mikołaj." *Polski Słownik Biograficzny,* 1960–1961, 263–64.
Majchrowski, Jacek M. "Hammerling, Ludwik Mikolaj." *Kto byl Kim w Drugiej Rzeczypospolitej.* Warsaw: Polska Oficyna Wydawnicza, Oficyna Wydawnicza BGW, 1994, 514.
Mościcki, Henryk and Włodzimierz Dzwonkowski. *Parlament Rzeczypospolitej Polskiej, 1919–1927.* Warsaw: L. Złotnicki, 1928.
Proceedings of the Anthracite Mine Strike Commission. Scranton: Scranton Tribune, 1902–1903.
R. L. Polk & Co. *1915 Trow General Directory of New York City.* Vol. 128. New York: n.p., 1915.
R. L. Polk & Co. *Wilkes-Barre Directory, 1904.* Wilkes-Barre, 1904.
R. L. Polk & Co. *Wilkes-Barre City Directory, 1908.* N.p, n.d.
Restriction of Immigration. Hearings before the Committee on Immigration and Naturalization. House of Representatives. Sixty-fourth Congress. First Session on H. R. 558. Friday, January 21, 1916. Statements of Mr. Louis N. Hammerling and Hon. Bourke Cockran of New York City. Washington, DC: Government Printing Office, 1916.
Senat Rzeczypospolitej Polskiej. Okres I. Sprawozdanie Stenograficzne z 18 posiedzenia Senata Rzeczypospolitej z dnia 19 kwietnia 1923r. Warsaw: Senat RP, 1923.

Senat Rzeczypospolitej Polskiej. Okres I. Sprawozdanie Stenograficzne z 23 posiedzenia Senata Rzeczypospolitej z dnia 15 czerwca 1923r. Warsaw: Senat RP, 1923.

Senat Rzeczypospolitej Polskiej. Okres I. Sprawozdanie Stenograficzne z 33 posiedzenia Senata Rzeczypospolitej z dnia 10 października 1923r. Warsaw: Senat RP, 1923.

Senat Rzeczypospolitej Polskiej. Okres I. Sprawozdanie Stenograficzne z 35 posiedzenia Senata Rzeczypospolitej z dnia 25 października 1923r. Warsaw: Senat RP, 1923.

Senat Rzeczypospolitej Polskiej. Okres I. Sprawozdanie Stenograficzne z 40 posiedzenia Senata Rzeczypospolitej z dnia 25 6 grudnia 1923r. Warsaw: Senat RP, 1923.

Senat Rzeczypospolitej Polskiej. Okres I. Sprawozdanie Stenograficzne z 67 posiedzenia Senata Rzeczypospolitej z dnia 24 lipca 1924r. Warsaw: Senat RP, 1924.

Senat Rzeczypospolitej Polskiej. Okres I. Sprawozdanie Stenograficzne z 1 posiedzenia Senata Rzeczypospolitej z dnia 28 października 1923r. Warsaw: Senat RP, 1923.

Thompson's Wilkes-Barre Directory for 1902. Wilkes-Barre: n.p, 1902.

Who Was Who in America? Vol. 1, 1897–1942. Chicago: Marquis Who's Who, 1966.

Williams' Wilkes-Barre City Directory. Scranton: n.p., 1903.

Memoirs, Letters, Diaries

Dębski, Jan, ed. *Maciej Rataj. Pamiętniki.* Warsaw: Ludowa Spółdzielnia Wydawnicza, 1965.

Dzendzel, Henryk. "U boku premiera Wincentego Witosa," in *Wspomnienia weteranów ruchu ludowego.* Warsaw: Ludowa Spółdzielnia Wydawnicza, 1968.

Jana Drohojowskiego Wspomnienia dyplomatyczne. Warsaw: Państwowy Instytut Wydawniczy, 1959.

Karczewski, Eugeniusz and Józef Ryszard Szaflik, eds. *Wincenty Witos, Moje Wspomnienia, Część II.* Warsaw: Ludowa Spółdzielnia Wydawnicza, 1990.

Madejczyk, Jan. *Wspomnienia.* Warsaw: Ludowa Spółdzielnia Wydawnicza, 1965.

McAdoo, William G. *Crowded Years.* New York: Houghton Mifflin, 1931.

Namier, Julia. *Lewis Namier: A Biography.* London: Oxford University Press, 1971.

Seton-Watson, R. W. *Masaryk in England.* Cambridge University Press, 1941.

Steed, Henry Wickham. *Through Thirty Years, 1892–1922: A Personal Narrative.* 2 vols. London: Heinemann, 1924.

Voska, Emmanuel Victor and Will Irwin. *Spy and Counter-Spy.* London: Doubleday, Doran, 1940.

Witos, Wincenty. *Moje Wspomnienia.* Vol. 3. Paris: Instytut Literacki, 1965.

SECONDARY SOURCES

Published Works

Ara, Angelo. *L'Austria-Ungheria nella politica Americana durante la prima Guerra mondiale.* Rome: Edizioni dell'Ateneo, 1973.

Biskupski, M. B. B. "Socialists, Spies, and Presbyterians: A Case Study of the Poles as Alien Enemies in World War I." In *Ethnicity, Culture, City,* edited by Thomas

Gladsky, Adam Walaszek, and Małgorzatka M. Wawrzykiewicz, 265–86. Warsaw: Oficyna Naukowa, 1998.

Biskupski, M. B. B. "Strategy, Politics and Suffering: The Wartime Relief of Belgium, Serbia, and Poland, 1914–1918." In *Ideology, Politics and Diplomacy in East Central Europe,* edited by M. B. B. Biskupski, 31–57. Rochester: University of Rochester Press, 2003.

Biskupski, M. B. B. *The United States and the Rebirth of Poland, 1914–1918.* Dordrecht, NL: Republic of Letters, 2012.

Blatz, Perry K. *Democratic Miners: Work and Labor Relations in the Anthracite Coal Industry, 1875–1925.* Albany: State University of New York Press, 1994.

Blum, John M. *Joe Tumulty and the Wilson Era.* Hamden, CT: Archon, 1969 [1951].

Calder, Kenneth J. *Britain and the Origins of the New Europe, 1914–1918.* Cambridge University Press, 1976.

Carsten, Oliver. "Ethnic particularism and class solidarity." *Theory and Society* 17 (1988): 431–50.

Devlin, Patrick. *Too Proud to Fight: Woodrow Wilson's Neutrality.* New York: Oxford University Press, 1975.

Doerries, Reinhard R. *Imperial Challenge: Ambassador Count Bernstorff and German-American Relations, 1908–1917.* Chapel Hill: University of North Carolina Press, 1989.

Durand, E. Dana. "The Anthracite Coal Strike and Its Settlement." *Political Science Quarterly* 18 (September 1903): 385–414.

Falcke, H. P. *Vor dem Eintritt Amerikas in dem Weltkrieg: Deutsche Propaganda in den Vereinigten Staaten von Amerika, 1914–1915.* Dresden: C. Reissner, 1928.

Gerson, Louis. *Woodrow Wilson and the Rebirth of Poland, 1914–1920: A Study in the Influence on American Policy of Minority Groups of Foreign Origin.* New Haven: Yale University Press, 1953.

Ginger, Ray. "Managerial Employees in Anthracite, 1902: A Study in Occupational Mobility." *Journal of Economic History* 14 (Spring 1954): 146–57.

Gowaskie, Joseph M. "John Mitchell and the Anthracite Coal Strike of 1902: A Century Later." In *The "Great Strike": Perspectives on the 1902 Anthracite Coal Strike,* edited by Kenneth C. Wolensky, 123–39. Easton, PA: Canal History and Technology Press, 2002.

Greene, Victor R. *The Slavic Community on Strike: Immigrant Labor in Pennsylvania Anthracite.* Notre Dame, IN: University of Notre Dame Press, 1968.

Hemmerling, Zygmunt. *PSL "Wyzwolenie" w parlementach II Rzeczypospolitej, 1919–1931.* Warsaw: Uniwersytet Warszawski, 1990.

Higham, John. *Strangers in the Land: Patterns of American Nativism, 1860–1925.* New Brunswick: Rutgers University Press, 1955.

Holzer, Jerzy. *Mozaika polityczna Drugiej Rzeczypospolitej.* Warsaw: Książka i Wiedza, 1974.

Hudson, Berkley and Karen Boyajy. "The Rise and Fall of an Ethnic Advocate and American Huckster," *Media History* 15, no. 3 (2009): 287–302.

Janosov, Robert A. "Beyond the 'Great Coal Strike': The Anthracite Coal Region in 1902." In *The "Great Strike": Perspectives on the 1902 Anthracite Coal Strike*, edited by Kenneth C. Wolensky, 1–29. Easton, PA: Canal History and Technology Press, 2002.

Kantowicz, Edward R. *Polish-American Politics in Chicago, 1888–1940*. Chicago: University of Chicago Press, 1975.

Klein, Philip Shriver and Ari Arthur Hoogenboom. *A History of Pennsylvania*. New York: McGraw, 1973.

Landau, Zbigniew. "Kucharski, Władysław." *Polski Słownik Biograficzny* 41 (1971): 54–57.

Lato, Stanisław. *Ruch Ludowy a Centrolew*. Warsaw: Ludowa Spółdzielnia Wydawnicza, 1965.

Link, Arthur S. *Woodrow Wilson and the Progressive Era, 1910–1917*. New York: Harper, 1954.

Lissak, Rivka Shpak. "The National Liberal Immigration League and Immigration Restriction, 1906–1917." *American Jewish Archives* 46, no. 2 (1994): 197–246.

Makulec, Louis. *Church of St. Stanislaus, Bishop and Martyr*. New York: The Roman Catholic Church of St. Stanislaus, B.M., 1954.

Marsh, Ben. "Continuity and Decline in the Anthracite Towns of Pennsylvania." *Annals of the Association of American Geographers* 77, no. 3 (September 1987): 337–52.

McDonough, Jack. *The Fire Down Below: The Great Anthracite Strike of 1902 and the People Who Made the Decisions*. Scranton: Avocado Productions, 1902.

McKerns, Joseph P. "The 'Faces' of John Mitchell: News Coverage of the Great Anthracite Strike of 1902 in the Regional and National Press." In *The "Great Strike": Perspectives on the 1902 Anthracite Coal Strike*, edited by Kenneth C. Wolensky, 29–43. Easton, PA: Canal History and Technology Press, 2002.

O'Grady, Joseph P., ed. *The Immigrants' Influence on Wilson's Peace Policies*. Lexington: University of Kentucky Press, 1967.

Olszański, Kazimierz. *Wojciech Kossak*. Wrocław: Ossolineum, 1976.

Osada, Stanisław and Adam Olszewski. *Historia Związku Narodowego Polskiego*. 4 vols. Chicago: Polish National Alliance, 1957–1963.

Park, Robert E. *The Immigrant Press and Its Control*. New York: Harper, 1922.

Pease, Neal. *Poland, the United States and the Stabilization of Europe, 1919–1933*. New York: Oxford University Press, 1986.

Peterson, H. C. *Propaganda for the War: The Campaign against American Neutrality, 1914–1917*. Norman: University of Oklahoma Press, 1939.

Petit, Jeanne D. *The Men and Women We Want: Gender, Race, and the Progressive Era Literary Test Debate*. Rochester: University of Rochester Press, 2010.

Phelan, Craig. *Divided Loyalties: The Public and Private Life of Labor Leader John Mitchell*. Albany: State University of New York Press, 1994.

Phelan, Craig. "The Making of a Labor Leader: John Mitchell and the Anthracite Strike of 1900." *Pennsylvania History* 63 (Winter 1996): 53–78.

Pienkos, Donald E. "Polish Americans in Milwaukee." In *Ethnic Politics in Urban America*, edited by Angela T. Pienkos. Chicago: Polish American Historical Association, 1978, 66–91.

Ręk, Tadeusz. *Chjeno-Piast, 1922–1926: W świetle obrad sejmu i senatu.* Warsaw: Ludowa Spółdzielnia Wydawnicza, 1955.

Roberts, Ellis W. *The Breaker Whistle Blows: Mining Disasters and Labor Leaders in the Anthracite Region.* Scranton: Anthracite Museum Press, 1984.

Rzepecki, Tadeusz and Witold Rzepecki. *Sejm i senat, 1922–1927.* Poznań: Wielkopolska księgarnia nakładowa Karola Rzepeckiego, 1923.

Seymour, Charles. *Woodrow Wilson and the World War: A Chronicle of Our Own Times.* New Haven: Yale University Press, 1921.

Stankiewicz, Witold. "Pakt Lanckoroński." *Roczniki dziejowa ruchu ludowego* 1 (1959): 196–216.

Szerer, Mieczysław. "Szlakami propagandy." *Przegląd dyplomatyczny* 3 (September-October 1921).

Wiebe, Robert H. "The Anthracite Strike of 1902: A Record of Confusion." *Mississippi Valley Historical Review* 48, no. 2 (September 1961): 229–51.

Witcover, Jules. *Sabotage at Black Tom: Imperial Germany's Secret War in America, 1914–1917.* Chapel Hill: Algonquin Books, 1989.

Wittke, Carl. *German-Americans and the World War.* Columbus: Ohio State Archaeological and Historical Society, 1936.

Zakrzewski, Andrzej, ed. *Sejmy Drugiej Rzeczypospolitej.* Warsaw: Ludowa Spółdzielnia Wydawnicza, 1990.

Zakrzewski, Andrzej. *Wincenty Witos: Chłopski polityk i mąż stanu.* Warsaw: Ludowa Spółdzielnia Wydawnicza, 1977.

Zeidel, Robert F. "Hayseed Immigration Policy: 'Uncle Joe' Cannon and the Immigration Question." *Illinois Historical Journal* 88 (Autumn 1995).

The Press

The American Courier [Milwaukee]
Ameryka-Echo [Toledo]
Altoona Mirror
The Atlanta Constitution
Brooklyn Eagle
The Chillicothe Constitution
The Democrat and Standard [Coshocton]
Dziennik Narodowy [Piotrków]
Fort Wayne Daily News
The Fort Wayne Sentinel
Głos [Warsaw]
Illustrowany Kurier Codzienny [Kraków]
Kurjer Polski [Warsaw]
Kurjer Poranny [Warsaw]
Kurjer Warszawski
Kuryer Narodowy [New York]
The Lima Times-Democrat

The Marion Daily Star
Národni List
The News [Frederick]
New-York Commercial Advertiser
The New York Times
New-York Tribune
New York World
New Yorker Staats-Zeitung
Pittsburgh Dispatch
Reno Evening Gazette
Sandusky Evening Star
The Scranton Times
The Sheboygan Daily Press
The Star and Sentinel [Gettysburg]
Telegram [Buffalo]
The Troy Budget [New York]
United Mine Workers Journal
The Warren Evening Times
The Washington Post
Wilkes-Barre Leader

Letters

Perry Blatz to author, August 26, 2011.
Joseph Giulietti [Calvary Cemetery] to author, July 13, 2004.
Judith Gold [Hammerling's granddaughter] to author, January 18, 2006.
Judith Gold to author, February 9, 2006.
Judith Gold to author, February 18, 2006.   .
Judith Gold to author, February 22, 2006.
Judith Gold to author, March 1, 2006.
Judith Gold to author, January 13, 2014.
Judith Gold to author, January 17, 2014.
Judith Gold to author, January 19, 2014.
James Renier Hammerling [Hammerling's grandson] to author, December 16, 1999.
James Renier Hammerling to author, February 24, 2000.
James Renier Hammerling to author, July 27, 2000.
James Renier Hammerling to author, August 8, 2000.
Louis N. Hammerling [Hammerling's grandson] to author, January 22, 2002.
Phillip Hammerling to author, February 1, 2006.
Jeane O'Donnell [Hammerling's granddaughter] to author, June 2, 2002.
James S. Pula to author, August 15, 2011.
Victoria Hammerling Rosenberg [Hammerling's granddaughter] to author, January 22, 2014.
Victoria Hammerling Rosenberg to author, February 6, 2014.
Witold Stankiewicz to author, January 8, 1996.

INDEX